CREATIVE FRICTIONS

ARTS LEADERSHIP, POLICY AND PRACTICE IN MULTICULTURAL AUSTRALIA

CREATIVE FRICTIONS

ARTS LEADERSHIP, POLICY AND PRACTICE IN MULTICULTURAL AUSTRALIA

CECELIA CMIELEWSKI

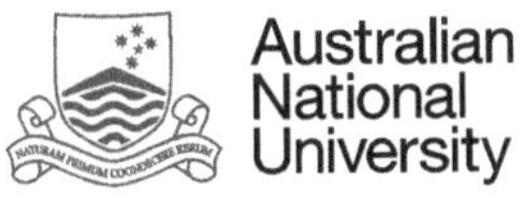

Australian National University

PRESS

This book is dedicated to my parents and my grandchildren.

To my parents, who together instilled in me their love of education and the arts.

To my mother, for continuing formal education through all stages of her life.
I walk in your footsteps.

To my father, for teaching me how to dance and refusing to teach me Polish,
which meant I had to learn it myself. I honour the gusto of your life as
a postwar migrant.

To my grandchildren, who are a constant source of joy.

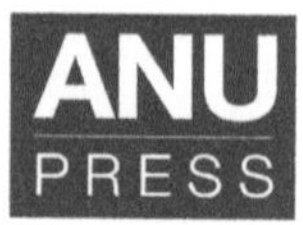

Published by ANU Press
The Australian National University
Acton ACT 2601, Australia
Email: anupress@anu.edu.au

Available to download for free at press.anu.edu.au

ISBN (print): 9781760464585
ISBN (online): 9781760464592

WorldCat (print): 1262786424
WorldCat (online): 1262785069

DOI: 10.22459/CF.2021

Cover design and layout by ANU Press

Cover Image: Hossein Valamanesh, *Untitled 1*, 2005. Cornus branches and wax varnish on paper, 11.5 cm diameter. Private collection, Adelaide. Photo: M. Kluvanek.

This book is published under the aegis of the Public Policy Editorial Board of the ANU Press.

Contents

Acknowledgements

I am grateful to all the artists and cultural practitioners who gave their precious time and told me what they *really* think and feel. I thank the artists for the persistence they bring to their creative practices, and the practitioners who have dedicated their careers to the discourse and advancement of multicultural arts in Australia. I hope this book goes some way to acknowledge your work and leaves a trail for others.

I owe a debt of thanks to Professor Greg Noble and Distinguished Professor Ien Ang for their incisive insights. I thank Greg for expanding my horizons and Ien for focusing them. I would especially like to acknowledge Ien for her vision and efforts in establishing the Institute for Culture and Society, which is a wonderfully rigorous, convivial and supportive environment.

I thank my husband, Nigel Helyer, for his remarkable belief in my ability to do this. I am grateful for the incredible energy that he dedicates to his art practice and for keeping the adventures happening over these recent years, whether through walking, kayaking, sailing or installing his ambitious art projects.

List of Tables

List of Illustrations

Acronyms

ABC	Australian Broadcasting Corporation
ABS	Australian Bureau of Statistics
ACE	Arts Council England
ACMAC	Australia Council Multicultural Advisory Committee
ACT	Australian Capital Territory
AHRC	Australian Human Rights Commission
AIATSIS	Australian Institute of Aboriginal and Torres Strait Islander Studies
ALP	Australian Labor Party
AMA	Arts in a Multicultural Australia
ATSIA	Aboriginal and Torres Strait Islander Arts
Australia Council	Australia Council for the Arts
BAME	Black, Asian and minority ethnic
CAAP	Contemporary Asian Australian Performance
CALD/CaLD	culturally and linguistically diverse
CCA	Canada Council for the Arts
CCAA	Centre for Contemporary Asian Art
CCDB	Community Cultural Development Board
CDC	Cultural Diversity Clusters
CEF	Cultural Engagement Framework
DARTS	Diversity Arts Australia
DCA	Department of Culture and the Arts
DCMS	Department for Culture, Media and Sport

EAC	Ethnic Arts Committee
ESB	English-speaking background
MAPD	Multicultural Arts Professional Development
MAV	Multicultural Arts Victoria
MONA	Museum of Old and New Art
MoU	Memorandum of understanding
MPA	major performing arts (companies)
MTC	Melbourne Theatre Company
NESB	non–English speaking background
NIDA	National Institute of Dramatic Arts
NPO	National portfolio organisations
NSW	New South Wales
PL	Performing Lines
PWA	Playwriting Australia
Qld	Queensland
S2M	small to medium
SME	small to medium enterprise
SA	South Australia
SBS	Special Broadcasting Service
UNESCO	United Nations Educational, Scientific and Cultural Organization
WA	Western Australia
Vic.	Victoria

Introduction

Despite over 30 years of arts and cultural policy attention to cultural diversity, the general public and artists alike continue to hold the view that Australia's creative production does not reflect our multicultural society (Australia Council 2016a; Screen Australia 2016). As well as fulfilling traditional roles of creative expression, art is called on to contribute to social questions of national identity, social cohesion and intercultural understanding (Van de Vyver and Abrams 2017), the importance of which often stems from local and global issues of social discord (Soutphommasane 2017). Artists and their practices of exploring cultural difference in Australia are central to my research, providing insights into the arts policies that have aimed to support them.

As Jakubowicz and Ho (2013, 286) argue, and this book examines, the key challenge that remains for the arts sector is to support 'creativity that is inclusive and produces absorbing and rich representations of the reality of Australian life'. Their comment, however, implicitly echoes a kind of utopianism, probably because of the 'utopian impulse or tendency present in many of our foundational works of art and literature' to the extent that many 'think art makes the world a better place' (Noble 2012, 12). The echo can also be found in individual experiences of migration:

> Once remembered cultural landscapes became increasingly reconstructed as social Utopias. In a process that shares similarities with Benedict Anderson's 'imagined communities', migrants used the past to consolidate contemporary identities and norms that offered empowerment in the Australian context. (Mason 2010, 7)

The 'imagined communities' went on to become a sociopolitical vision 'of multiculturalism that contained an implicit form of cosmopolitan humanism—which Lippman [founding chair of Ethnic Communities Council of Victoria] defined in terms of "empathy of interaction"' (Papastergiadis 2013a, 6).

Various modes of leadership that enable the interactions of arts practice and cultural difference are explored in this book. It is valuable to think about identity beyond the simple evocations of the nation found in much cultural policy such as *Creative Australia* (Parliament of Australia 2013). For example, most of the Australia Council's 'multicultural arts' policies were aspirational statements to elicit a vision of artistic participation that was informed by, and reflected, society. The theme of leadership frames an exploration of the relationship between experience, practice and policy, and the environment that surrounds artists of non–English speaking backgrounds (NESB) and their work.

My starting point is the premise that artistic participation is not simply a matter of individual artists' intentions or having better policy documents per se, but involves big questions of leadership and collaboration within the sector. The fostering of an arts policy and practice that captures the aesthetic and symbolic expressions of a multicultural society is not necessarily a 'smooth' process. Critiquing the notion of 'unity-in-diversity', Ang (2003a, 33, original emphasis) suggests paying 'detailed attention to the very *process* of creating a sense of "we" in the face of our heterogeneity'. My intention is that, by attending to the processes of art-making and multicultural arts policymaking across three distinct domains of leadership, an ethos of inclusion within the arts can be fostered.

The Australian Human Rights Commission estimates that '32 per cent of Australians are from non-Anglo-Celtic backgrounds' (Soutphommasane 2016). However, the participation rates of NESB artists are half those of NESB employees in the general workforce (Throsby and Petetskaya 2017, 143). This question of under-representation should certainly be a management issue in the arts sector, but the question of representation would also benefit from being understood more broadly, rather than in the narrow sense of multiculturalism as a tool to manage cultural difference (Rizvi 2003, 231–33). Despite their low presence in the arts, NESB (a problematic term discussed more fully below) artists find and generate support through the creative, institutional and organisational environments in which they practice. Therefore, it is valuable to consider creative, institutional and organisational leadership—domains that are critical for effecting sustained change in the arts environment as they encapsulate most arts activity.

Creative leadership refers to artists who generate new developments in creative content and expand the potential for others to do so. Institutional leadership occurs through government and their agencies, in this case the Australia Council, specifically their policies towards the arts in a multicultural Australia and the disbursement of funds. Organisational leadership refers to those in positions of influence in arts organisations funded by the Australia Council and how resources and support are made available for NESB artists—the most significant producers in the area of multicultural arts.

Throughout this book, I explore the relationship between Australian arts and cultural policies and the fostering of NESB artists' creative practices, particularly in relation to the federal government's arts agency, the Australia Council for the Arts, and their 2000 and 2006 Arts in a Multicultural Australia (AMA) policies. I approach this relationship through creative use of the idea of 'friction' and the ways in which gaining 'trust' can generate the 'traction' to increase culturally diverse art practice. I also explore whether Australian multicultural arts policies enabled the 'mainstream' to change, and whether NESB artists continue to work in marginalised spaces. 'Mainstream' in this context refers to those, usually, major arts organisations within the subsidised arts sector who receive the bulk of government and philanthropic funds and whose programming is generally drawn from the 'Western' artistic 'heritage' canon. I also analyse the range of creative tensions and artistic opportunities that are produced in an Australian multicultural society that has increasingly become the social 'mainstream' (Ang et al. 2002, 4). At a deeper level, 'mainstream' points to the 'workings of power and privilege [within] prevailing structural norms' (Rizvi 2003, 234) that, in the arts, are viewed as '"establishment" arts organisations' (Khan 2010, 184). Khan (2010, 190) identifies the issue of multicultural arts within the 'mainstream' context as a 'normative and problematic one [that] complicates questions of what multicultural arts are, and who they are ultimately for'. The relationship to the 'mainstream', in turn, prompts questions about the ways in which NESB artists maintain their arts practices and how they draw on their hybrid and multiple identities to describe, influence and/or critique Australia's cultural landscape.

Research Context

Published research has paid attention to broader questions of the arts in a multicultural Australia in the 1990s (Gunew and Rizvi 1994; Hawkins 1993, 86–88; Blonski 1992) and to culturally diverse audience development strategies in the 2000s (Kapetopoulos 2004; Rentschler 2006). Artists face issues in terms of their identity, creative production and relationship to their discipline fields and organisational infrastructures, all of which are further complicated by a perception that 'multicultural arts' are pigeonholed by 'mainstream' organisations as 'community arts'. Kalantzis and Cope (1994, 13) detail the impact of confusions and contradictions of the range of terminologies around 'excellence' in the arts, 'showing the concept of excellence in the arts to be a contested one' because elite art was considered the domain of Anglo-Australians. Their hope that Australia was at a crucial turning point towards cultural inclusion in the arts 20 years ago is yet to be realised. Since 2000, there has been limited research published on the connections between national multicultural arts policy and the fostering of multicultural arts practices.

The text unfolds around my discussions with artists, cultural practitioners, former Australia Council Multicultural Advisory Committee (ACMAC) members, and senior arts bureaucrats. There emerged a focus on the experiences of creative practitioners, an examination of institutional practices, and an analysis of the effectiveness and impact of policy aims. A bureaucrat at the Australia Council may see the policy as imperfect but effective, but cultural practitioners may point to the lack of diversity in the arts available to the public, while artists working in multicultural arts may express frustration at the slow pace of change in the arts sector when it comes to normalising their inclusion.

The resulting tensions paint a picture of a lack of comprehension and/or relevance of multicultural arts policy within the creative sector. This includes the apparent cyclical nature (not unlike a vicious cycle) of debate around the naming, strategic focus and positioning (mainstream or not) of multicultural arts. The public record of attempts to address issues across multicultural arts is incomplete. This uneven documentation results in limited historical memory or legacy in the field. National research with a dedicated focus on NESB artists and the arts in a multicultural Australia has not been published since 1994 (Gunew and Rizvi 1994). By reprising the work undertaken through the 2000 and 2006 AMA policies, I aim to address that gap. Further, by exploring the current state of multicultural arts practices in Australia, and critiquing the relevance of past and present arts policies, I intend to unravel some of the complexities that NESB artists encounter, and profile their creative and strategic responses.

The issues of intermittent leadership and paucity of historical knowledge in the development of multicultural arts practices in Australia continues a cycle of frustration at the lack of recognition of, and engagement with, artists working in this sphere. Via a framework of creative, institutional and organisational leadership, this book aims to provide ways to think through some of the 'messes' that frequently accompany multicultural arts policies. I entwine elements of art-making and policymaking together, and consider whether cultural policies have embraced 'multiculturalism as an aesthetic issue' (Rizvi 2003, 135). I also ask whether the complexity of multiculturalism challenges a 'smooth' arts policy process.

Exploring the Issues

Due to the 'lag' between arts policy and practitioner experience, NESB artists are required to navigate their practices with determination and creative persistence. Tsing describes the need for dynamic small gestures among groups and individuals to disrupt the large-scale demise of the planet. Addressing cosmopolitanism and complexity, she notes that the 'challenge of cultural analysis is to address both the spreading interconnections and locatedness of culture' (Tsing 2005, 122). Modes of leadership are used in this text to explore the agency of artists who connect across cultures to 'locate' their multicultural art practices.

Creative, Institutional and Organisational Leadership

Three domains of leadership are considered useful for examining the challenges and opportunities in the relationship between the arts and cultural difference. These domains provide a way to analyse the possibilities that enhance a milieu that is more supportive of artists whose work contributes to 'multicultural arts' practice. The three domains—creative, institutional and organisational—entail a range of leadership modes, such as transactional, transformative, distributed and relational leadership

(Hewison and Holden 2011, 28–40). I explore how those modes are used in conjunction with processes of 'accompaniment' (Lynd and Lynd 2009, 93) and 'attunement' (Gibson 2005, 272–73), and how they are relevant to many NESB artists in their collaborative practices.

Friction, Trust and Traction

Notions of friction, trust and traction are used as conceptual tools to discuss the issues and aspirations encountered by artists across creative, institutional and organisational domains of the arts. These ideas emerged throughout the empirical research and reviews of federal policies directed towards the arts in a multicultural Australia. The agency of the artists and cultural practitioners who exercise and/or experience creative, institutional and organisational leadership is explored through how they exploit frictions and gain trust to generate longer-term traction. I suggest that translating the friction into longer-term traction sees trust act as a hinge to enable change across the arts.

This book explores constraints experienced by NESB artists who, in their creative leadership roles, can be typecast on stage and within their artform practice. I explore how the friction arising from these constraints is used to develop intercultural practices that strive for creative and cultural autonomy. The notion of trust is also explored across all three domains as a marker of how artists and cultural practitioners engage and participate in multicultural arts. The moments of change towards greater support for the arts in a multicultural Australia are identified through the notion of traction.

The theme of friction and its role in generating creativity addresses both the political and the experiential context. Friction is a multidimensional force caused by the 'rubbing of two bodies (physical and mechanical); the resistance a body encounters when moving over one another; clash of wills, temperaments, opinions' (*Concise Oxford Dictionary* 1982, 393). In innovation and management studies, friction as a 'discomfort' is seen to aid innovation because divergent views can create new solutions. Innovation is a synthesis of fresh ideas into new forms of production that resonate within contemporary society. Friction in organisations can also signal when things are being made 'too hard to do' (Sutton and Seelig 2017).

Trust, by way of contrast, is established 'when you do what you say you would do' (Punt and Bateman 2018, 39). This includes fulfilling those aims ethically and confirming whether the 'processes, platforms and people' are in place to achieve those aims (Punt and Bateman 2018, 39). It is arguable that the past decades of friction, whether experienced as an NESB artist, arts sector, government or its agencies, have produced a lack of mutual trust. Trust, succinctly defined as a 'specific solution to risk' (Luhmann 2000, 95), is required when faced with an unfamiliar situation from which 'a bad outcome would make you regret your action' (Luhmann 2000, 98). The relationship between trust and risk relates to the establishment of a multicultural arts milieu. To encourage the culturally unfamiliar (the risky) would open up new creative possibilities, and the allocation of (or trust with) resources would provide adequate support for the unfamiliar.

Traction relies upon friction between components or agents in a system and, if used tactically, can produce a trajectory towards a desired outcome. I use traction to indicate movement towards a more supportive multicultural arts milieu. Traction in this sense is a result of a cultural and social understanding of the friction arising from the constraints and opportunities experienced by NESB artists and multicultural arts organisations. To enliven a multicultural arts milieu, issues of 'trust' (how to *generate* it) and 'friction' (how to *exploit* it to gain traction) are central.

Who is a Non–English Speaking Background Artist?

The issue of terminology is a vexed one for artists and institutions working broadly in the area of 'multicultural arts'. Artists can hold significant ambivalence towards different types of labels, including NESB (which, at times, has distinguished between migrants ['NESB1'] and children of migrants ['NESB2']) and multicultural arts. I have made the deliberate decision to employ these 'unfashionable' terms (i.e. NESB and multicultural arts) throughout this book.

The term NESB was introduced in the 1970s; although it has been abandoned by many in recent decades, it remains useful as a description. It is a category that is contested both in itself and as an artefact of social practices and government policies. It is problematic because it frames people in the 'negative'—that is, by identifying a person only via a language that is not their first tongue. It becomes even more problematic when considering that their children who were born in Australia (i.e. NESB2) may only speak English. The phrase 'language background other than English' (or LBOTE) is preferred by education departments, while the government's most widely used term is 'culturally and linguistically diverse' (CALD or CaLD). CALD is problematic because, while it ostensibly refers to diversity across populations (i.e. everyone), it has come to stand for groups of 'non-mainstream' or 'culturally diverse' people in the same way that 'ethnic' or NESB might have been used in the past. Artists' ambivalence about their NESB classification also stems from perceived expectations that they should fit into a prescribed, at times simplistic, creative mould. Many migrant artists (and children of migrants) identify themselves through their 'hyphenated' and 'ethnic minority' backgrounds such as Greek-Australian or Polish-Australian, which can also encompass the generational aspect of migration. While the hyphen is appropriate for individuals and groups of ethnically similar artists, such as those from Arabic-Australian backgrounds, it cannot be applied more broadly. The collective genres can be described broadly as 'multicultural arts' but individuals are rarely comfortable being referred to as 'multicultural artists'.

A recurring challenge for the development of multicultural arts policies is based in the fluidity of artists' identities and the dynamic evolving nature of Australian society through emerging ethnic groups. By contrast, other demographic groups to receive attention for 'inclusion' in the arts are somewhat fixed and more easily identified. A young person is defined as under 26, a regional artist is defined by their residential postcode, an artist with a disability can choose to identify as such, gender options have increased to incorporate a broad range of possibilities, and an Indigenous (or 'First Nation') artist is recognised through their tribal lineage and peers (AIATSIS n.d.).

One criticism of the term NESB is that it reinforces 'othering' because it positions people in a negative category—by lacking the 'positive' attribute of having English as a first language. Babacan suggests that this leads to a form of 'relative exclusion' from access to resources and the associated cultural sense of belonging to the general community (quoted in Sawrikar and Katz 2009, 4). The term is also criticised for combining those who are economically disadvantaged with those who are not and, as such, for not assisting with the monitoring of resource distribution with a view to ensuring social justice outcomes (Sawrikar and Katz 2009). Confusion can also arise when Indigenous language speakers are considered because many do not use English as their first language; this means that the NESB label can equally incorporate First Nations artists, adding an extra dimension of complexity. A further complicating factor is that people with English-speaking backgrounds are uniformly positioned as 'white', which leaves non-white English speakers querying how they might be 'included'.

An alternative view that supports the term NESB suggests that it remains a useful category because it is factual: it states the power differential in play. English is clearly identified as the source of power, and those without it are considered to be lacking, although this becomes problematic for NESB2 artists whose first language may be English.

Shifting identities (Ang 2011) that defy and complicate any satisfactory description are part of the fluid cultural milieu within which NESB artists operate. Initially, artists who were migrants from non-Protestant, non-Anglo origins (Gertsakis 1994) were called 'migrant', 'ethnic', 'multicultural', then NESB and now CALD. While these terms have each been derided and critiqued in turn, the absence of any term at all is less than ideal, particularly with regards to a multicultural arts policy framework. In considering the option to abandon the (at the time, current) term of NESB, Papastergiadis, Gunew and Blonski sought to establish the value of a name.

> A name is like a container that one can accept and work within,
> or rebel against. To have no name is to be dropped into a vacuum;
> to wallow without markers. It disables rather than enables cultural
> intervention (Papastergiadis, Gunew and Blonski 1994, 128).

The authors pursued the option to reclaim the term NESB so as to 'reinscribe the negativity' (128). This process aimed to identify the excluded category; legitimise viewpoints, experiences and practices that are not part of the dominant arts discourse; transform the cultural base through critical interpretations and new agendas; and indicate cultural change by acting as a bridge between the 'invisible and visible forms within a national culture' (129).

Papastergiadis, Gunew and Blonski value the distinguishing terms of NESB1, those born overseas, and NESB2, who are descendants of immigrants and who maintain the linguistic and cultural links of their parents. They evoke the trope of the journey to explain a continual process of change. For NESB1 artists, they claim the journey is associated with other dichotomies such as 'home/exile; severance/reconciliation'. They describe the NESB2 artist as inhabiting:

> A more ambiguous zone of neither home nor exile. If we could say that the perspective of NESB1 is predominantly bi-focal, then we would say that NESB2 is multivalent. Their pattern of engagement will be more complex, subtle, layered with identity formation no longer emanating primarily from the decision to leave one place, but from a mixture of inherited values and projected stereotypes. (Papastergiadis, Gunew and Blonski 1994, 130)

This description captures the sense of the intergenerational processes that contribute to a dynamic, multicultural Australia. It is a depiction yet to be captured by alternative terms.

'Migrant' could be used, as it is also an accurate term. Ang (2003b, 9) describes Hall and Gilroy, two key UK thinkers, as 'post-colonial migrants'. However, in Australia, this term is less accurate, as the majority of migrants have historically arrived from the UK as native English speakers. This led to the introduction of the term 'ethnic' and its artistic equivalent 'folkloric' into bureaucracies, both of which became derogatory terms in contemporary arts lexicon (Khan, Wyatt and Yue 2014, 7).

The term CALD, which came into official use in 1996, was developed to address some of the issues arising from the 'negative' positioning of NESB (Sawrikar and Katz 2009, 2). The perception is that CALD 'does not fix a characteristic from which minority ethnic groups deviate, and so it can avoid the relational exclusion and divisiveness NESB may produce for minority ethnic groups' (3). Sawrikar and Katz suggest that CALD differentiates the range of cultural and linguistic groups in Australia. However, the term can also be seen as not providing any real level of nuance, because CALD, by its very openness, includes everyone who has a culture and a language.

CALD's acknowledgment of the uniqueness of different (minority) groups detracts from the fact that, in its common use, the term still refers to the same groups as NESB—those who are different from the majority; it is simply less transparent about the fact that there is a majority from which others are seen to differ (Sawrikar and Katz 2009, 6). Curiously, Sawrikar and Katz (2009, 10) suggest an even clumsier term, 'Australians ethnically diverse and different from the majority (AEDDM)', to address issues of inclusion. However, this term faces the same issues, as it identifies people on the basis of being 'different from the majority'. Trying to identify a subject by tying the language into knots compounds the frustration for the subject and does little to creatively engage the general population, decision-makers or bureaucrats.

The simple term 'minority' has merit, in part because it is not an acronym, but also because it is more easily understood and acknowledges difference as distinct from the mainstream majority of a population. It appears to be less awkward because it does not draw attention to the specific characteristics of a person. However, this is also where the term can generate confusion because it does not specifically identify the ways in which someone is a minority.

For example, 'minority' can include people with different physical and intellectual abilities, or those who live outside urban centres. It carries similar overtones to the term 'cultural diversity'—in that it is used to describe many groupings and situations and have come to be equated with multiculturalism. As Gunew (2003, 178) observes, however, the function of the term 'cultural diversity' is one of assimilation; it obviates the need for understanding because it 'signals a refusal to examine difference in terms of incommensurability'. She suggests Homi Bhabha's term 'cultural difference' as a useful alternative (178). Yet this has the potential to create confusion within the arts context, because artforms produce cultural diversity of *form* as they evolve. This is why I use the term 'multicultural arts' to indicate arts practices that arise out of the creative potential afforded by multicultural Australia.

At times, the term 'diaspora' (Ang 2003b) has been deployed in the service of the arts (*Artlink* 2011) to refer to artists caught up in global migration flows. It is useful to consider this term because it suggests the productive potential of members of the diaspora, as well as the complex relationships that must be navigated across multiple locations. However, while it encompasses the global experience for many, it does not explain the service delivery needs of specific settler groups and their particular situations within an arts context. As Ang (2003b: 8) suggests, the idea of the 'diaspora' may not incorporate the possibilities of local dynamics:

> The hybridising context of the global city brings out the intrinsic contradiction locked into the concept of diaspora, which, logically, depends on the maintenance of an apparently natural essential identity to secure its imagined status as a coherent community.

In Australia, most migrant NESB artists work as individuals or in small groups, and are rarely part of a 'coherent' ethnic group through which their 'marginal' status might be maintained. Two examples of organisations with broad ethnic bases (that also retain some specificity) are the Centre for Contemporary Asian Art (CCAA) and Contemporary Asian Australian Performance (CAAP). Rather than emphasise their 'hyphenated identities', these groups highlight their contemporary practices (4A Centre for Contemporary Asian Art; CAAP 2017).

A term that has yet to be matched in Australia, *métissage* is derived from the Caribbean critic Edouard Glissant's 'concept of braiding diverse cultural forms' (Gunew 2003, 190). When applied to the arts, *métissage* poetically evokes the interweaving of cultural difference through art practices, but still does not quite address the issue of terminology to describe individual artists.

NESB remains in circulation in Australia and, for some, enables self-identification for such purposes as monitoring levels of participation and assessing the distribution of resources. The cultural economist David Throsby, for example, uses NESB in longitudinal research into artists' incomes in Australia to maintain consistency in research parameters, and also because it is technically accurate (Throsby and Hollister 2003; Throsby and Zednick 2010; Throsby and Petetskaya 2017). Similarly, Sawrikar and Katz (2009, 5–6) argue that:

> The word 'diverse' in the term CALD carries an emotive valence for people which the factual 'language in country of origin' does not. This valence is arguably detrimental to Australia's capacity to embrace itself as a multicultural nation.

I chose to use the 'unfashionable' term 'NESB artist'. With this choice, I intend to incorporate those artists who are either born overseas whose first language is not English (NESB1: first generation) or have at least one parent whose first language is not English (NESB2: second generation). This term is less confusing and cumbersome than some of the other, more generalised descriptors. But one of my key reasons is that, like the pejorative colloquial term 'wog', NESB 'reinscribes the negativity'

(Papastergiadis, Gunew and Blonski 1994, 129). Similarly, in writing of 'multicultural arts', I refer to art produced by a majority of first- or second-generation NESB artists. In particular, I am keen to be able to experience on any given day, in any given venue, the work of individual artists whose non-Anglo creative heritage and ways of creating are able to be expressed. I prefer to see more NESB artists with creative control in multicultural, cross-cultural and intercultural creative pursuits. These issues contribute to what I describe as a 'multicultural arts milieu'—an alternative to arts policy that encompasses elements that can be conducive, or not, in support of multicultural arts practices. This concept assists with the aim of identifying possible models that develop a supportive milieu.

Method

My mixed research method included sourcing published and unpublished data, and semi-structured interviews. Quantitative data was drawn from the Australia Council's published annual reports, strategy planning documents and commissioned longitudinal studies into artists' incomes. Multiple requests submitted to the Australia Council for data on grants paid to NESB artists and multicultural arts organisations were declined. As one of the designers of the system to collect, enter, store and extract data, I am aware that accessing these data should have been eminently possible. However, rather than lodge a freedom of information request, I decided to extrapolate data from information that the institution was prepared to publish. The textual data relevant to the 2000 and 2006 AMA policies included Australia Council annual reports and unpublished internal reports, such as those provided by consultants commissioned to review policy and direction. I knew of the existence of these reports because I was involved in commissioning them; and I knew also that they provide a rich archive that attests to the levels of activity over the two final AMA policies.

The Research Participants

The interview data provided the experiences and insights of NESB artists, cultural practitioners, policymakers and arts managers. The artists interviewed indicate the spectrum of the art disciplines and provide some national overview. I chose to concentrate on performing artists, as the issues of participation based on language and identity appeared more significant for them, borne out by arts participation research (Throsby and Hollister 2003). The interviews took place during 2015 in a range of locations chosen by the interviewee, such as artists' studios, coffee shops and offices; four interviews were conducted via telephone to London, Canberra and Darwin. Six former ACMAC members responded to my email inviting them to reflect on their experiences, as did Annette Blonski, who documented multicultural arts in the early 1990s.

The range of backgrounds of each of the interviewees reflects their diverse cultural heritages as well as the diversity of their arts practices. Many of them juggle 'portfolio' careers, including a variety of casual employment roles, in order to manage and support their artistic careers (Stevenson et al. 2017, 11). Eight established and four emerging independent artists from different disciplines gave generously of their time to be interviewed. Each artist has had a unique trajectory, many arcing over decades, yet their experiences often coalesced around similar concerns. A further nine interviews with bureaucrats, cultural practitioners and a consultant capture a diverse range of ethnicities and professional perspectives on the relationship between the 2000 and 2006 AMA policies and the fostering of NESB artists. All biographies are listed in Appendix A.

My Role at the Australia Council

My personal interest in this research is based on over 25 years working in the national arts sector and my experience as an advocate and policymaker in the area of multicultural film and arts practice. I was employed by the South Australian Media Resource Centre from 1990 to 1998 to increase the participation of multicultural practitioners and audiences, and then at the Australia Council from 1998 to 2011 to develop and implement AMA policy. I managed the cycles of the 2000 and 2006 AMA policies. My personal contacts in this space are wide-ranging, and I am encouraged by the genuine interest in this research shown by former colleagues and the many artists I encountered. I am in a unique position to articulate the context and content of the two AMA policy cycles but, rather than discuss this information from an autobiographical perspective, I chose to gather the reflections and experiences of those artists who remain active in the multicultural arts sector, and to aerate the reports and initiatives that appear to have lain dormant for the past several years.

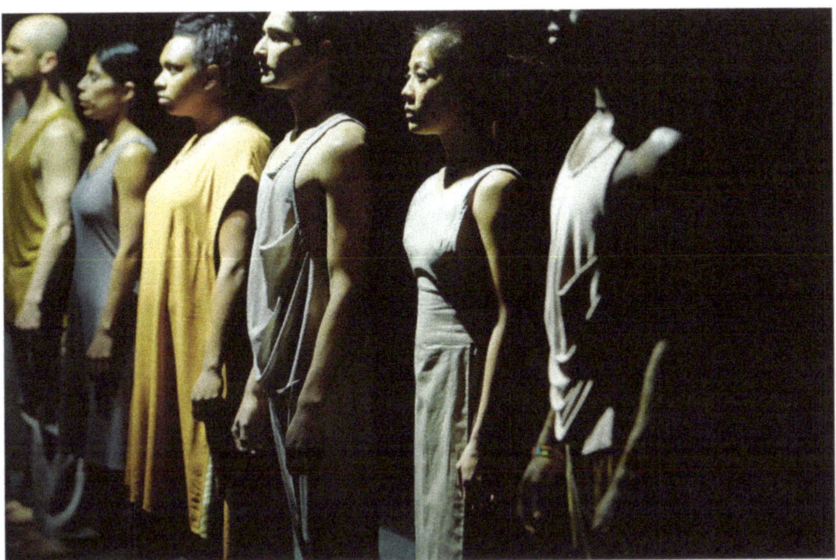

Image 1: Annalouise Paul, *Mother Tongue*, 2014
Photographer: Shane Rozario

My ease of access to, and communication with, the artists and cultural practitioners who provided the empirical data was possible due to my many years of working in the field—as a visual and media artist, curator and arts administrator, and, for over a decade, as a senior policy officer and researcher at the Australia Council. The interviewees were very forthcoming, reflecting the collegiate and decades-long relationships we had developed. Similarly, I was able to establish a quick rapport with the emerging artists I had not previously met by finding common ground based on the trusting relationships I had had with their mentors.

I count myself fortunate to have been able to work directly with four chairs of ACMAC and more than 50 artists who took on engaged governance roles as ACMAC members during my time with the Australia Council. These experiences are complemented by my understanding of the roles played by the consultants and commentators with whom I worked to develop and review the effectiveness of AMA. This knowledge puts me in an exceptional position to be able draw on the generosity of those contacts and to incorporate unique internal content to inform this research. The impetus for me to undertake this research, four years after having left that career, came from a curiosity about whether any of that work had been effective. What began as a curiosity was buoyed by the interest from the multicultural arts sector, especially my interviewees' repeated concerns about a lack of change and their view that it was important for this research to be done.

Overview

Chapter 1, 'Advancing Multicultural Arts: Policies, Problems and Practice', sets the social and cultural frame of multicultural arts, the case for addressing multiculturalism in the arts, and discusses how the UK, Canada and Australia have approached this policy area. The issues of creativity and the participation rates of NESB artists are discussed, including a detailed description of the range of art practices that have emerged as innovative responses to multicultural Australia.

Chapter 2, 'Leading for the Arts in a Multicultural Australia', explores a repertoire of leadership modes that have the potential to improve the situations of NESB artists and their multicultural arts practices. The themes of friction, trust and traction are expanded upon, followed by an analysis of the three domains of creative, institutional and organisational leadership.

In the third chapter, 'Shaping the Discourse of Arts in a Multicultural Australia', I analyse the issues around policy formation and present a brief history and context of AMA. The 2000 and 2006 AMA policies are reviewed, along with a close reading of the structural role of ACMAC. This chapter fills in the historical gaps in multicultural arts policy and finds that AMA 2006 appears to be the last AMA policy following the adoption of the Cultural Engagement Framework.

Chapter 4, 'Creative Leadership: The Agency of the NESB Artist', brings the research into the present and delves into the issues still being experienced by NESB artists. It explores the ways they articulate the need for trust and the role of network formation as a way to sustain and extend their practices. A case study of *Mother Tongue* by choreographer and dancer Annalouise Paul illustrates creative persistence and experimentation of intercultural performance (see Image 1).

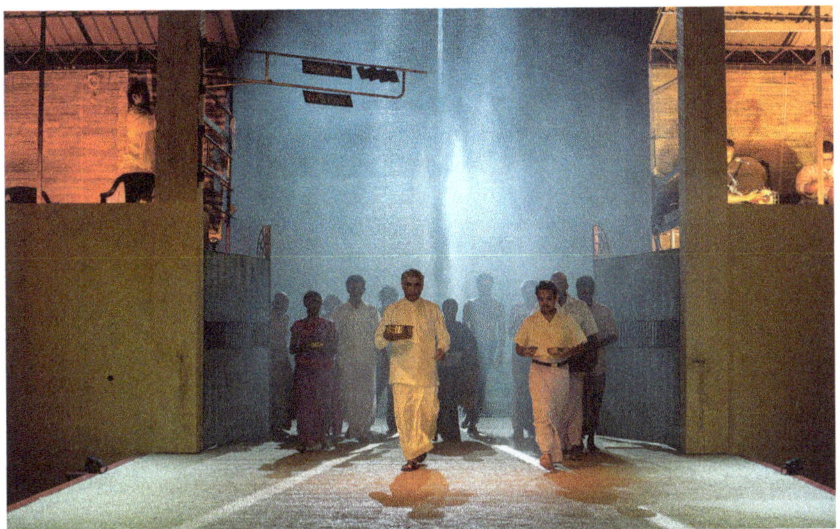

Image 2: *Counting and Cracking*, Belvoir Street Theatre, 2019
Photographer: © Brett Boardman

Chapter 5, 'Challenges of Institutional Leadership: Reluctance in the Australia Council', analyses some of the issues experienced by NESB artists who participate in governance roles at the Australia Council. The chapter examines the challenging demands of post-ACMAC peer roles, as well as the issues of grant allocations to CALD artists and organisations. In this chapter, the valuable role held by ACMAC of stimulating critical discourse about multicultural arts practices is reviewed, as are the failed attempts to establish a flagship company for the multicultural arts sector.

The sixth chapter, 'Organisational Leadership: Expanding the Multicultural Arts Milieu', highlights the ways in which two forms of creative and organisational leadership working in tandem have the capacity to generate longer-term traction for a supportive multicultural arts milieu. Three cases form the backbone of this chapter: Shakthidharan's epic award-winning play *Counting and Cracking* with Belvoir Street Theatre and Co-Curious (see Image 2); the multicultural arts touring work of kultour; and the shining example of the Lotus Playwriting Project (CAAP 2017), a partnership between CAAP and Playwriting Australia, which demonstrates that change can occur relatively quickly. The findings in this chapter include a 'road map' of stages to achieve positive change.

Both individuals and groups of artists contribute significantly to an Australian multicultural arts milieu. This in turn generates and creates the space and provenance for more art to be made and seen. This is how a genre like multicultural arts either maintains its autonomy or moves into the mainstream. A continuous history of production and presentation can shift the boundaries of, in this case, multicultural arts, to become the 'mainstream'. It could, but does not yet, follow that, because we are a multicultural society, the art that is produced here reflects our society. This book details several processes that can be scaled up or down and are found in the persistence of artists and arts organisations that focus on multicultural arts practices to improve the multicultural arts milieu.

1

Advancing Multicultural Arts: Policies, Problems and Practice

The global reality is one in which shifting identities, mass migration and refugee movements are the norm. Since World War II, about 7 million immigrants from over 150 countries have settled in Australia, resulting in a linguistic and cultural diversity that is among the highest in the developed world, and this population trend looks set to continue. There are over 300 languages spoken in Australia with more than one-fifth (21 per cent) of the population speaking a language other than English at home (ABS 2017). It is estimated that 32 per cent of Australians are now from non–Anglo Celtic backgrounds (Soutphommasane 2016).

Policies of multiculturalism were developed in response to rapid demographic changes in Australia's population and have been distinguished by three distinct approaches (Ho 2013, 31). The social justice approach focuses on the disadvantages experienced by migrants whose first language was not English; it saw, among other things, the establishment of migrant resource centres and the Special Broadcasting Service (SBS) as the multilingual broadcaster. The productive diversity approach promotes the value of a culturally diverse workforce, such as language skills, intercultural and cross-cultural communication competencies, access to international markets and business knowledge (Ho 2013, 36). Social cohesion promotes the concept of a 'mainstream'—an undefined concept of what it means to be Australian and to which migrants are supposed to aspire (Ho 2013, 38). A detailed account of the development of government policies of multiculturalism can be found in work by van Teeseling (2011).

The policies of multiculturalism underscore the tensions that are held in play between plurality and cohesion, the economic advantages afforded by migrants and the cultural aspects of citizenship. These issues regarding multicultural Australia remain topical and contested and, arguably, are among the most important issues to resolve in the context of global migrations. Australian Human Rights Commissioner Dr Tim Soutphommasane (2017) sees the arts as crucial to contributing to conversations about issues of identity and belonging:

> It goes to the mission of the arts when they flourish: to nurture creativity, to foster exchange, to encourage understanding and respect. For those of you working for diversity in the arts, this task has become more urgent than ever.

Australia's multicultural society carries with it the potential to create genuinely dynamic arts and cultural spaces in which artists may explore some of the consequences, and offer opportunities to increase understandings, of multiculturalism in action. This chapter presents an historical and sociological overview of multicultural Australia and the artistic expression that arises from this cultural diversity.

The diversity of Australia's population includes a wide range of artistic traditions. Yet, there is a disparity between the socio-demographic aspects of multicultural Australia and cultural and artistic participation. Despite decades of policy directed towards increasing cultural participation, the diversity of the Australian population is not reflected in the country's cultural production (Screen Australia 2016; Australia Council 2014a; Khan et al. 2017, 1). Consequently, there exists enormous potential for artistic gestures and symbols to be explored:

> A diversity of cultural expressions is intrinsic to social experience in all contemporary societies. Cultural difference is not something 'out there', outside of us, but part of who we are, irrespective of our cultural or ancestral background. Artistic work can express this intrinsic diversity by mobilising the unpredictable interfaces of intercultural exchange, which can be found everywhere. (Mar and Ang 2015, 8)

Artists thrive on working with unpredictability and many non–English speaking background (NESB) artists take up the potential offered through intercultural exchange as a point of departure in their creative process. The issue is whether these artists experience adequate support to be able take up the challenges and opportunities presented through a multicultural Australia. This chapter presents demographic data about, and some approaches to, the experiences of Australians living in a multicultural Australia, as well as several arts policy responses. A consideration of those of Arts Council England (ACE)—the organisational body on which the Australia Council for the Arts was modelled—provides an international perspective alongside those of the Canada Council for the Arts (CCA), whose history of colonisation and multiculturalism is similar to Australia's. Australia's national makeup includes six states and two territories, of which arts strategies from four states will briefly be touched upon. A discussion of creativity and types of multicultural arts practices brings the focus to artists.

Multiculturalism as a Social and Cultural Issue

Multicultural Australia

According to the 2016 Census, 49 per cent of Australians were either born overseas (first generation of migrants) or have either one or both parents born overseas (the second generation) (ABS 2017). The countries of origin of recent arrivals are changing. There has been a decline in migration from longstanding source countries such as the UK (3.9 per cent as a proportion of total population). In 2017, 2.2 per cent of the Australian population was born in China and 1.9 per cent was born in India (ABS 2017).

The degree of demographic diversity varies significantly across Australian locations. The five mainland state capitals' average populations include 34 per cent of Australians born overseas, as compared to 12 per cent in rural areas. At the suburban level, the data are more dramatic: 88 per cent were born overseas in Haymarket at the southern end of the Sydney central business district in NSW, with the majority born in China, Indonesia and Thailand. In Harris Farm near Parramatta, NSW, 77 per cent were born overseas, mainly (46 per cent) in India. In Clayton, an outer suburb of Melbourne, Victoria, 77 per cent were born overseas and are mainly students from China, India and Malaysia (ABS 2013). Australians' social and cultural experiences of multiculturalism through diversity and migration, therefore, are varied and characterised by dynamic change.

Language and national origin form part of the portrait of Australia's demographic diversity. The dynamics of Australian society are made up of multiple intersecting identities that incorporate any combination of race, ethnicity, class and geographic demography. Shifting enthusiasms and increasing scepticism about the value and success of multiculturalism make negotiations of identity particularly complex and ambiguous for NESB artists. Part of this ambivalence is because Australia is no longer made up of discrete ethnic groups that can be readily identified and essentialised and thus more easily represented (Ang 2011, 24; Vertovec 2010, 94).

The evolution of Australia's diverse makeup is caused by widescale immigration, which is now in greater numbers than following World War II. This leads to what Vertovec (2010, 94) calls 'super-diversity', whereby migrants and their families possess a 'plurality of affiliations'. Such 'post-multicultural' (Vertovec 2010, 94) discourse suggests that ethnicity is no longer the single most important marker of identity. Noble (2009, 45) argues that Australia is 'hyper-diverse', characterised by the development of 'poly-ethnic neighbourhoods', which result in relations and interactions that produce 'a diversification of this diversity'. The ways in which Australians work at engaging with this level of diversity in their daily lives produce different types of experiences of cultural diversity— which everyone experiences and produces differently. Noble (2009, 51) makes the point that this is work: unpaid work that requires 'sustained practices of accommodation and negotiation' to produce conviviality. Art is also work, and is similarly rarely recognised as such (Gerber 2017). In particular, the role of the artist in delivering different ways to approach cultural difference carries those practices of accommodation and negotiation to a wider sphere.

Research into Australian responses to multiculturalism and cultural diversity over the past decade affirm support for migration into Australia. A study undertaken in 2002 found that only about 10 per cent of Australians had a negative view of multiculturalism and cultural diversity (Ang et al. 2002, 5). These findings are challenged by more recent data in the Scanlon Foundation's social cohesion report, completed in 2017. Over the course of the 10-year project, Australians expressed their overwhelming acceptance of multiculturalism, although there has been a recent decline. In 2017, 75 per cent of Australians either agreed or strongly agreed that multiculturalism had been good for Australia, whereas that agreement had previously been consistent across the 83–86 per cent range (Markus 2017, 1). This drop was buffered by the positive response from 94 per cent of younger Australians aged between 18 and 24 (Markus 2017, 72). The decline, however, is reinforced by the doubled increase of those who 'reported experience of discrimination "because of your skin colour, ethnic origin or religion"' from 9 per cent in 2007 to 20 per cent in 2017 (Markus 2017, 3). These figures suggest a chafing between the experiences of the population and the ability to accommodate changes in society. Markus (2017, 3) posits that this indicates that, in 2017, Australia was 'less resilient than the Australia of 10 years earlier, less able to deal with economic and other crises that may eventuate in coming years'.

Markus's findings improve upon, but are not dissimilar to, those generated by SBS at the beginning of the century. In 2001 SBS commissioned research to assist them in formulating their future directions. This found that:

> The overall picture is one of a fluid, plural and complex society, with a majority of the population positively accepting of the cultural diversity that is an increasingly routine part of Australian life, although a third is still uncertain or ambivalent about cultural diversity. (Ang et al. 2002, 4)

Follow-up research in 2006 identified 'practical tolerance' as the main approach adopted by Australians to manage their everyday experience of cultural differences (Ang et al. 2006, 37). This research included a focus on intergenerational responses to multiculturalism and found that younger Australians of culturally diverse backgrounds do not feel completely accepted by mainstream society; and yet, paradoxically, what the researchers describe as 'interactive diversity' is becoming an everyday experience:

> Many of these Australians have experienced or observed instances of prejudice, discrimination and intolerance first hand. However … interactive cultural diversity is becoming increasingly mainstream. Younger Australians of culturally diverse backgrounds are more comfortable interacting with others of different cultural backgrounds and feel that multiculturalism in Australia has progressed a lot in the past 30 years. (Ang et al. 2006, 9)

Many of the younger people interviewed for the SBS study tacitly accepted the Anglo-Australian core as the cultural norm. They expressed concern about separated and 'siloed' ethnic cultural groups, which was said to reflect a desire for 'intercultural connection' (Ang et al. 2006, 19). This acceptance was characterised as one in which Australians 'live and breathe' cultural diversity through their everyday lives. The ambivalence expressed by a significant minority is consistent with the 2017 Scanlon Foundation findings. Both sets of research uncovered concerns about living in a multicultural Australia. However, the Scanlon Foundation noted a starker contrast between the experiences of migrants and the general population, and identified 'trust' as one of the measures of inclusion expressed as a sense of belonging. The foundation's 2015 survey found that, among those who had arrived in Australia since 2001, indications of trust in others was 37 per cent, compared with 50 per cent at the national level (Markus 2016, 46). When the findings of both reports are taken together, it can be established that an increase in intercultural connectedness can generate a sense of belonging and inclusion. Processes that enable intercultural connectedness include those of multicultural arts practices.

Everyday Multiculturalism, Conviviality and Interculturality

Terms such as 'post-multicultural' and 'cosmopolitanism' are relevant to the multiple roles of the artist, as they provide different frames for understanding the daily experiences of living in a multicultural society (Noble 2011, 2009; Papastergiadis 2013b, 2013c). Rather than viewing cosmopolitanism (and other seemingly outmoded phases such as assimilation and cohesion) as a linear historical process, it can be experienced on any given day—at the corner shop, on the train, in the park, at the cinema and, occasionally, in the art gallery. However, the policy version of multiculturalism often bears little relationship to everyday experiences because of the increasing versions of difference that no longer conform to essential views of ethnicity:

> This differentiation of difference makes the reified categories of ethnicity celebrated by multicultural policies increasingly unviable and, because of this, often results in social anxieties because this differentiation challenges how we manage differences. (Noble 2011, 830)

Those everyday experiences can be described as cosmopolitanism. Cosmopolitanism comes from the original Greek meaning 'citizen of the cosmos' and has been refined to include the manner in which the citizen engages in the world as well as a moral imperative to do so:

> Cosmopolitanism can be defined as a global politics that, firstly, projects a sociality of common political engagement among all human beings across the globe, and, secondly, suggests that this sociality should be either ethically or organisationally privileged over other forms of sociality. (James 2014, x)

Regardless of its scope (whether local or global), this ability to move between cultures is an acquired skill based on experience and proximity to others and, as such, is one of the competencies to help navigate difference:

> The internationalist outlook of cosmopolitan multiculturalism enhances people's resilience in such a world. A cosmopolitan orientation to life entails openness towards different cultures, peoples and a general willingness to engage with 'the other'. (Ang, Hawkins and Dabboussy 2008, 21)

Many NESB artists are particularly well placed to adopt such an outlook and competency.

The ability to engage is receiving research attention, and is providing an alternative to the dystopic narratives around the 'failure' of multiculturalism generally presented in academic research (Wise and Velayutham 2013). This alternative comes from the observations that an 'ease' in everyday relations between ethnic and mainstream groups, or conviviality, is 'the processes of cohabitation and interaction that have made multiculture an ordinary feature of urban life in Britain' (Gilroy, quoted in Wise and Velayutham 2013, 407). This critiques 'fixed' notions of difference based on race and identity to go beyond the colonial position and 'carnivale multiculturalism'—the occasional celebratory showcase of difference. Wise and Velayutham suggest that Gilroy offers a resilient approach to living multiculturally because he highlights the satisfaction generated by small daily events that come from the 'creative, intuitive capacity among ordinary people who manage tensions' (Gilroy quoted in Wise and Velayutham, 2013, 407). This could also be described as a form of social resilience that exceeds the incapacity of those who simply tolerate, because the people Gilroy observes show the capacity to interact with each other.

In *Friction*, Tsing (2005) describes the dynamic small gestures that groups and individuals use to disrupt the large-scale demise of the planet. In addressing cosmopolitanism and complexity, she reflects that: 'The challenge of cultural analysis is to address both the spreading interconnections and locatedness of culture' (122). The relevance of this challenge for arts practitioners can be seen both as a technique to make use of connections and as an inspirational form for artists navigating their multicultural arts practices.

Noble (2011, 827) attributes navigational agency to members of Australia's multicultural society because he sees that cultural difference is not juxtaposed, as in the 'mosaic' metaphor for multiculturalism, but is 'negotiated'. Social and cultural possibilities are presented as a dynamic relationship of 'interactive interculturality' (Ang et al. 2006, 23) that is more than an 'awareness' of difference, and is 'seen in the multiple forms of adaptation and mixing that mark the process of settlement, intermarriage, intergenerational change and the plural social contexts in which difference is negotiated' (Noble 2011, 827).

The issue of competence, however, sits at the centre of a successful engagement with such opportunities. Those with cosmopolitan awareness display their credentials by showing up in the first place, and by these appearances suggest that they have already developed a level of confidence to navigate and, if necessary, negotiate culturally complex events that require diverse 'transactional competencies' (Noble 2011, 838). Those who are not interested in acquiring the competency to act 'in-between' or do not feel confident in navigating cross-cultural events may choose not to participate. Herewith lies the 'friction' that is at the heart of the multicultural reality: the range of differences include different attitudes to engaging with difference. Art can be one of the vehicles to assist in exposure to difference and may in turn open up spaces for dialogue between differences.

The Case for Addressing the Cultural Issue of Difference in the Arts

Young adults of migrant parents have described themselves as having 'hybrid' cosmopolitan identities but, in a 2011 study, they did not tend to describe themselves as Australian (Collins 2013, 144). Nor did they recognise themselves as being visibly represented as Australians. Instead, they equated their ethnicity with social and cultural credentials attained through their diasporic families and capacity to engage through the internet and social media. Five years on, similar statements were expressed by the young artists interviewed for this book. The right to be represented as belonging to the nation and as national subjects has been one of the core areas of friction in the policy development of multiculturalism. As Cope and Kalantzis (1997, 264) observed 20 years ago:

> Those custodians of the symbolic nationhood, the media, the arts and education, have been slowest and the most combative when faced with the need to modify norms, canons or representational imagery. This is now a critical challenge. For too long those interested in change have drawn a dichotomy between the economic-political and the symbolic. It is time to bring them together.

To bring the economic-political and symbolic together remains a critical challenge in Australia. Symbols are at the heart of cultural production and must be handled with care because of their potential power. Whose symbols and how new ones emerge are core issues that face artists, including those artists concerned with ethnic minority identities.

Stuart Hall (1997, 4) identifies the cultural role of the symbolic as crucial, both because it goes to the heart of social life, and because culture 'permeates all of society'. He explains that language, in the broad sense of the term (encompassing images, objects, gestures, texts, data and materials, etc.), constructs and transmits meaning. For Hall (1997, 4), language is the 'privileged' medium for the construction of meaning across 'all facets of the cultural circuit—in the construction of identity and the marking of difference, in production and consumption, as well as in the regulation of social conduct'.

The question of how to produce cultural representation varies according to context. *The SBS Story* by Ang, Hawkins and Dabboussy (2008) offers an in-depth description and analysis of the intricate politics and complexities of inclusion within Australian cultural production. It documents how Australia's national multicultural radio and television broadcaster, SBS, negotiates and presents Australia's multicultural society. Examining the challenges of cultural diversity in which multiple aspects of identity are clearly articulated, it argues that:

> For many people, ethnicity is not the all-important determinant
> of their sense of self. Arguably the capacity for individuals to
> explore their own place in society, irrespective of their cultural
> background, is one of the hallmarks of a successful multicultural
> society. (Ang, Hawkins and Dabboussy 2008, 46)

The authors, quoting former SBS Managing Director Malcolm Long's claim that, 'in the world that is coming, if you can't navigate difference, you've had it', present a succinct rationale for the benefits of cultural inclusion. They distinguish three phases in SBS's multicultural representation: ethno-multiculturalism, cosmopolitan multiculturalism and popular multiculturalism (Ang, Hawkins and Dabboussy 2008, 22). From the late 1990s, 'popular multiculturalism' positioned multiculturalism as the cultural norm, claiming it as the mainstream rather than the marginal (20). The concept of popular multiculturalism is of key relevance to this research and appears to have been a premature cultural claim given the continued low levels of participation in the arts by culturally diverse Australians.

Francois Matarasso (2010), a UK-based cultural researcher, speaks of shaping cultural identity—and having it be recognised by others—as being:

> Central to human dignity and liberty. If people can't represent
> themselves culturally, how can they do so politically? If people are
> only imagined and portrayed by others, how can they be equal,
> autonomous and active members of society?

Matarasso (2010) suggests that a solution can be found in the arts because 'art is a great tool for intervening in culture'. There is also heightened interest and research in how the role of art leads to increased sociality. One recent study observed (in this case via music) the transformation of 'personal subjective experiences into collective collaboration' (Sorsa et al. 2017, 1). Similarly, an affirmative link between a sense of belonging and culturally diverse artistic expression is inferred in research into cultural citizenship (Khan et al. 2017, 1).

According to the Australia Council, Australian audiences wish to see a fuller artistic expression of the country's cultural diversity. Australian audiences want cultural diversity in what they see, listen to and read, and less than two-thirds of people think the arts 'reflect the diversity of Australian cultures' (Australia Council 2014a). In 2016 Australia Council data analysed by market research company Morris Hargreaves Macintyre

(2013) indicated that 75 per cent now held this view (Australia Council 2017e, 12). Further, Australia Council data from 2017 suggest that 64 per cent of respondents think the arts have a big or very big impact on our understanding of other people and cultures (Australia Council 2017c). These varied results highlight the mercurial nature of cultural statistics, yet also bring to the fore the desire for cultural production that is relevant to Australian society. The data also raise questions about the effectiveness of the policies developed to address the imbalance of NESB artists' production, dissemination and audience development.

United Kingdom and Canada: Issues and Responses to Cultural Diversity in the Arts

The development of arts policy responses to cultural diversity takes place internationally. The UK, for example, regularly revises its equity legislation through its *Equality Act 2010*, in part because of its European Union commitments. The similarities between Australian and Canadian histories of indigeneity, colonialism and migration, which have resulted in highly culturally diverse populations, makes a comparison of arts policies in the two countries prudent.

Arts Council England

Established in 1946, ACE is an agency of the Department for Culture, Media and Sport (DCMS) and has had equity policies, including for Black, Asian and minority ethnic artists (BAME), in place since the 1970s (ACE 2011, 5). The Australia Council for the Arts is modelled on ACE. As part of a regular review of ACE, DCMS commissioned former Edinburgh festival director Brian McMaster to report on the most effective use of public funds towards the arts. He identified:

> The profound value of arts and culture. Just as the new society we live in has immense potential for the creation of art, so art has never before been so needed to understand the deep complexities of Britain today. (McMaster 2008, 5)

The need for art to contribute to understanding society is often cited as a beginning point for such reports; however, the McMaster report reinforces this point by articulating diversity as one of eight key areas of recommendations. McMaster (2008, 9) 'refutes' the association of excellence in the arts with exclusivity, heritage and elitism, instead viewing it as a process that 'takes and combines complex meanings, gives us new insights and new understandings of the world around us and is relevant to every single one of us'.

McMaster (2008, 11) perceives that, to be relevant, a commitment to diversity 'must run through' the concepts of excellence, innovation risk-taking and participation:

> The diverse nature of 21st century Britain is the perfect catalyst for ever greater innovation in culture and I would like to see diversity put at the heart of everything cultural. We live in one of the most diverse societies the world has ever seen, yet this is not reflected in the culture we produce, or in who is producing it. Out of this society, the greatest culture could grow. Culture can only be excellent when it is relevant, and thus nothing can be excellent without reflecting the society which produces and experiences it.

These statements are akin to Australian discourse regarding the yet to be realised potential that cultural diversity offers to a vibrant culture. The claim to inspire change occurs by placing diversity as a central tenet of art and cultural production.

Taking up the process to amplify issues of diversity, in 2009 ACE commissioned *Third Text* to heighten the debate 'about diversity and the arts to a new and different level' (ACE 2011, 4). *Third Text* is a longstanding journal dedicated to issues of the arts and diversity edited by Rasheed Araeen. There are two other longstanding UK 'flagship' companies: Rich Mix (Mirza 2009), which is dedicated to diversity in performing arts; and iniva (Institute for International Visual Art), which is dedicated to diversity programming and discourse in the visual arts. These two companies lead the production and critique of work by BAME artists. The resulting report, *Beyond Cultural Diversity: The Case for Creativity*, included claims from UK-based critical thinkers and writers that Britain's state-sponsored policy of cultural diversity had failed (Appignanesi 2010, 5): 'Some of us in Britain are being cast as outsiders who require a domestically engineered foreign policy'. The report called for a 'culturally integrated future' that surpassed cultural diversity, included government statements on leadership within the frame of the arts, and promoted an 'arts and artists-led approach to diversity and equality' (ACE 2011, 16).

Arts professionals were asked to own and creatively adapt ACE policies on diversity and equality and to 'probe (and) innovate creative approaches and solutions' (ACE 2011, 16).

Diversity is seen as a core driver of creativity by ACE, and no longer as a deficit burden, drawing from business models that connect the 'characteristics of resilient organisations and the embracing of creative diversity' (Nwachukwu and Robinson 2011, 5). This link to resilience echoes the concerns of the 2017 Scanlon Foundation report discussed earlier. *The Creative Case for Diversity* (hereafter *Creative Case*), launched in 2011, is ACE's diversity policy based on equality, recognition and a new vision. The new vision moves from a deficit model to one that articulates 'an approach that encompasses the ways in which diversity has been and remains an intrinsic and dynamic part of the creative process' (ACE 2011, 4).

ACE's approach affects all subsidised sectors of the arts and, in particular, supports those who excel at incorporating diverse influences and practices relevant to British populations. Activities across six themes identify whether subsidised national portfolio organisations (NPOs) are actively pursuing the *Creative Case*. The themes relate to artistic programs, talent development, barriers to artistic involvement, resourcing and monitoring, self-evaluation and sector leadership. ACE (n.d.-a) positions diversity at the centre of the *Creative Case* as a sustainable strategy for the arts, because its view is that diversity is able to:

> Address other challenges and opportunities in audience development, public engagement, workforce and leadership. Our funded organisations are expected to show how they contribute to the Creative Case for Diversity through the work they produce and present.

This expectation follows through in ACE's funding decisions for 2018–22. The Bush Theatre, based in the culturally diverse London suburb of Shephard's Bush and known for its creative direction and BAME development under Madani Younis, received a 20 per cent increase, while Hampstead Theatre, which has not produced work across the equity areas, had a 14 per cent decrease in funding. This is seen to reflect:

> That in the 21st century who you choose to work with, and how you work with them, is part and parcel of artistic policy. Arts organisations can't continue to work on outdated models and expect to secure funding. (Gardner 2017)

Part of ACE's 'new vision' is to support the companies whose traction for diversity is evident. ACE also has clear equity objectives for BAME, disability, gender and sexual orientation across artistic outcomes, workforce and governance participation (ACE 2016, 6). The *Creative Case* recognises diversity as the central tenet for innovation to which UK£11 million strategic funds have been allocated—approximately 10 per cent of the country's annual expenditure (ACE 2016, 6; n.d.-b).

The *Creative Case* sits inside the British Government's Equity Policy, whereby each department must deliver equitable inclusion and demonstrate accountability across a range of measures, including equity in employment and governance roles. To this end, ACE publishes the employment data generated by arts organisations. They report that BAME employment in the arts is now at 17 per cent compared to an average of 15 per cent in broader employment contexts (ACE 2016, 7). The implication that, since 2011, BAME artists and organisations have been leading in terms of the cultural diversity of the workforce lends credibility to ACE's claim as to the effectiveness of an arts-centred approach to diversity.

Another ACE strategy allocated UK£5.3 million to 'elevate' (ACE's words) the many small organisations that have always had diversity as their creative focus by building their capacity to successfully apply for more substantial funds in the future, thereby increasing the diversity of the organisations supported through NPO funds (ACE n.d.-c). In this manner, *Creative Case for Diversity* addresses the structural barriers faced by artist-run small companies that create important access spaces that enable diverse participation.

Arts sector debate is enabled in various ways: for example, through live interactive webcasts of conferences—such as Creative Case: Leading Diverse Futures, which included presentations from the chair of ACE, artists, bureaucrats and administrators (ACE 2018); and through Arts Professional, an online arts news and information resource, which featured a series of monthly debates on diversity for organisations and practitioners in 2017 (Richens 2017). In addition, ACE develops resources to inform companies about how they can increase diversity in their sphere of the arts: tool kits for governance (e.g. how to produce an 'Equity Plan'), tool kits for increasing diversity in creative projects (e.g. how to attract talent and leaders from diverse backgrounds) and equity data on diversity employment in each funded company (ACE 2016, 2018). The striking element about ACE's approach, particularly over the past decade, is that

Creative Case systematically addresses structural barriers to diversity by tying funding agreements to outcomes that increase diverse participation, creative content, employment and governance.

Canada Council for the Arts

The CCA was established in 1957 'to foster and promote the study and enjoyment of, and the production of works in, the arts'. Interestingly, and creatively, the minister responsible for the arts is also responsible for Canadian heritage and multiculturalism, which places art within a strong cultural environment (CCA 2018). This sends a different signal of importance to that of Australia, where the federal arts portfolio is usually associated with communication or entertainment activities. Another distinction is that the CCA is responsible for the Canadian Commission for UNESCO. The commission's aims are to encourage a Canadian society in which knowledge and learning is shared, locally and globally, so as to 'build peaceful, equitable and sustainable futures' (CCA 2018). As in Australia, the CCA 'firmly believes' in the effectiveness of peer assessment to allocate funds and works cooperatively across various governing jurisdictions. The four commitments of the CCA are to increase support to artists, amplify Canadian art through digital means, renew the relationship between indigenous artists and audiences, and raise the international profile of Canadian artists (CCA 2018).

The following brief analysis is drawn from the CCA's policy statements and published critiques, which suggest that similar frissons between artists and the workings of the council occur in Canada and Australia. The 2017 CCA *Equity Policy* specifies an understanding of, and approach to, the term 'cultural equity'. The preamble positions the CCA's approach squarely within UNESCO's (2001) sustainability agenda and rights-based diversity of cultural expressions:

> Cultural diversity is not only a necessary element in the development of the arts, but also an essential factor in developing sustainable human societies. This diversity needs to be reflected in the arts to counter homogenization of artistic expressions and inequitable distribution of resources, so the next generation of citizens can fully achieve their artistic potential and exercise their cultural rights. (CCA 2017, 9)

Like the Australia Council, the CCA has responded to ongoing concerns of equal representation. Such pressures have come from within the institution as well as advocacy by First Nations artists and artists of colour (Fatona 2011, 108). Yet, it was government intervention that generated deeper awareness:

> The practices of government, including multiculturalism and its policies, found their way into the Council, highlighting the ways in which the state and the social and political are intertwined and are difficult to disentangle. (Fatona 2011, 116)

It was not until the early 1990s that the need for a policy was instituted at the CCA and, again, as with the Australia Council, the work had been established mainly through the 'community arts' funding section. In the case of the CCA, this was known as the 'Explorations Program', which worked with ethnic and minority cultures within the arts:

> We were doing what they called multicultural work at the time in the Explorations Program recalls [former CCA staff member] Creighton-Kelly … 'In a sense, the genesis of work directly concerned with cultural diversity occurred in the Explorations Program'. (Fatona 2011, 154)

The policy recognises that marginalised cultures, because of 'cultural differences, systemic barriers and uneven resources', deserve 'financial, infrastructural and public policy support *comparable to the dominant culture of a society*' (CCA 2017, 9, emphasis added). The idea of comparable investment is bold, yet raises a number of issues and challenges, such as defining the scope of 'comparable', understanding the means to achieve 'comparable' and resourcing a proportionate level of investment.

The most obvious difference between Australia and Canada is the lived reality of bilingualism; however, bilingualism results in similar issues as multilingualism, as 'Francophone and Anglophone cultures assume dominance over other cultures' (Fatona 2011, 108). The resonance of multilingual streetscapes also hovers across both countries.

As regards policy, the CCA adopts the umbrella term of 'equity-seeking groups' to define who may benefit from, and seek, 'specific measures to improve access to programs and funding support' (CCA 2017, 7). The term is striking in its apparent simplicity, yet it holds the suggestion of a lack and the desire to participate in the 'mainstream', a quasi-condition that could concern some artists who wish to remain marginal. The CCA names the groups it includes as 'equity-seeking' as 'visible minorities', and uses the term 'culturally diverse' to 'respectfully identify racialized groups. These are Canadians of African, Asian, Latin American, Middle Eastern and mixed racial heritages' (CCA 2017, 7).

As in Australia, indigenous artists are considered separately and also have diverse heritages, being First Nations, Inuit and Métis peoples (CCA 2017, 8). There are specifically articulated policy statements regarding who the groups are and why they are supported for equity considerations. Notably, unlike the Australia Council, the CCA allocates resources to implement strategic initiatives dedicated to realising equity policy intentions (CCA 2017, 14).

Committees continue to form the structure for monitoring, reporting and strategic directions. In the 1990s, not dissimilar to the Australia Council Multicultural Advisory Committee (ACMAC), a Racial Equity Committee that included 'racialized artists' assisted a consultant to undertake policy development. A 'First Peoples Advisory Committee' was subsequently formed in recognition that their similar issues 'diverged because of historical differences in the groups' relationship to the Canadian nation-state'. Fatona (2011, 110, 113) notes that addressing 'equity, access and new practices' has been seen as an urgent requirement. By addressing these needs together, the potential for the stigma of equity and access may in some way be ameliorated when associated with 'new practices' of digital arts.

In 2019 the CCA Board was made up of artists, arts company heads, mining and financial industry members, and a First Nations filmmaker (CCA n.d.). The CCA's investment in arts grants is aligned to their strategic priorities. The external jurors or grant assessors are reminded of these at the beginning of the process:

> They give you a list of the council's priorities. I think there were about five priorities last time I was there. And they're very typical ones; they're like we should take into consideration cultural diversity, for example. (D'Andrea 2017, 251)

Attention to cultural diversity appears to have gained traction. The CCA's 2019 annual report notes that the council's support for indigenous artists, groups and organisations increased by 35 per cent; for culturally diverse and 'official language minority communities' by 24 per cent; and for deaf and disabled artists by 48 per cent (CCA 2019, 16). In 2018–19, the CCA allocated CA$242.7 million, of which CA$49.2 million went to individual artists; of that, a very encouraging 842 grants were awarded to 'culturally diverse artists', totalling more than CA$25 million (CCA 2019, 24).

ACE, the CCA and the Australia Council all claim that demographic diversity is the defining element of their identities, and that arts and culture benefit from this diversity in terms of creative expression and innovation. They each face challenges to fully realise these creative expressions in an equitable way, as do artists in these countries who strive against the wheels of a Western canon. The CCA's investment in culturally diverse artists is 'encouraging' to use their term. My focus on the Australian context gives pause to reflect on the benefits yet to be garnered from a shared international discourse on these issues.

Australian Cultural Policy

Australian National Cultural Policy

The policy to tie Australian funding to particular outcomes is one that wanes far more than it waxes in the arts. Government support for the arts has been slow and limited. Committees, such as the Commonwealth Literary Fund (1908) were established in Australia at the time of Federation or soon after, but it would take 65 years before a government agency was established. The Australian Council for the Arts, based on the British and Canadian model of 'arm's length' or distance from government interference, was established in 1973 by Prime Minister Gough Whitlam, who noted the lack of an Australian cultural policy, which would take a further 20 years to be tabled (Gardiner-Garden 1994). The Australia Council has, from 1975 onwards, had a history of awkward relationships with governments and oppositions alike, experiencing administrative and funding shifts on a regular basis. Even the almost sacred tenant of 'arm's length' decision-making has been critiqued for neither adequately 'insulating' the Australia Council from political demands, nor providing a valuable firm presence in Cabinet (Macdonnell 1992). The 1988 Coalition shadow minister Chris Puplick saw it as an 'excuse for Ministers to avoid their responsibilities to define and promote a national arts policy' (Gardiner-Garden 1994, 35).

There have been two, albeit short-lived, federal cultural and arts policy statements, both of which established connections between cultural diversity and creative expression: *Creative Nation* in 1994 and *Creative Australia* in 2013. As the federal arts agency, the Australia Council developed specific multicultural arts policies that built on, and reshaped, the 1970s era of ethnic arts that 'remained trapped within the rhetoric of welfare' (Hawkins 1993, 120). The Australia Council's policy statements on Arts in a Multicultural Australia (AMA) in 1993, 1996, 2000 and 2006 stand out as periods of policy attentiveness and resourced activity.

Creative Nation (Department of Communications and the Arts 1994), launched by the Keating Labor Government in 1994, promoted a broad approach to culture that included areas such as film, media, libraries and heritage. Framed by this creative pluralism, it is important to note this document's direct reference to Indigenous and migrant cultures as central in shaping Australia's domestic and exported identity. But, as Stevenson (2000) notes, the arts agenda continued to inadequately deal with the creative priorities of ethnic minorities. *Creative Australia*, launched almost 20 years later (Parliament of Australia 2013), made similar connections, but compounded the sense that political leaders are ambivalent about multicultural arts practices. Khan, Wyatt and Yue (2014, 1) commented that:

> *Creative Australia* contains very limited references to multicultural arts, and outlines no policies explicitly directed at expanding the participation of migrant or ethnic communities in the nation's arts and cultural sectors. Instead, cultural difference in the arts is referenced obliquely within a broader category of 'diversity'.

Developed out of the national consultation process of the 2020 Summit, *Creative Australia* generated high expectations in the arts sector for clear direction and leadership. The 101 members of the 'Towards a Creative Australia' reference group included a handful of NESB artists and arts workers; however, it is not clear how influential the group was in formulating the five main goals of the final policy document. These goals included recognising Aboriginal and Torres Strait Islander culture, supporting excellence and innovation, and expanding capacity in 'all aspects of national life'. The second goal was expressed in the least active language: to 'reflect' the diversity of Australian citizens, including 'cultural background, location and social circumstance' (Parliament of

Australia 2013). According to Khan et al. (2013, 28), the *Creative Australia* policy dissipated multicultural objectives 'via the language of diversity, into a range of economic, social and cultural governmental agendas'.

Ambiguity about who or what was meant by 'diversity' steered the focus away from identifying specific groups. This had the effect of confusing arts organisations as to where their 'inclusion' agenda, if they had one, could be directed:

> Drawing multicultural policy back into an instrumentalist, welfarist agenda that is also targeted at 'community' has the effect of decentring it from narratives of the nation state. This displacement means that the language of 'multiculturalism' no longer carries the same symbolic status it did in *Creative Nation*, where it was explicitly incorporated into a vision of Australian society. (Khan et al. 2013, 29)

The *Creative Australia* policy disappeared with the change of government following the September 2013 federal election. Australia's cultural policy was in limbo, in effect leaving the 2006 AMA statement as the policy on multicultural arts under the umbrella of the Australia Council's strategic plan of May 2014. The unexpected and fractious budget reallocation to the Arts Ministry announced in May 2015 caused a significant rupture between the major performing arts (MPA) companies quarantined from cuts to the Australia Council budget, and increased competition between artists, especially smaller and medium-sized organisations. The Turnbull government (from September 2015) continued the call for 'excellence' as the fundament for the arts, and stipulated a quarantine from funding cuts to MPA companies. This being the only word from the current government on funding to the arts, by default, it must be read as the Coalition's current cultural policy.

State Cultural Policy Statements

The national context provides additional layers of policy. Australian state and territory governments enact their own arts and cultural policies that also interact with their local government areas and the federal government's arts agency. The strategic directions of four state arts departments provide insight into the positioning of the arts in a multicultural context. Moving from west to east, the Department of Culture and the Arts (DCA) in

Western Australia released its *Strategic Directions 2016–2031* in 2016. This document views multiculturalism in WA as 'an obvious asset' in their challenge to 'attract and retain' artists:

> The role of our State and community collections in reflecting our identity, culture and environment will become increasingly important for full citizen engagement to contribute to social cohesion, authentic Western Australian branding and meaningful storytelling around a shared identity. How we include our most creative people into our civic decisions will be one of the most important challenges in reaching 2031. (DCA 2016, 16)

Notwithstanding this compelling role, the action to 'better [reflect] our multicultural population in our artistic and cultural output' (DCA 2016, 32) sits as one among 30 actions despite it being one of their most important issues.

South Australia is the next state moving eastwards and their *Arts and Culture Plan South Australia 2019–2024* was launched in 2019. It refers to 'new communities of people from a range of cultural backgrounds, including growing international student communities, [that] represent opportunities for diverse forms of cultural engagement and dialogue across all ages' (Department of the Premier and Cabinet 2019, 11). One of the plan's four values is: 'Embracing diversity—promoting inclusion and encouraging new voices and approaches across all demographics' (6). The intention of this value, without being specified as such, must be to attach to each of the six goals that, aside from a focus on Aboriginal and Torres Islander arts, do not detail multicultural engagement.

Creative Victoria's *Creative Industries Strategy 2016–2020* provides specific detail around how it will continue to improve its 'Access and Diversity' goal. This goal faces the challenge that there is 'still work to be done to ensure that diversity in our cultural products and experiences reflects the diversity of our population' (Creative Victoria 2016, xx). To address these challenges, Creative Victoria flags its serious intentions by dedicating funds and articulating strategies. AU$32.15 million was allocated over four years to 'improve access to, and participation in, cultural activities', which includes audience engagement as well as employment in the arts (27). This strategy extends to awareness training in the creative sectors that receive government funds. In conjunction with peak organisations including Arts Access Victoria, Aboriginal Victoria and the Office of Multicultural Affairs and Citizenship, the expectation is that funded creative organisations will develop 'appropriate access, diversity and inclusion plans as well as the requisite training to improve workforce diversity and engender greater diversity in programming and participation' (28).

The most eastern and populous state is New South Wales. Its state arts department, Create NSW, released its 10 year *Arts and Cultural Policy Framework* in 2015 and, similar to the Australia Council's 2000 and 2006 AMA policies, it defines multicultural NSW as a strength of its innovation goal: 'New pathways and opportunities will draw upon NSW's great strength—our cultural and linguistic diversity' (Create NSW 2015, 10). Create NSW also articulates the need for leadership for institutional and organisational governance, cultural programming and employment:

> The State Cultural Institutions will also work to reflect the diversity of NSW's population in all aspects of their organisations, including more culturally relevant programming. Arts NSW will work with funded organisations to promote a workforce that reflects the diversity of NSW's population. (Create NSW 2015, 36)

The NSW framework, as with other states, includes case studies of creative projects. In the case of NSW, the artworks provide dynamic insight into the creative work that stems from the state's multicultural artists.

A consistent theme surfaces across these four states about the relevance and importance of demographic diversity to a creative future. However, Victoria is the only state from this brief analysis to attach financial investment to realise an increase in participation.

The Role of the Australia Council: Multicultural Arts Policy

The Australia Council began taking an interest in the structural inclusion of ethnic groups in the mid-1970s, eventually leading to the establishment of ACMAC (Blonski 1992, 10; 1994, 202–03). The first meeting of the Australia Council's Migrant Committee in 1975 considered two models for the inclusion of 'migrant artists' into the remit of the Australia Council. The Aboriginal Arts Board's 'parallel' model or a distributed model in which all boards took on responsibility for 'reflecting "the multicultural reality of Australian society"' (Blonski 1992, 15). This issue of the positioning of multicultural arts within the institution would be a recurring theme for the council and its advisers (see Appendix B). The Migrant Committee recommended increased membership from a wide range of ethnic groups, advertising programs in ethnic media, consistent financial and advisory programs, and that their title be changed to 'Ethnic Arts Committee' (EAC) to better reflect their role (Blonski 1992, 15). The relationship with Aboriginal and Torres Strait Islander Arts (ATSIA) was also on the committee's agenda from its inception. After several years, ATSIA joined the EAC to present a united presence supporting difference in the arts.

One of the key issues faced by EAC and ATSIA was the schism between practices of cultural maintenance and new art production based on a criteria of 'excellence'. The assumption was that 'cultural maintenance' falls outside the regime of excellence. Kalantzis and Cope (1994, 13) elucidate the impact of confusions and contradictions in this criterion, 'showing the concept of excellence in the arts to be a contested one ... linked to particular ideological positions'.

Decisions about excellence as one of the 'elite' systems of exclusion are discussed in *Access to Excellence* (Kalantzis, Castles and Cope 1993). This series foregrounded the barriers and reviewed the means by which access is denied based on a narrow perspective of what constitutes excellence in the arts. Tim Rowse (1985) suggests that, despite Australia Council Chair Dr Timothy Pascoe questioning the use of 'excellence' as an assessment criterion, the early days of the Australia Council are imbued with a narrow perspective. Rowse (1985, 33) sees excellence as a 'language of the powerful, which effaces the social basis of that power' and argues, presciently, that it will 'probably continue to be a persistent rhetoric'. He explores the way this rhetoric is established as myth—as utopian in the homogeneity of its single scale of values—and contends that the notion of excellence attempts to distance art from 'grubby' politics and monetisation (Rowse 1985, 34).

A third utopian element can now be added to Rowse's discussion. The Australia Council's stated mission is to move away from 'homogeneity', suggesting that Australian society should be reflected in the participation and engagement in the arts as 'arts without borders' (Australia Council 2017b, 10). However, this means nothing if the funds and the structural mechanisms are not present, and are not centre and front of the institution. Historical accounts of the arts in a multicultural Australia challenge the rhetoric of inclusion that the arts will, in a regular and normalised manner, fully reflect multicultural Australia.

The two most recent Australia Council policies that focus on multicultural arts are those of 2000 and 2006. AMA 2000 highlighted the roles of tradition and innovation in creativity and profiled individual artists' practices as well as their roles in community settings. By taking this focus, the policy attempted to alter the perception that multicultural artists were relevant only in a community setting, with its attendant lower status in the arts world. AMA 2006 highlighted the need to incorporate 'the diversity of our cultures' through leadership, participation and creative production, including cross-cultural exchange between Indigenous and NESB artists. Since 2008, the AMA policy has been subsumed under the umbrella of the Australia Council's Cultural Engagement Framework.

Multicultural Arts Practices

Issues of Creativity

Creativity is considered to be the profound and defining characteristic of humanity. It is the 'innate quest for originality' and can be 'judged by the magnitude of the emotional response it evokes' (Wilson 2017, 3). The concept of originality carries with it subjective recognition as to what constitutes the 'new' and the potential for challenges to be generated in society because of that newness:

> Whether on the temporal, phenomenal, or social plane—the new is not objectively existing, but it always depends on schemes of interpretation, which are more often than not controversial. Social regimes of the new, as they are characteristic of modern societies, do both: they observe the new and they prefer it to the old. (Reckwitz 2014, 25)

Using this lens, Reckwitz could conceivably be writing about the challenges faced by NESB artists when raising the issue of 'interpretation' and who decides what is new, and, therefore, of value. This may include social challenges, such as a lack of understanding about, and support for, NESB artists' work by mainstream arts agencies, and creative challenges, such as when NESB artists bring traditional forms, usually associated with their ethnicity, into conjunction with contemporary art practices. The newness, or 'unexpected[ness]', brought about through creativity is also seen to stem from the recognisable (Hastrup quoted in Svašek and Meyer 2016, 3). Those wishing to make the new 'cannot escape the intertwining of past, present and future' (Derrida quoted in Svašek and Meyer 2016, 3).

Art is even more elusive to define. The following is among my favourite contemporary descriptions because it evokes the potential, risk and power of symbols that endure:

> I can't tell you what art does and how it does it, but I know that art has often judged the judges, pleaded revenge to the innocent and shown to the future what the past has suffered, so that it has never been forgotten. I know too that the powerful fear art, whatever its form, when it does this, and that amongst the people such art sometimes runs like a rumour and a legend because it makes sense of what life's brutalities cannot, a sense that unites us, for it is inseparable from a justice at last. Art, when it functions like this, becomes a meeting place of the invisible, the irreducible, the enduring, guts and honour. (Berger 1992, 9)

The 'meeting place of the invisible' conjures, for me, the sites of multicultural arts breaking through into visibility regardless of which medium the work stirs from. A more direct definition suggests that 'art is a powerful tool to redress and reimagine our world' (BDL Museum 2018). This definition also sits comfortably with how NESB artists may develop their practice.

British-based art theorist Araeen describes the difficulty and importance of creating and presenting culturally diverse artwork:

> An enormous confusion reigns about cultural diversity, which has obscured both the question of its necessity to society and also its relationship to creativity … Only when people have freedom to think, to reflect and contemplate, can they confront the norms that have become fixed dogmas, and so reactivate society's creative energy. In other words, new ideas produced by individual creativity, underpinned by freedom of thought, create a society able to change and transform itself into a dynamic force in history. (Araeen 2013, 95)

Araeen's claims of transformation based on cultural diversity resonate with the McMaster report, placing diversity at the centre of innovation. Both are advocacy documents written for a range of art decision-makers and artists. Each type of discourse reinforces the central themes of the other and points to the influence that cultural theorists and bureaucrats can garner to make the social and cultural case for diversity in the arts. The ways this transformation can occur are multi-platform and multi-sited, building upon opportunities and creative constraints.

Participation by NESB Artists

Cultural economists recognise that a measure of culturally inclusive multiculturalism rests on the participation of artists in contributing to cultural formation:

> One of the most important roles for the arts in this country is in celebrating the cultural diversity of contemporary Australian society. There are many professional artists in Australia who specialise in creating and re-creating art derived from a wide range of cultures, especially in the performing arts of music, dance and theatre. Artists from a non-English speaking background (NESB artists) also pursue their professional practice in the mainstream, often enriching their contribution through the influence of their particular cultural heritage. All of this activity is a vital element in the evolution of Australia as a truly multicultural society. (Throsby and Hollister 2003, 71)

The 30-year longitudinal study into artists' incomes in Australia, *Making Art Work: An Economic Study of Professional Artists in Australia*, reveals some improvement in the circumstances of NESB artists (Throsby and Hollister 2003; Throsby and Zednick 2010; Throsby and Petetskaya 2017). Yet, the capacity of the arts to contribute to this rich diversity is circumscribed by economic and other factors. In 2017, 10 per cent (an increase from 8 per cent) of professional artists were of a non–English speaking background, compared to 18 per cent in the general workforce (Throsby and Petetskaya 2017, 143). By comparison, the proportion of English-speaking background (ESB) artists (78 per cent) was higher than the proportion of ESB employees in the general workforce (73 per cent) (Throsby and Zednick, 2010). The slight increase in NESB artists professional participation—from 8 to 10 per cent—does not translate as an arts specific increase, because it has kept pace with the 2 per cent increase of NESB participation in the general workforce—from 16 to 18 per cent (Throsby and Zednick 2010, 23; Throsby and Petetskaya 2017, 142).

More detailed data reveal that visual arts and craft maintain the highest proportion of professional NESB artists at 16 and 14 per cent, respectively; composers make up 8 per cent; musicians and community arts and cultural development (CACD) workers make up 7 per cent; and writers comprise the lowest proportion at 6 per cent (Throsby and Petetskaya 2017, 143). The most significant increase is that of acting and directing in live theatre, which, at 13 per cent, is up from 5 per cent in 2009. Language-based arts, such as writing and acting, are considered to be the most challenging for NESB artists, and CACD work is considered to be the most accessible due to local councils' use of arts in communicating with their 'multicultural communities' (Throsby and Hollister 2003, 23; Throsby and Zednick 2010, 23). Historically, 'ethnic' artists were 'allowed' into the arts sector via the community arts door (Blonski 1992, 1994; Hawkins 1993, 86–88). The most recent data on the proportion of NESB artists across artform professions is shown in Table 1.

Table 1: Proportion of professional NESB artists in each artistic field, 2009 and 2015

Survey year	Visual artist	Craft	Actor/ director	Dancer	Composer	Writer	Musician	CACD
2009*	14%	14%	5%	10%	4%	4%	6%	3%
2015**	16%	14%	13%	13%	8%	7%	6%	7%

* Throsby and Zednick (2010, 24).

** Throsby and Petetskaya (2017, 147).

NESB artists mostly work in visual arts and crafts; however, there has been a notable rise in the performing arts since 2009 when distinctions between artform practices were first published. The perception that NESB practitioners are mainly employed in CACD roles is challenged by the data. Table 1 indicates that NESB artists are not primarily found in CACD and that participation remains relatively low compared with other artforms. This result may reflect more robust research techniques, a high level of volunteering by NESB artists in CACD and/or a general decline in CACD practice (Throsby and Petetskaya 2017, 7). It may also reflect an upward trend in participation across the range of artforms.

The income gap from creative practice and arts-related activities (mainly teaching) between ESB and NESB artists has also shifted. In the 2002 and 2009 *Making Art Work* studies, NESB artists earnt 36 per cent less than the AU$22,000 average creative income of their ESB colleagues (Throsby and Zednick 2010, 83). In the 2017 study, the income from creative practice increased to 95 per cent for NESB artists when compared to ESB artists (Throsby and Petetskaya 2017, 142). Earnings from arts-related activities were 18 per cent higher for NESB artists in 2009 but, in 2017, were 27 per cent lower than their ESB colleagues (Throsby and Zednick 2010, 83; Throsby and Petetskaya 2017, 145). Shifts such as these highlight the precarity of the portfolio careers that artists must engage with in Australia, and the agility with which artists must manoeuvre to maintain their practice. While it is heartening to see that creative income is reaching parity, it is cause for concern when NESB artists' ability to subsidise their income and have a broad presence across Australian arts reduced by 45 per cent between 2009 and 2017.

Levels of public funding are another measure to gauge support to artists. In 2017, 18 per cent of NESB artists claimed that the largest barrier to their practice was the 'lack of access to funding or other financial support' (Throsby and Petetskaya 2017, 147)—a rise of 5 per cent (Throsby and Hollister 2003, 74). This links to the finding that, compared with ESB artists, 'fewer applications made for a grant, fellowship, residence, prize or funding are successful'—even though NESB artists had more success in grant applications at the Australia Council than with state art departments or local councils (Throsby and Petetskaya 2017, 147). The Australia Council claims an improved success rate of culturally and linguistically diverse (CALD) applicants. In March 2015, 20 per cent of all applicants identified as CALD and, of those, 19 per cent were successful; in March 2017, 23 per cent of all applicants identified as CALD and, of those, 29 per cent were successful, which indicates an increased success rate of 10 per cent over two years when compared within the CALD cohort (Australia Council 2017d, 17). These success rates indicate the high calibre of applications in the very competitive arena of arts grants. However, if these data are used to compare success across all applicants, the 29 per cent cohort of CALD artists' success represents an overall success rate of 5.8 per cent.

Despite their leaner economic position in the arts, in an earlier *Making Art Work* study, 60 per cent of first-generation NESB artists felt that their ethnic backgrounds benefited their careers while 15 per cent cited a negative impact (Throsby and Zednick 2010, 24). In 2017, 54 per cent identified an overall positive impact with an increase to 19 per cent of those who experienced an overall negative impact (Throsby and Petetskaya 2017, 145). For one-fifth of an artist population to identify negative consequences suggests significant issues are preventing their full participation.

These published data provide a detailed view of the situation for NESB artists and those organisations dedicated to their support and promotion. The picture that emerges is one of consistent underemployment in the arts of NESB artists when compared to the rest of the NESB population, and lower levels of arts grant funding across all categories in comparison to ESB colleagues. These data suggests that, should Australians wish to see cultural diversity in the art produced and experienced in this country, a policy response could improve the situation. Rowe et al. (2016, 12) observe that 'policy provides the articulation of field problems and solutions by setting and shifting agendas, validating actors and directing funding and technological resources'. Therefore, it is useful to look at the relationship between multicultural demographics and arts policies that aim to encompass and support the range and types of multicultural arts practices.

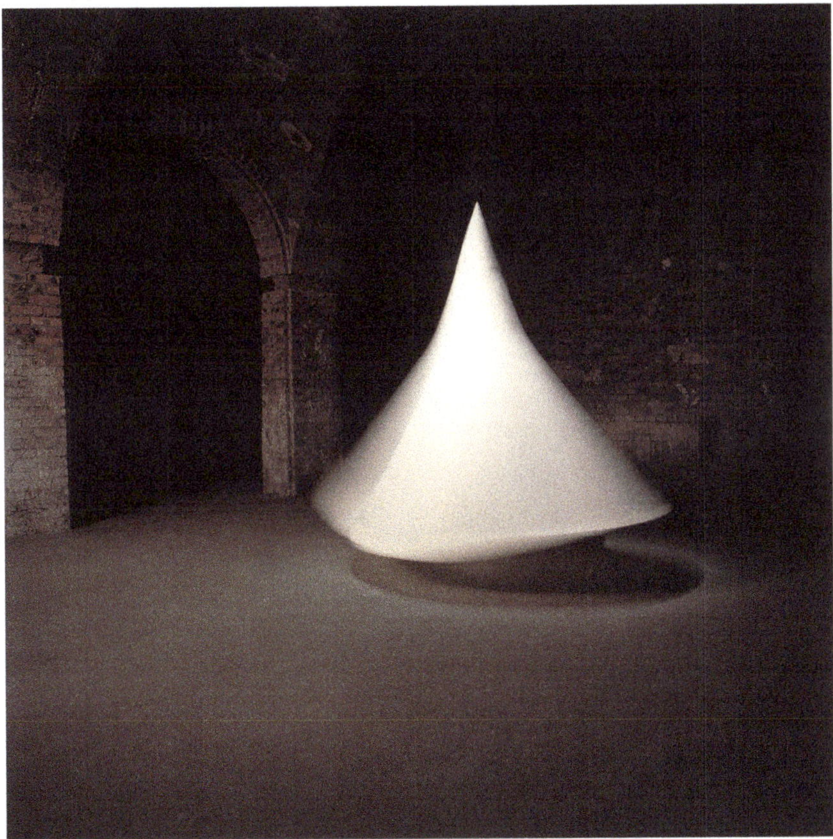

Image 3: Hossein Valamanesh, *The Lover Circles His Own Heart*, 1993
Silk, electric motor
Collection: Museum of Contemporary Art Sydney
Photographers: M. Michalski and B. Wojcik

Types of Multicultural Arts

There is an inherent creative response in all migration: through 'an internal dialogue, the migrant compares the old home with the new, making with luck some creative novum out of their disparities' (Cubitt 2005, 315). All artists have a desire to make works that are affective and potentially transformative to individual audiences and, for some, to social groups as well. There are artists who choose to concentrate on their individual practice and accept the constraints and opportunities afforded by existing contemporary art infrastructure. Many of the artists interviewed for this study describe their need to be able adapt to, or stretch beyond, the systemic barriers they can face in the arts in Australia, some working within existing structures and others devising their own. Interdisciplinary or intercultural elements and collaborations are often considered as a foundation for creating environments to encourage innovation, and have emerged as the most contemporary ways in which artists navigate their presence into the arts scene. There is, however, an apparent tension that emerges when a claim is made for the potential for innovation because of a multicultural context.

Historically, 'multicultural arts' has been relegated to the sidelines as outdated and, by implication, mediocre, because of the association with cultural maintenance that sets it aside (Blonski 1992, 1994; Hawkins 1993; Khan, Wyatt and Yue 2014). It could be argued that, as a response to this kind of criticism (as simplistic) and perception (as static), NESB artists have developed a spectrum of creative processes to increase the possibilities of artistic innovation. The spectrum includes ethno-specific, intra-cultural, bicultural, intercultural, cross-cultural and, in more recent years, transcultural categories. These different processes come together under the umbrella of multicultural arts and the more general descriptor of 'hybrid'.

Ethno-specific refers to ethnic and linguistic groups who share the same race and ethnicity. When used artistically, the term points to the cultural traditions of specific ethnic groups and implies maintenance of those cultural 'traditions'. Hawkins (1993, 87) describes the inaugural funding for 'ethnic arts' through the community arts program of the Australia Council as having a focus that was:

> Almost exclusively on support for the folk or traditional arts activities of non-English speaking groups … the discourse of ethnic arts invoked tradition in a way that restricted the possibility of connections with other artforms and practices. It implied that migrants were essentially cultured and that their cultural expressions were pure and original.

According to Hawkins (1993, 86), this resulted in a 'narrow cultural ghetto for migrants'. It also may have contributed to the double-bind narrative that migrants are both valorised for their 'stories' and inherent knowledge of what constitutes 'culture', while simultaneously being shunned by creative peers for not being 'contemporary'.

In Australia in 2018, ethno-specific artists are most likely to be musicians, singers or visual artists and, if successful in gaining attention and an audience, tend to be slotted into the 'world music' or 'global art' genre. Ajak Kwai is a singer and storyteller who migrated from South Sudan to Tasmania and now lives in Melbourne. In 2006 she toured as part of the kultour program, which romantically described her performances as 'songs of the timeless musical traditions of her people, the Dinka of Southern Sudan' (MAV 2006a). This stage of her career is an example of multicultural arts as 'ethnic showcasing'—often perceived as a narrow view of multiculturalism that is static and limits cultural exchanges (Shigayuki quoted in Mar and Ang 2015, 9). Yet, as we see below, ethno-specific arts can also leverage from their traditional base into dynamic, creative shifts that alter the artists' work.

Rebetika, a form of jazz/blues first performed between the 1920s and the 1950s in Greece, is an ethno-specific artform that uses traditional instruments such as bouzouki. A group of Greek-Australian musicians and musicologists were part of the revival of this musical form in the 1980s, eventually receiving international recognition for their performances. A successful play was developed through a Multicultural Arts Professional Development project that celebrated this subcultural milieu. *Café Rebetika*, directed by Stephen Helper, toured Australia with kultour in 2011. Regular performer Demeter Tsounis appreciates Greek music and wants to 'have the opportunity to keep exploring and rediscovering it and performing it because it is such a treasure' (Tsounis quoted in Karavas 2009).

Intra-cultural processes occur between artists of similar cultural backgrounds that may reinforce cultural traditions but can also lead to adjustments within a cultural form, depending on the context. Artists who perform cultural forms of traditional dance and music may be said to work intra-culturally. The Tawadros brothers use intra-cultural processes as composers and musicians. Joseph Tawadros is an oud player trained in Egypt who, it is claimed, 'single-handedly popularized the ancient instrument' (Radio National 2015). Joseph mainly plays with his brother James, both of whom live in Australia. Similarly, brothers Slava and Leonard Grigoryan are accomplished Australian guitarists originally from Kazakhstan. When these two sets of brothers perform together as Band of Brothers they present a more intercultural or bicultural process to their music.

Visual artist Hossein Valamanesh works in a minimalist contemporary style using materials from the earth to make two and three dimensional works that evoke his Iranian heritage. His use of materials, which could be from an Australian as well as Iranian landscape, and the motifs he employs—such as the twirling shape of a dervish, or items, such as oil lamps—lead to adjustments in the cultural form of contemporary painting and sculpture (see Image 3). Mar and Ang (2015, 8) argue that 'truly relevant and energetic creative work will come from working across cultures' when considering the diversity of cultural expression. There are several practices that arise from this process to generate art that has a more contemporary look and feel as well as having a closer context to much of contemporary life.

Bicultural creative processes link two (usually distinguishable) cultures or perhaps subcultures. Ajak Kwai fuses her musical sources in a bicultural process to (what appears to be) great success, performing at WOMADelaide, the National Folk Festival and the Melbourne Festival:

> Whether Ajak is singing in Arabic, Sudanese or English she leaves you in no doubt as to the depth and richness of her Dinka roots. Music is the vehicle for her experiences as a refugee, exiled from her home town. Ajak and her songs take us on a journey deeply feminine, unique from the Upper Nile to gospel singing in Cairo to Melbourne where she has successfully fused her African roots with the grassroots of Australian music. (Kwai n.d.)

Doppio Teatro, a South Australian–based Italo-Australian theatre company established by Teresa Crea and Christopher Bell in 1983, demonstrates the move from ethno-specific (originally they presented bilingual theatre by Italian playwrights) to bicultural writing in presenting theatre about the experiences of Italo-Australians. Crea explains:

> The idea behind Doppio is to underline the duality that exists here in Australia for many people who have two cultures within them— or rather, who have culture of origin plus their confrontation with the dominant culture, which is the common code we live by, the Anglo Australian culture. (quoted in Mitchell 1998, 133)

Doppio Teatro was known for its quality production values and also for its ability to respond to the changes in society through the influences that were included in their productions. It reinvented its purpose from a bicultural theatre company to one that explored cross-cultural themes.

Cross-cultural implies a number of cultures in 'dialogue', crossing their boundaries to generate artistic development. Cross-cultural experiences are ones in which cultural forms and identities are reshaped and give way to form new creative entities. This is complex and difficult to articulate on a stage. Nevertheless, in 1997, showing bold, creative leadership, Doppio Teatro rethought their purpose to become Doppio para//elo and:

> Expanded its range of activities under the para//elo banner, giving them the 'space to work more broadly from a bicultural platform to a cross cultural platform'. Their work now draws on the group's Italian heritage as one of many ingredients in a contemporary global perspective. They are broadening the definition of what multiculturalism means to include to work on parallel cultural experiences in the context of global Internet communications. (Cope, Kalantzis and Ziguras 2003, 25)

Intercultural creative production occurs between artists of two or more linguistic and/or cultural backgrounds and, when successful, is often evident where collaborative processes are used to develop creative works. It is similar to cross-cultural production and has come into vogue with artists working in the multicultural space as a way of contemporising their creative practice. Intercultural does not necessarily require equality of creative input; however, in contemporary arts, it is often used to imply that all artists have some equality of creative input to effect a creative collaboration. This process is very challenging for artists more accustomed to their own practice.

In discussing the influence of cultural diversity, performance artist Brian Fuata (2011, 22) describes the 'patchy and tentative' knowledge that led to his performances exploring his feminine role in Samoan society as a fa'a fafine:

> It is a lived rather than known experience, a nickname, a family context, a child's drag act, someone else, a cultural ascription, a cyber friendship, a short film, a passing meeting, a google search, a wrong classification, an islander body. I know nothing more theoretical, official or definite.

Working collaboratively with other artists, Fuata works interculturally and, perhaps, trans-culturally—across cultural understandings and iconographies. This mode shows that artists have become more adept and less constrained in how they interact with each other's practices. According to Fuata (2011, 23), 'in relation to a notion of identity and the cultural diversity thereof, such a project reflects a contemporary arts society that is inherently diversified and acknowledging of that'. This artist is making a group effort with one artist at a time, and generating their own peer support network in the process of their practice. The scope of culturally diverse forms is, therefore, vast—definitely not a ghetto—and continues to morph as artists seek out the new while grounding their work in something they find familiar.

I argue that the potential for creative practices emerging from Australia's multicultural society has yet to be fully realised or supported to the extent it warrants. Further, there is an expectation that NESB artists have a particular role and capacity to stimulate social transformation, in part through the scope of their practices if they can work interculturally.

Conclusion

This historical and sociological overview of the fields that inform multicultural arts has considered the conditions that support the practices of NESB artists. The similarity of critical and government discourse between the UK and Australia about diversity is clear; however, the UK has gone further to implement tied funding to achieve diversity outcomes. The British Government has positioned diversity in a critical role to generate a flourishing culture and, through ACE, is rewarding those companies that demonstrate their capability to deliver that role. The CCA is also investing in programs to stimulate that progress.

By contrast, in Australia, the history of targeted funds from the 1970s onwards has witnessed bitter disagreements among art boards that have been expected to support the artistic work of migrants. These periods of friction have led to short productive phases of traction and change for the arts in a multicultural Australia. Key productive moments have occurred in 1982–86, 1993–96 and 2000–05, and are associated with articulate and politically astute ACMAC leadership, members and staff who recognise the importance of critical debate about multicultural issues within the arts.

The structural quandary of where migrant, ethnic, multicultural arts or AMA policy should be located at the Australia Council underlines the issue of a lack of trust in the art that has been produced by so-called ethnic artists. Their work has been labelled as 'amateur', has been associated with cultural maintenance and has been seen as being in direct opposition to artform codes of 'excellence'. Their role, as designated by the Australia Council, was to uphold traditional arts and crafts, which in turn raised questions regarding their capacity to be artists with contemporary practices. This higher moral ground about the suitability of the label 'contemporary' is mainly applied to ethnic artists.

That the majority of the Australia Council's funds support the performance of European classical 'heritage' arts (Blonski 1994, 199) is an irony that seems to have escaped the council's notice. Indigenous arts are supported for cultural maintenance as well as contemporary arts reasons. The history of multicultural arts practices highlights a range of tensions around issues of trust and leadership in terms of eligible creative endeavours and questionable aesthetic assumptions on the part of some decision-makers at the Australia Council.

2

Leading for the Arts in a Multicultural Australia

Creative, institutional and organisational leaders are all part of the process to enliven opportunities for the arts in a multicultural Australia. These opportunities adapt or lead to new forms of art production for artists and can generate wider audience demographic attendance, which can also foster greater social cooperation (Van de Vyver and Abrams 2017). To realise these opportunities, policies need to be in place to address prevalent and long-term issues such as underemployment of, and low funding to, non–English speaking background (NESB) artists (see Chapter 1). To this end, institutional and organisational champions implement policies by directing funds and resources while artists in the field spearhead the change that policy is designed to generate.

Leadership can be seen as operating like a well-oiled or rusty hinge, opening up or closing down opportunities. Arts leadership in practice is frequently located within, and contextualised by, a complex set of political and administrative structures around funding and policy; the decisions made within these structures often affect artistic practice, but are usually made outside the realms of any individual artist's input. However, beyond this 'institutional' level of leadership, the arts are also characterised by a loose amalgam of artist networks through which creative aspects—ideas, techniques and influences—are disseminated, discussed, challenged and altered. Informal relations of established and emerging artists constitute forms of creative leadership that may often be in tension with administrative hierarchies and organisational forms of leadership. Therefore, it is helpful to understand forms of leadership practices from a range of disciplines and how they appear within an artistic milieu.

NESB artists frequently call for more effective leadership from agencies and mainstream organisations to address their varying levels of support and lack of inclusion in the arts environments they wish to experience (Castagna 2017). This brings into question different kinds of leadership and how they can best manifest to generate the changes that many agree need to occur. The qualities of leaders who cultivate culturally diverse artistic content in the Australian arts sector demonstrate distributed, relational, transformative and transactional leadership styles.

The arts sector's interest in leadership is matched by organisations such as the Australia Council. The 2000 Arts in a Multicultural Australia (AMA) policy established the Multicultural Arts Professional Development program, an annual university and foundation partnership-based leadership program, that combined creative production and audience development in a very practical approach for the arts in a multicultural Australia, and that ran successfully for eight years (Kape Communications 2010). The Australia Council now funds separate courses for established and emerging leaders—usually employed in arts organisations—that include diversity, but do not appear to be tailored to the needs of NESB artists or multicultural arts practitioners (Australia Council n.d.-c). Therefore, while those who work in arts organisations have something of a pathway of courses for leadership and development, NESB artist leadership opportunities have arguably been more ad hoc. This chapter explores several modes of leadership relevant to NESB artists and the roles of friction and trust in generating the traction towards a supportive multicultural arts milieu.

Modes of Leadership

Leadership is valued as an area for research as much for its role in society as for the ongoing debates that attempt at a definition (Jackson and Parry 2011, 14). Discourse on leadership follows, and occasionally leads, changes in social organisation. As Grint (2005, 9) puts it: 'If our future world is very dynamic, competitive and unstable, then we "need" to provide flexible and decentralized leadership systems'. By connecting a dynamic environment and a decentralised mode of leadership, Grint evokes the symbiotic relationship between the need for foresight about that environment and the best way to adapt to the opportunities it presents. Contemporary leadership theories often focus on collective approaches to achieve common goals (Sorenson, Goethals and Haber 2011; Hewison and Holden 2011; Jackson and Parry 2011) and advocate the need 'to move beyond the leader-follower-shared goal conversation, and make room for more organic, systemic, and integrative ideas and approaches' (Sorenson Goethals and Haber 2011, 36).

The concept of 'integrative ideas and approaches' aims to address systemic issues by including those people affected by any given situation into processes of generating solutions and modes of implementation. These methods are at the forefront of current leadership management discourse and are useful when considering the ways in which many artists and cultural practitioners are working to improve multicultural inclusion in the arts.

Leadership in organisational contexts is also discussed in terms of leadership and management—roles that are often unclear in the workplace. Peter Drucker (quoted in Holmes, Marra and Vine 2011, 6) argues that 'the only definition of a leader is one who has followers', and that leadership provides 'inspiration and setting new directions for an organisation, whereas management involves planning and organising to implement the objectives'. Reconsidering the traditional view of a leader at the top of a hierarchy opens up a spectrum of definitions. At one end of the spectrum, Stogdill (quoted in Holmes, Marra and Vine 2011, 12) views leadership as a process to influence the 'activities of an organised group in its efforts toward goal setting and goal achievement'. At the other end of the spectrum, Peter and Austin provide a wider and emotive definition:

> Leadership means vision, cheerleading, enthusiasm, love, trust, verve, passion, obsession, consistency, the use of symbols, paying attention, out-and-out drama (and the management thereof), creating heroes at all levels, coaching, effectively wandering around. Leadership must be present at all levels in the organisation. It depends on a million little things done with obsession, consistency and care, but all of those million little things add up to nothing if the trust, vision and basic belief are not there. (quoted in Jackson and Parry 2011, 12–13)

The conventional image of leadership entrusted to the 'hero', 'heroine' or 'charismatic' figure embodied in one particular individual as the head is shifting to a more reflective role as the 'soul' (or 'moral' centre) of an organisation (Mendonca and Kanungo 2007, 3). Mendonca and Kanungo (2007) claim that it is the moral principles of the leader that lend credibility and legitimate the vision for the organisation. This leadership style intertwines management and leadership but, significantly, encourages the talents of those in the organisation to flourish (e.g. by mentoring and collaborating).

An issue for the arts regarding shifting notions of leadership is the prevalent image of the artist as working solo, or as a solo entrepreneur, striving to make their own work:

> Part of the problem in the cultural world is that the dominant tradition focuses on the individual artist and their work, failing to see that creativity in the arts depends on a network of cooperation among many people. Similarly, in the wider creative industries, much attention is given to the individual entrepreneur, whereas in fact, as in the arts, teamwork, networking, peer competition and cooperation are vital. (Hewison and Holden 2011, 32)

The issue here is that artists need highly developed communication and cooperation skills to be able to effectively compete, collaborate and network with their colleagues. Within theatre and music ensembles, for example, the tendency in the arts is to valorise the 'star' talents of individuals at the expense of acknowledging those who work as part of a group or within a 'community' of artists. Grint (2005, 33) suggests that the 'ship' (or community) has been forgotten, and organisations need to reconfigure the environment in and around the 'ship' and move away from the sole focus on the leader. This concept does not acknowledge, but is reminiscent of, Foucault's discussions of government that use the metaphor of a ship:

> What does it mean to govern a ship? It means clearly to take charge of the sailors, but also of the boat and its cargo; to take care of the ship means to reckon with winds, rocks and storms; and it consists in that activity of establishing a relation between the sailors and the ship which is to be taken care of. (Foucault 1991, 93–94)

Governing is seen as 'establishing a relationship'. It has a management role to ensure the safe delivery of sailors, ship and cargo, and evokes leadership when speaking of establishing relationships in a context-dependent environment of the unexpected.

Grint (2005, 15) equates management to 'deja vu', which relates to responding appropriately to a familiar situation, and conceptualises leadership as 'vu jade', meaning to be able to respond to novel or completely unfamiliar situations or experiences. The lack of—or, at best, intermittent—leadership within mainstream arts organisations with regard to cultural diversity generates the sense of (in this case, negative) deja vu far more frequently than that of 'vu jade' in the experience of NESB artists. This presents opportunities for managers to reinforce what has worked in the past and to combine with leaders who attempt new approaches. This interplay between the familiar and the unexpected, even risky, suggests a push–pull friction between the myriad calibrations that the NESB artist faces in the context of the wider arts environment.

Leadership Repertoire for Multicultural Arts

The types of leadership pertinent to the arts in a multicultural Australia link to the roles discussed in this book: the creative role of the artist, the multicultural arts advocates within institutions and the leaders who establish partnerships between arts organisations. Given that there are no major national multicultural arts companies in Australia, in this book I emphasise the individual artist and small multicultural arts organisations who take on leadership roles that may stretch beyond their capacity. These individuals and groups interact to varying degrees with bureaucrats at the government arts agency, the Australia Council, as well as with cultural practitioners in small to medium (S2M) and major arts organisations. The range of interactions that may lead to change in the arts environment for multicultural arts can usefully draw on the modes of distributed, relational, transformative and transactional leadership.

Distributed leadership integrates ideas and approaches by sharing lead responsibilities within a team, either as co-leaders or by switching the lead role depending on the skills required at the time (Burke, Diaz-Granados and Sales 2011, 342). This is a flexible mode that requires high-level trust and understanding between each member so that the work keeps flowing. It also requires reflexiveness in the team members to 'authorise' each other as leaders. The relevance of this style of institutional leadership for multicultural arts policy development and implementation is that it enables multiple players to take a lead role in delivering a broad scope of structural changes. For example, the previous institutional role of the Australia Council Multicultural Advisory Committee (ACMAC) utilised the particular expertise or insight of its artist members in constructive debate to produce well-considered strategies and policy advice across the different artform areas of the institution and within the arts sector (Australia Council 2002, 12). Distributive leadership is found in creative and organisational leadership and can be seen in how media arts organisation CuriousWorks creates 'multi-year, national, large-scale artistic initiatives that celebrate Australia's cultural diversity' (CuriousWorks 2021a), for example. CuriousWorks engages with and educates emerging artists from diverse cultural backgrounds through its production of digital media works, the dissemination of which strongly adopts all social media forms. The company resources numbers of emerging artists, called 'Curious Creators', to co-lead projects that produce work that 'defies' mainstream stereotypical narratives (CuriousWorks 2021b). This distributed form of leadership provides opportunities for Curious Creators with different skills to step into creative and organisational lead roles in which their skill sets can come to the fore. The notion of distributed leadership in this instance provides a hands-on approach to fast-tracked professional development within a supportive environment.

Relational leadership also stresses relationships between people rather than power over them. Hosking (2011, 460–61, original emphasis) characterises the relational perspective as one based in *ethics and local (interconnected and extended) pragmatics* and demonstrated through open dialogue. This type of leadership requires ongoing abilities to listen attentively and non-judgementally. A sense of 'relational responsibility (rather than blaming others)' generates 'space for improvisation' (Hosking 2011, 461). Generating space for improvisation is a creative act that forms the basis of collaborative artistic work. The delicacy and temporal elements of this process cannot be underestimated, particularly when cross-cultural exchange is taken into account. Such an approach evokes the ways many NESB artists and multicultural organisations conduct their work and presents a process that builds cultural capability through cross-cultural partnerships.

Transformative leaders are perceived as charismatic and are valued for leading change in organisations because they generate trust in their vision (Hewison and Holden 2011, 31). This type of leader holds positional power and maintains it by persuasive and inspirational behaviours. Charismatic leadership was first used in a secular manner by sociologist Max Weber to describe the authority given to those who are perceived as 'extraordinary individuals [who offer] a transcendent purpose as their mission' (Conger 2011, 86). Artists who use their 'charisma' to transform how the world is perceived are often described as 'extraordinary'. The risk within institutions or organisations is that a charismatic leader's legacy for change can be short-lived. This is particularly an issue for leadership succession in multicultural arts. Alongside economic constraints, lower NESB participation rates in the arts suggest that there may be fewer opportunities to gain institutional or organisational roles as leaders.

Transactional leadership, on the other hand, is based on a transaction. To transact is to agree on an exchange. Transactional business leaders depend on their position and role within a company and tend towards a management style of leadership (Hewison and Holden 2011, 116). While transactional leadership is considered to be less nuanced because of its direct approach, undertaking effective negotiations that generate satisfactory transactions requires a certain amount of flair for influential communication. The useful side of transactional leadership, particularly given the precarity of the arts, is that the implied 'contract' requires explicit terms of agreement. Greater transactional leadership from arts funding institutions, for example, would satisfy calls for increased accountability from major arts organisations who need to demonstrate diversity as part of their funding agreement.

Activating Networks

These modes of leadership share a common factor. The quality of an influential leader is increasingly based on the ability to activate networks (Grint 2005). Each of the leadership styles above have in common the potential to develop and activate networks. One of the key qualities of leadership is the ability to broker relationships that form networks. Castells (2010, xxxvi), in his observation of the 'network society', finds that, despite the ubiquity and rapid proliferation of technological mediated communication systems, 'the intangible factor is still access to the micro-networks located in certain selective places, in what I named "milieus"'.

The value of the 'micro-network' is applicable to the NESB artist and the small multicultural arts organisation not only because of their size and the potential for extended international relationships, but also for the role they play in a multicultural arts milieu. In this respect, networks can be open or closed, and are closed when they are perceived as a clique with a tightly held membership (Carmichael 2011, 43). This can apply to both multicultural 'micro-networks', especially those that are ethno-specific, and the perception that some mainstream arts organisations are a 'closed circuit'.

A network is made up of people who support and influence each other through 'brokers as key actors [who] enable different patterns of social capital to develop' (Burt quoted in Carmichael 2011, 43). Social capital is widely recognised as the value attached to belonging to social groups and the ability to extend those groups. Putnam (2000, 19) defines it as the 'connections among individuals—social networks and the norms of reciprocity and trustworthiness that arise from them'. He distinguishes two forms of social capital: bonding capital that functions like 'superglue' to hold groups together, and bridging capital that enables people to work together. Bourdieu includes an institutional component, articulating the functional level of positional influence to his definition:

> Social capital is the sum of the resources, actual or virtual, that accrue to an individual or group by virtue of possessing a durable network of more or less institutional relationships of mutual acquaintance and recognition. (Bourdieu and Wacquant 1992, 119)

Both concepts of social capital concern the outcomes of effective leadership and participation, but with a different emphasis. Putnam focuses on the social aspect of exchange and trust, while Bourdieu emphasises the capital aspect of resources and influence. When viewed together, these offer insight into the role of the broker in network formation relevant to cross-cultural and intercultural arts practice. International case studies from arts institutions and S2M companies suggest that a new form of leadership is emerging in the UK that is inclusive and network-based, and recognises that 'the notion of "aesthetic leadership", requires new distributed leadership models' (Glow 2013, 132). Here, the link between creative practice, shared vision and responsibility, and the capacity to create, expand and maintain productive networks, articulates how the arts sector can remain relevant and reflexive in the work they produce.

Different levels of skills are needed at different times: for example, in navigating turbulence in arts funding and at the various stages of policy and artistic development cycles. This requires insight on the part of the leader to consult appropriately and foresight on the part of the manager to put programs in place that respond accordingly and to implement them effectively. Within the multicultural arts policy context, change is further complicated by shifts in political as well as demographic realities, requiring a high level of flexibility to respond to different political environments, social changes and artistic experimentation as they arise.

'Situated, strategic … transactional' (Noble 2009, 51) and cross-cultural capabilities are important attributes for navigating cultural difference. For those who champion and implement the arts in a multicultural Australia, they are essential skills. These skills would be variously nuanced based on whether the leader was in a creative, institutional or organisational position.

Creative Leadership

Creative leaders are artists recognised by their peers and the public as artists who generate new developments in creative content to explore—in this case—diversity arising from multicultural Australia. So as to be able explore that diversity, their roles as cultural brokers require cosmopolitan and cross-cultural competencies that are recognised/advocated as essential skills to creativity in a 'hyper-diverse' multicultural Australia (Mar and Ang 2015; Noble 2009). These skills are demonstrated by the artists I interviewed, yet, at times, their identities or artworks continue to meet resistance within arts systems. This resistance raises questions as to whether each aspect of the 'culture cycles' in the UNESCO Convention on the Protection and Promotion of the Diversity of Cultural Expressions (the Convention) can be found in Australia. Such 'culture cycles' represent a value chain encompassing the multiple phases in art production from education through to production and distribution (Mar and Ang 2015, 7). The low rates of employment in arts-related sectors indicates that NESB artists are absent from many of the decision-making areas within culture cycles. Yet, it is often these same artists who must generate their own opportunities as the main producers of content to explore and interpret a multicultural Australia. While these abilities reflect the entrepreneurial traits of NESB artists, we need to be cautious when sole responsibility is placed onto underpaid multicultural artists to creatively contribute to more complex understandings of Australian society (Keating, Bertone and Leahy n.d., 13).

Nevertheless, new modes of creative leadership develop despite, or perhaps in part from, systemic constraints. The new creative modes recognise 'cultural diversity as an inescapable interactive context to which arts and cultural workers respond in their working processes' (Mar and Ang 2015, 8). The NESB artist works 'in-between' here in some ways. The context of the arts system may constrain, yet the multicultural society may inspire, and vice versa. It is through navigating and creatively activating these complex relationships that a supportive multicultural arts milieu becomes more palpable.

Intercultural Practice

One process that activates complex relationships is intercultural creative practice because it can co-produce spaces for change through such elements as traditional knowledge exchanges as well as experimentation. Intercultural practice facilitates and promotes creative results from cultural diversity, presenting challenges and opportunities. As Mar and Ang (2015, 8) observe: 'Artistic work can express this intrinsic diversity by mobilising the unpredictable interfaces of intercultural exchange, which can be found everywhere'. Risky and messy (unpredictable interfaces) and potentially hugely productive (found everywhere), creative innovation and diversity are thus linked.

Creative responses are often prompted by the tensions that exist between 'traditional' and 'contemporary' binaries in art discourse; frequently defined as 'hybrid', these form the basis of the creative trajectories of many NESB artists. This trajectory is a form of what Papastergiadis (2010, 7) terms 'translation', whereby cultural innovation becomes apparent through a 'robust process' that mutates, appropriates and reconfigures. This process involves a creative dialectical between forms and concepts that require rigorous inquiry and resolution to be 'robust'. In the context of migration and diversity, 'hybridising' is viewed as occurring 'when an entanglement and cultural mix is produced'; this facilitates 'innovating' when 'the entanglement enlightens a creative cultural innovation' (Chan Kwok-bun quoted in Morató, Zarlenga and Zamorano 2015, 4).

As I suggest below, this 'friction' generates energy that illuminates and encourages new ways of understanding different knowledge systems that enliven the arts.

In Australia, the visual arts and music have historically provided accessible forms of 'enlightened entanglement', in part because they can transcend language (Throsby and Hollister 2003, 23). Visual arts have the highest proportion of professional NESB artists at 16 per cent, while 8 per cent of NESB artists are composers and 7 per cent are writers (Throsby and Petetskaya 2017, 143). However, the artists and cultural practitioners that make up these data reach beyond issues of linguistics to encompass a 'language of representation … [that deals with] inclusions and exclusion in the narratives of the nation' (Gunew 2004, 19).

Cultural Brokers

Not all creative practitioners are in a position to engage in national narratives. The cultural broker holds a delicately balanced role in activating those all-important networks in the arts and cultural sectors. Cultural brokers originally worked with people to conserve the artefacts and processes celebrated as 'folk life', safeguarding intangible heritage (Jacobs 2014). Richard Kurin (1997, 17) of the Smithsonian Institute views the role as an institutional intermediary within the museum context. For him, cultural brokers engage in a specialised form of audience development, bringing audiences and what he calls 'culture bearers' together to translate and negotiate new and different cultural meanings. Kapetopoulos (2009, 13) depicts this as essential: in his view, arts administrators and marketers need to become cultural brokers, or seek out cultural brokers, when trying to reach Australia's multicultural audiences. The role of the broker in the arts becomes innovative in this example of audience development. This innovation also extends back to the artists themselves who, although not always acknowledged as such, are the primary cultural brokers (Babacan 2011, 18). Brokering can be reasonably direct through artist exchanges, yet can readily expand to encompass a vastly complex network. Elaborating on the complex scope of the role within a broad multicultural arts context, Gibson (2005, 272) explains that such a person needs to be able to:

> Broker combinations of cultural, cognitive, aesthetic and political factors; mesh a profusion of genres, individuals and communities; braid different strands of government and systems of power, different valences of allowance and impediment.

This lays out the daunting scope of work and articulates beautifully the set of relationships and factors that require attention, increasing our understanding of what contributes to 'relational' and 'distributive' leadership. These are the skills of creative leaders that NESB artists accumulate as cultural brokers. They form networks and articulate the need for access to other influential networks to further their practice (Stevenson et al. 2017; Gonsalves 2017). Thus, the broker, as artist or producer, lubricates the social, cultural, economic, political and, especially, creative realms of the arts towards a multicultural arts milieu.

Creative and Cultural Autonomy

The NESB artist, in carrying out brokering roles, moves between creating and interpreting, each of which carries a form of responsibility. At some point, the artist will try to assert autonomy over their practice. Creative and cultural autonomy here refers to the level of artistic control the artist can achieve through what is mostly an intercultural creative practice. The need to establish and maintain such autonomy is a key challenge faced by NESB artists, in large part because of the stereotyping, tensions and 'dumbing' down that result from limits placed on diversity in cultural representation that 'exclude more complex dynamics' (Mar and Ang 2015, 7). One of these limits is the artist's position as a representative of an ethnic group because it denies:

> The relative aesthetic autonomy that is understood by white artists to be their right, an autonomy that takes as its core the idea of art and art's entire history, not a narrow anthropological notion of culture. (Fisher 2010, 64–65)

The discourse of creative practice typically positions NESB artists within the community arts sector (Hawkins 1993, 86–88; Blonski 1994, 199) to the extent that multicultural arts have been seen to equate to 'community arts', which sits outside the perceived canon of 'excellence' (Kalantzis and Cope 1994, 14–19). Notwithstanding the fact that only 7 per cent of NESB artists work in a professional capacity in community and cultural development, some NESB artists still find this perception attached to them (Throsby and Petetskaya 2017, 143). At the 2017 Beyond Tick Boxes symposium, NESB artists expressed the concern that:

> Their culturally specific art practices are difficult to articulate to grant assessors, art galleries and theatre producers who see their artform as part of a cultural practice, better suited to the community arts realm than the mainstream arts world. (Castagna 2017)

Clearly, some ambiguity still exists regarding what is recognised as a professional arts practice and some residual stigma is still attached to ethno-specific arts practices. Regardless of their practice, NESB artists and arts workers must be consummate networkers across creative disciplines and sector structures. To work creatively 'across cultures', therefore, requires confidence and empathy: confidence in one's creative pursuits, confidence to address the structures of the creative sector, and empathy to engage and communicate cross-culturally.

Institutional Leadership

The institutions in the creative sector (state, territory and federal government funding agencies) form a crucial part of the system of state patronage in the arts, particularly in the Australian context, which has limited philanthropic engagement in the creative sector. The Australian subsidised arts sector is closely aligned with the funding and advisory role of the institution of the Australia Council, the key federal government arts funding agency. Institutional leadership in this context refers to how staff and artist peers might lead the policy and grant decision processes of the Australia Council.

Intermediaries

The internal cultures of these arts ministries and the Australia Council form their own microcosms—internal and external networks that broker resources into the sector. They make and facilitate decisions about the allocation of resources. Within these microcosms are 'intermediaries who "connect or disconnect" people to resources from the common purse': 'people who assess works of art, who select media programs, film projects or edit news' (Totaro 1991, 4). As Totaro (1991, 4) explains, such people 'need to be able to understand a cultural milieu of increasing diversity and complexity. How do our institutions expand their corporate knowledge and understanding of cultural diversity?'

Recognition and inclusion of NESB artists as professionals needs to go hand in hand with the professionalisation of institutions. Institutions need to be diverse in their programming, governance and staff at all levels; they need staff who not only understand but also accept their roles as institutional intermediaries. Ahmed (2012) suggests that this is a form of 'institutional will', referring to the future tense in which the institution articulates what it 'is willing to do' by allocating an additional investment. The process to reach institutional commitment can be a cause of friction but contains within it the potential to be 'transformational' (Ahmed 2012, 128).

However, transactional leadership is more frequently found in bureaucracies with their vertical, hierarchical structures. These types of leaders occasionally provide charismatic and even transformational leadership, but are usually associated with stability; to briefly return to Foucault's metaphor, they keep the ship on course and the shop in profit. The impetus in bureaucracies is to maintain the status quo, as Machiavelli (quoted in Nadon 2013, 4) observed:

> There is no more delicate matter to take in hand, nor more dangerous to conduct, nor more doubtful in its success, than to set up as the leader in the introduction of changes.

Transactional leaders are likely to use 'coercive' power on occasion to drive organisational change (Grint 2005, 28). A transactional business relationship relevant to multicultural arts would be one in which Australia Council funding included conditions tied explicitly to cultural diversity outcomes in staff employment and artistic content. This approach is similar to the type of contractual arrangement operating at Arts Council England. There are some precedents in the Australian arts context. Screen Australia has included specific gender and diversity considerations in their assessment criteria (Screen Australia 2017). Specific protocols for non-Indigenous artists to work with Indigenous artists have also been developed by the Australia Council (Janke 2016). Protocols via formal mechanisms such as these generate a simulacrum of trust or lead to an environment in which trust can occur, because many of the issues regarding the relationship and outcomes have been considered and clarified. In these instances, 'transparency' is a mechanism that establishes trust.

Being Diverse

Another way to gauge an institution's internal commitment to cultural diversity is through employment data published in annual reports, because staff of diverse heritages demonstrate *being diversity* (Ahmed 2012, 49, original emphasis). Recent data suggests a drop from 15.4 per cent in 2014–15 to 11.2 per cent in 2016–17 of Australia Council staff who 'identify as culturally and linguistically diverse' (CALD), the current term favoured by government (Australia Council 2017a, 90). The Australia Council reports that 700 peers were registered in 2016–17 to assess grant applications and, of those, 21 per cent identified as CALD. In comparison, 25 per cent were regional and remotely based (Australia Council 2017b, 50), 18 per cent were Aboriginal or Torres Strait Islanders, and 6 per cent identified as living with a disability (Australia Council 2017b, 90). These staff figures indicate a decline in staff diversity while the peer figures show that efforts have been made to include culturally diverse artist peers, and suggests that the internal responsibilities to ensure peer appointments has generated traction over time to become a matter of course within the agency.

The Australia Council can consult with, and incorporate, its constituency in the process of forming policy and actions. For example, until 2008, the Australia Council sought expert advice on the arts in a multicultural Australia from ACMAC. Ahmed (2012, 31) describes two relationships between people and committees established for advocacy and change: one aims to attract and keep diversity advocates on important committees and the other seeks to have influential people on diversity committees. This duality presents a strategically durable way to influence change across an institution and is relevant to its governance.

Organisational Leadership

Within the multicultural arts focus of this book, organisational leadership refers to those in positions of influence in arts organisations funded by the Australia Council who seek to include and support NESB artists through the use of creative and financial resources. Arts organisations span the unevenly subsided arts sector. They range from S2M arts companies, including a handful of multicultural arts organisations, to major performing arts companies or major visual arts museums. Arts organisations may have a broad 'mainstream' remit or they may be dedicated to the specific promotion of NESB artists. Calls for mainstream organisations to demonstrate cultural diversity in their people and programs are also underpinned by questions of how they allocate their resources (Castagna 2017). The issue of the ability of mainstream arts to 'multiculturalise'—a useful alternative term akin to 'multiculturalization' (Noble 2011, 833)—comes to the fore in discussions of large flagship arts organisations, and, by the same token, the issue of marginalisation comes to the fore in discussions of smaller multicultural arts organisations. Multiculturalising can be considered a cautious process that avoids creative exchanges and being 'usurped by elite culture while the peripheries remain precisely where they are' (Gertsakis 1994, 45). The danger is that of 'inscribing one knowledge at the obliterative expense of another' (Gibson 2005, 273). In describing their framework for 'utopian co-production' between academia and community, Bell and Pahl (2018, 108) are wary of practices in which 'forms of knowledge co-production are diluted or repressed'. These concerns highlight the issues around 'shared' knowledge and critique some of the results of so-called mainstreaming to increase the visibility of cultural difference in the arts. Notions of mainstreaming must be treated cautiously because organisations:

> Are not ready for it: to act as if mainstreaming is the case, because it should be the case, can be counterproductive because the conditions are not available in the present *to make it the case.* (Ahmed 2012, 138, original emphasis)

Here, the issues of timeliness, context and organisational culture are necessary precursors to an organisation's values and programs being able to accept cultural difference. However, both mainstream and multicultural organisations have different roles and must be accommodated and supported for their respective roles. The leadership skills within mainstream arts organisations bring resources to a broader presentation of the work. Multicultural arts organisations (although few in number) bring resources to develop the creative potential of artists. Both types of organisation have the potential to establish, develop and maintain partnerships that aim to alter the balance of artworks that influence and contribute to an understanding of multicultural Australia.

The relational mode offers the potential for more creative leadership when cross-cultural, intercultural and intra-cultural art is being developed, and is appropriate when new approaches to an issue involve that issue's stakeholders. This has the potential to result in longer-term social change:

> Leadership as a social process can be defined as a process of dynamic collaboration, where individuals and authorised members authorize themselves and others to interact in ways that experiment with new forms of intellectual and emotional meaning. (Gemmill and Oakley quoted in Grint 2005, 28)

This social process is most likely to be adopted by 'relational' leaders who emphasise the 'quality of the relationship between the leader and the led … seen in terms of a group of people moving forward together' (Hewison and Holden 2011, 31).

The concept of 'accompaniment' is also relevant here because it builds on the relational process and adroitly avers the artificial notion of the leader and the led. The ethos of 'leadership as accompaniment' stems from the theology of liberation and Archbishop Òscar Romero's work with the campesinos of El Salvador. As Tomlinson and Lipsitz (2013, 9) explain: 'Accompaniment is a disposition, a sensibility, and a pattern of behavior. It is both a commitment and a capacity that can be cultivated'. Accompaniment is viewed as a partnership whereby professionally trained people share their skills and the people needing such skills 'offer lessons of a different kind of experience' (Lynd and Lynd 2009, 93). Accompaniment resonates with the creative pursuits of music, voice or performance of any kind. The use of accompaniment is apt to address issues of isolation, lack of access to the mainstream and increasing professional artistic practice for NESB artists because it is based in shared experience. There is also a resonance with community and cultural development practices that engage with community issues through creative exchange with a view to social and cultural change—to make the world a 'better place'. Accompaniment aims to create 'new social relationships that enacted the utopian hopes that religion and radical politics had previously only envisioned' (Tomlinson and Lipsitz 2013, 11).

Gibson's notion of 'attunement' takes us further along this concept as a way to specifically address the range of practices, protocols and 'babble of languages' that may be found in projects that are co-produced by any number of diverse artists. For Gibson (2005, 272–73), attunement is a 'patient and experimental process of listening and signalling, listening and altering … [to form] hybrid knowledge'. These two concepts (accompaniment and attunement) resonate with how those in creative and organisational roles may co-produce an expanded multicultural arts milieu.

Navigating towards a Multicultural Arts Milieu

It could, but does not yet, follow that, because we are a multicultural society, the art that is produced here reflects the complexity of our society. A multicultural arts milieu could engage with the creative potential afforded by a multicultural society. French philosophers Deleuze and

Guattari combine the three French meanings of 'milieu'—'"surroundings", "medium" [as in chemistry] and "middle"' (Massumi quoted in Deleuze and Guattari 1987, ix). One of their propositions is that 'rhythm is the milieu's answer to chaos' (Deleuze and Guattari 1987, 314). Their depiction of milieu suggests that it temporarily arranges a constantly dynamic world. Bourdieu and Wacquant (1992, 144), on the other hand, consider that a milieu is created through social relations of those in positions of power or influence to 'mirror' each back to the other: 'The relation to the social world is not the mechanical causality between 'milieu' and a consciousness, but rather a sort of ontological complicity'. Both of these depictions of milieu are appropriate for my purposes. 'Milieu' is the social context in which one finds oneself and one's peers, including systems to encourage or constrain a positive creative environment.

This ideal milieu would be aided by imaginative policy that views 'multiculturalism as an aesthetic issue' (Rizvi 2003, 135). Our dynamic and hybrid social realities mean that there is no one group of experts to hold the breadth of knowledge about multicultural arts practices across all artforms. Systems can be put in place to enable contributions to the governance of arts policy by NESB artists. As Mosquera (2003, 23) observes in the debates around cultural diversity, a 'key point is who exerts the cultural decision and on whose benefit it is taken'.

It is NESB artists' persistence that makes up an Australian multicultural arts scene; this, in turn, re-generates and creates the space and provenance to widen that milieu, enabling a set of practices to move into circulation (Ahmed 2012, 29–32). A continuous and contiguous history of production and presentation alters, permeates and shifts the boundaries of how multicultural arts 'circulate' and may generate a more supportive multicultural arts milieu.

For the individual practitioner, a cosmopolitan outlook can be viewed as a personal attribute; however, to produce a multicultural arts milieu, it is valuable to consider cosmopolitanism as a set of practices that can 'habituate open-ness to others' or, indeed, produce sites that 'foster forms of intercultural belonging' (Noble 2009, 51). Artist processes and presentations that are relevant to a multicultural Australia contribute to the production of such sites, which in turn foster the environment for multicultural arts practices. In order to foster such sites and practices, artists and multicultural arts organisations bring a cooperative approach to their cross-cultural creative work and involve their creative and ethnic networks.

It is reasonable to expect that the one (NESB artists making the work) will flow into the other (a general arts experience that describes a multicultural Australia). This is similar to the difference between intellectual and academic work as viewed by UK cultural theorist and activist, Stuart Hall (quoted in Ang 2015, 31): 'they overlap, they abut each other, they feed off one another, the one provides you with the means to do the other. But they are not the same thing'. Although describing a different set of worlds and practices, this could be seen to parallel the relationship between artist as activist and multicultural creative production as organisational change. The artist develops the organisation that provides the chance for the artist and future generations to keep on developing. Ideally, this could create a supportive milieu formed from relationships between artists, 'academies', agencies of government, arts organisations and audiences.

Constraints to the Ideal

A recurring historical narrative that hinders a flourishing multicultural arts milieu is the perception that multicultural arts comes from NESB artists working as community arts workers (Hawkins 1993; Blonski 1992, 1994; Gunew and Rizvi 1994). While recognised as the door through which the 'ethnic artist' could participate in subsidised arts, Community Arts and Cultural Development (CACD) processes are rarely valued as artistically 'excellent' because the benefits to the specific 'community' take precedence over artistic outcomes. The general public have limited access to the work, which limits wider recognition and creative traction. The perception that NESB artists are prevalent in CACD employment is challenged by data that show that only 7 per cent work in this area. Nevertheless, these associations may well be activated and reinvigorated as local governments increase support to arts and culture. *Edge of Elsewhere*, a multi-year and multi-sited international and intercultural visual arts project at Campbelltown Arts Centre in Western Sydney and 4A (now the Centre for Contemporary Asian Australia Arts) in inner Sydney, brought NESB and Indigenous artists into collaboration with community members to produce high-quality visual arts (Edge of Elsewhere n.d.). The creative outcomes of this ambitious project were made possible, in part, because of the '30 years of socially engaged arts activity in western Sydney' (Mar and Ang 2015, 55). The same is true with regard to Asian-Australian visual artists. Both point to the value of continuous organisational leadership in multicultural arts.

The support of family peers and networks are also essential to the systems that independent artists create around themselves to shore up their precarious existence and precarious art practice:

> Precarity is the condition of being vulnerable to others. Unpredictable encounters transform us; we are not in control, even of ourselves. Unable to rely on a stable structure of community, we are thrown into shifting assemblages, which remake us as well as our others. (Tsing 2015, 20)

Tsing elucidates precarity beyond unequal economic scenarios and emphasises the productive connections that can potentially occur between those very different to us. The existence of networks that build trust across those interfaces contribute to successful multicultural art projects. Permission from the family, for example, emerged as an important factor for second-generation NESB artists in their career path regardless of their ethnic background or class status; this mirrors the findings specific to Arab-Australian male artists (Idriss 2018).

The value of peer support and networks is a common issue: for example, 50 per cent of NESB respondents identified their most important need as being the opportunity to meet other artists (Stevenson et al. 2017, 54). An isolated artist cannot share their experiences and often internalises a sense of inadequacy. The response by artists to the Beyond Tick Boxes workshop organised by Diversity Arts Australia in 2017 raised this issue and attests to the need for artists to have opportunities to come together and try to make sense of their experiences. A multicultural arts milieu would see these opportunities at national, state and local levels regularly established in the arts calendar, similar to the bi-annual national regional arts conference.

A persistent issue encountered by the individual artist, and one that also plays out in public, is that of typecasting and stereotyping. Being typecast, stereotyped, cast in minority roles or not cast at all is a longstanding issue for NESB actors in theatre and on screen in Australia (Bertone, Keating and Mullaly 1998, xi). Twenty years on, a lack of opportunity remains the common experience for many NESB actors (Screen Australia 2017). Lewis (2007) sparked controversy around the lack of multicultural actors (adopting Hage's [2000] term of 'Third-World Looking People') on Australian stages and screens. This situation, if changed, would help to reframe the representation of Australia's national identity. Lewis (2007, 41) argues that the frequency with which NESB actors are cast in minority roles is 'akin to [the] spatial marginalisation of ethnic groups in cities'. Linking these two forms of cultural and spatial ghettos crystallises the sense of invisibility experienced by many actors.

Critical Appraisal and Appreciation

All artists want exposure for their work, yet access to extended networks and avenues of support to facilitate that exposure is often absent for NESB artists. Art criticism is interpretation and evaluation of an art project made public. Critical appreciation is extremely difficult to achieve in Australia because, as arts critic and writer Alison Croggon (2016a) observes, public discourse about art prefers 'to shore up the status quo rather than to question, to expand, to educate, to inquire, to imagine better'. There may also be resistance to writing about NESB artists, and, when such writing occurs, often a snide comment undermines the multicultural aspect of the work. In a critique of a review of *Fragments*, a book of poetry by Antigone Kefala (2016) in the *Sydney Review of Books*, Sneja Gunew argues that the reviewer takes an ill-informed standpoint from which to provide an impoverished review that, without basis, dismisses Kefala's work. Gunew (2017a) sees this as an example of the 'stereotypic methods … [by which] many Australian writers of non-Anglo-Celtic background get treated by the gatekeepers of Australian literature'.

Edge of Elsewhere raised the level of critical debate through a range of media and events. The project was afforded public circulation and attention through its inclusion in three annual programs of the popular Sydney Festival of the Arts, demonstrating how the general public can be brought into dialogue with culturally diverse practices. The processes and resources dedicated to this project and the longevity of practice in the local area points to what a momentary supportive multicultural arts milieu generates, and, in parallel, exemplifies the 'whole cycle' of the UNESCO Convention (Mar and Ang 2015, 60).

The Role of Friction, Trust and Traction

The preceding discussion suggests that the metaphors of friction, trust and traction provide a way to consider how to extend a multicultural arts milieu beyond the momentary.

Encountering Friction

Friction is a force that has several dimensions. It is the 'rubbing of two bodies (physical and mechanical); the resistance a body encounters when moving over one another; clash of wills, temperaments, opinions' (*Concise Oxford Dictionary* 1982, 393). For example, sandpaper rubbing over wood results in the alteration of both materials, oil is used to reduce friction in an engine, and disagreements or conflict can cause friction between people. All energetic exchanges will produce friction generating 'heat' as a by-product. In innovation and management studies, friction is seen to aid innovation through 'abrasion', whereby people are brought onto a project because they cause 'discomfort' and can present divergent views that may lead to new solutions. Friction in organisations can also help to identify when things are being made 'too hard to do' (Sutton and Seelig 2017).

The positioning of NESB artists and multicultural arts production within the Australia Council can be characterised by the type of friction that makes things 'hard to do' (Sutton and Seelig 2017). The causes of such friction can arise from pressure from multiple sources, including federal government policies on multiculturalism; arts funding; migrant constituencies; council staff and board members; and the perceptions of, and by, NESB artists. There has, at times, been fierce, internal resistance as to the need for 'special treatment' of migrants, ethnics or NESB artists (depending on the terms of the day) that has required articulate and influential leadership on the part of those wanting to encourage arts practices that reflect Australia's multicultural reality (Blonski 1992; Hawkins 1993; Sammers 1999).

The theme of friction and its role in generating creativity emerged through my analysis of AMA policies and the refrains of my interviewees who complained about the lack of change in the arts sector and the typecasting of artists in terms of their background. The processes of intercultural practice and negotiation for creative and cultural autonomy reflect how artists respond to those constraints. Anna Tsing (2005, 4–5), writing on 'contingent encounters', argues that 'cultures are continually co-produced in the intersections I call 'friction': the awkward, unequal, unstable and creative qualities of interconnection across difference'. Navigating the 'awkward, unequal' and competing aspects of innovation and maintenance of cultural heritage encapsulates the practices of some NESB artists. Innovation is a synthesis of fresh ideas into new forms of production that resonate within contemporary society. Cultural heritage is 'collective memory made tangible' that surfaces through forms of 'expression, maintenance, representation, recognition and renewal' (Anheier and Isar 2007, 30). These characteristics are frequently positioned as mutually exclusive binaries for multicultural arts practices, yet they present valuable opportunities through the capacity to generate creative responses.

The slow pace of change regarding representation is a 'glacial' friction that grinds over and eventually alters the landscape. The outer edges (or margins) at times move more quickly and generate greater friction and heat to produce some change in the landscape, while the centre (or the mainstream) moves far more slowly. The pertinent simile for NESB creative leadership in this scenario is that the margins 'melt' into a new fluid form more readily than the more static centre.

Establishing Trust

Trust is established 'when you do what you say you would do' (Punt and Bateman 2018, 39). This includes fulfilling those aims ethically and confirming whether the 'processes, platforms and people' are in place to achieve those aims (Punt and Bateman 2018, 39). It is arguable that past decades of friction, whether experienced by NESB artists, the arts sector or government (or its agencies), have produced a lack of mutual trust. Trust can be succinctly defined as a 'specific solution to risk' required when faced with an unfamiliar situation from which 'a bad outcome would make you regret your action' (Luhmann 2000, 95, 98). Arts funding institutions develop complicated procedures to assess and weed out risky clients, including those whose work is unfamiliar. If the artist is trusted (with the resources) and delivers on their grant obligations, their chances for repeat opportunities increase. This relationship between trust and risk is pertinent to the establishment of a multicultural arts milieu in several ways. The encouragement of the culturally unfamiliar would open up new creative possibilities and the allocation of (or trust with) resources would provide adequate support for the unfamiliar.

Weltecke also suggests that trust can be developed to reduce risk. While 'culturally constructed', trust may lead to an 'efficiency' of cooperation:

> 'Trust' can be seen as a specific combination of cultural practices, of emotional and rational phenomena, and of specific ideas and values connected with these practices and phenomena. Theories of trust might serve as a tool to become aware of the human ability to cooperate. (Weltecke 2008, 391)

Trust, therefore, becomes a multifaceted issue for some NESB artists that can be developed through the process of 'attunement' (Gibson 2005). Trust must be developed and present for an intergenerational, intercultural understanding that takes into account respect for knowledge holders and, as outlined above, manages that knowledge effectively to develop 'beyond' ethno-specific norms and contexts. Mutual trust for multicultural arts needs to be evident in many directions—from Australia Council staff and advisers to ethnic, migrant or NESB artists, arts organisations and vice versa, as well as the general public. If mutual trust becomes evident between these parties, the possibilities for a broader multicultural arts milieu increase.

Generating Traction

Traction describes the process whereby things can move in a desired direction by employing friction at the interface between two or more elements. Traction relies upon friction between these components or agents in a system and, if used tactically, can produce a trajectory towards a desired outcome. I use traction here to indicate movement towards a more supportive multicultural arts milieu. Traction in this sense is a result of a cultural and social understanding of the friction arising from the constraints and opportunities experienced by NESB artists and arts organisations.

The issue is how to manage exchanges that generate 'heat' towards a positive outcome while avoiding a destructive one. The process of establishing trust can determine the trajectory in a creative manner and, in time, generate traction towards something more stable and robust. The role of trust acts as a hinge that articulates and enables communication between the range of players in any given multicultural art project. There are many moments in that process where trust needs to be evident or established for an entire project to be successfully realised. Trust is publicly established when the artwork engages with, and is relevant for, diverse audiences. Contributions to those processes of developing traction include research that aims to educate artists and arts professionals alike. Such research includes *The World is Your Audience* (Migliorino 1998), *Who Goes There* (Kapetopoulos 2004), *Adjust Your View Toolkit* (Kapetopoulos 2009) and the Multicultural Arts Marketing Ambassadors program (Australia Council 2001, 21). Presenting culturally diverse content indicates attentiveness to culturally diverse audiences, which can have the effect of increasing the trust between creative work, presenters and audiences. These relationships enliven a multicultural arts milieu.

Conclusion

Despite investment in leadership courses by agencies such as the Australia Council, members of the arts sector, including NESB artists, continue to call for 'better leadership' (Castagna 2017; Gonsalves 2017; Badami 2017). A 'traditional' view is that leaders require a vision or direction, the capacity to engender trust in that vision and the ability to influence the group (of whatever size) to achieve their goal. The calls for better arts sector leadership raise questions about the ways in which directions for the arts are determined or led, and how any policies arising from those directions are implemented or managed.

Such calls suggest leadership styles that acknowledge the crucial role of relationships and reflect and assist the interconnected nature of contemporary society. Distributed leadership, for example, identifies how different skill sets in members of a group are activated to lead depending on the circumstances (Hewison and Holden 2011, 39). Relational leadership promotes open dialogue that shares responsibility between the people involved to generate innovative ideas. This approach suits a creative practice that innovates particularly between a range of cultures because it opens dialogue and shuts down judgement (30). Transformative leaders are charismatic and able to galvanise people to trust in their vision. These types of leaders are possibly more prevalent in creative arts organisations, as the arts often attracts those who wish to, or are comfortable to, 'stand out'. When the charismatic leader leaves, however, their galvanising abilities leave with them—often before their changes have been fully implemented (29–30). Transactional leadership, on the other hand, is a useful option, as it can provide a more explicit contractual basis to tie conditions of arts funding, thereby moving beyond personal preference to public expectation (29).

NESB artists and cultural practitioners are leading the arts in a multicultural Australia, in particular those who create new meanings through their relations with cultural groups. Their need to be adaptive and develop trust so as to be able to generate collaborations responds to the constraints of persistent under-representation and lower funding allocations (Keating, Bertone and Leahy n.d.). In this regard, each of the leadership styles discussed in this chapter are relevant at particular times in the full realisation of the UNESCO 'culture cycles' that will nurture a supportive, broader multicultural arts milieu. Crucially, it is also through the establishment of, and access to, networks for NESB artists and cultural practitioners that they will find themselves in a more generative environment. In that regard, the processes of 'accompaniment' (Lynd and Lynd 2009; Tomlinson and Lipsitz 2013) and 'attunement' (Gibson 2005) are skills worth cultivating. In all these instances, issues of 'trust' (how to *generate* it) and 'friction' (how to *exploit* it to gain traction) are central.

3

Shaping the Discourse of Arts in a Multicultural Australia

Since the 1970s, the discourse of Australia's multicultural arts policies has been shaped through interactions of government, government agencies (principally the Australia Council), arts bureaucrats, artists and cultural practitioners. This discourse has generated several Arts in a Multicultural Australia (AMA) policies and bursts of intense productive activity. However, the history of positioning non–English speaking background (NESB) artists and multicultural arts content within the Australia Council has been characterised by frictions that are often generated by issues around 'trust' that can limit any traction. This characterisation suggests that there are limits to multicultural arts policies, and questions whether the processes and debates within the Australia Council are able 'to go well beyond the instrumental' (Blonski 1992, 3). This chapter discusses barriers to policy effectiveness and locates the last two AMA policies of 2000 and 2006 within those histories of productive moments and the longer embattled and fractured narratives that characterise the arts in a multicultural Australia.

Policies and Their Problems

The aims of government policy are to responsibly address issues in their spheres of influence by articulating problems through research and agenda-setting, and offering solutions with key players and adequate resources (Rowe et al. 2016, 12). As a statutory agency of the Australian Government, the Australia Council is expected to develop arts-focused policies that relate to priorities set by the government. The need for a multicultural arts agenda is evident in the low levels of grant allocations to, and employment of, NESB artists, their lack of representation in the arts, and their increasing perception that their ethnicity can impact negatively on their arts careers. That these issues persist despite several decades of multicultural arts policies suggests that they may not be 'solvable' at the policy level alone and/or that policy implementation to date has been flawed. The leadership characteristics that contribute to effective development and implementation of the multicultural arts agenda can be found in cross-cultural competencies, relational and transactional leadership styles, and the capacity to activate networks.

Rittel and Webber's (1973, 155) typology of problems differentiates between those that are 'tame' (solvable) and those that are 'wicked' (intractable). A tame problem is complicated but can be addressed by research, strategy and 'established techniques and processes' and solved by management responses (Grint 2005, 9). In contrast, a 'wicked' problem is complex, 'novel, embod[ies] no obvious resolution point … depend[s] on the viewpoint of the stakeholder and is embedded in another similar problem' (Grint 2005, 9). Wicked problems are often 'ingrained' social problems, 'ill-defined' by government as a consequence of relying upon 'elusive political judgement' and considered unsolvable: 'at best they are only re-solved—over and over again' (Rittel and Webber 1973, 160). The paradox between these types of problems is that multiculturalism is often perceived as a managerial approach to diverse populations when perhaps a wider consideration applies.

According to Rittel and Webber (1973, 155), wicked problems appeared after the industrial revolution in the late eighteenth century because of the increase in the diversity of populations, the causes of their mobility and a wider range of group allegiances. While the arts are not viewed as an 'ingrained' social 'problem', the concept could apply when issues of the arts in a multicultural Australia are considered:

> Wicked problems often crop up when organisations have to face constant change or unprecedented challenges. They occur in a social context; the greater the disagreement among stakeholders, the more wicked the problem. In fact, it's the social *complexity of wicked problems as much as their technical difficulties that make*

> *them tough to manage* … confusion, discord, and lack of progress
> are tell-tale signs that an issue might be wicked. (Camillus 2008, 4,
> emphasis added)

Socially complex multicultural arts policy has received technical attention, which can be measured quantitatively, and is usually limited to the distribution of funds. However, from a purely creative perspective, the objectives of art are measured qualitatively. This is a challenge for a government arts agency, as success is always considered from a perspective other than the creative outcomes used by artists (Macdonnell 1992).

The other challenge facing the arts is that Australia currently has no national cultural policy. The two policies that had been developed and published were short-lived due to changes of government. *Creative Nation*, developed under Prime Minister Paul Keating in 1994, promoted a broad approach to culture that included film, media, libraries and heritage. Framed by this creative pluralism, the policy recognised Indigenous and migrant cultures as central in shaping Australia's domestic and exported identity. Twenty years later, *Creative Australia* muted this recognition:

> *Creative Australia* contains very limited reference to multicultural
> arts, and outlines no policies explicitly directed at expanding the
> participation of migrant or ethnic communities in the nation's
> arts and cultural sectors. Instead, cultural difference in the arts
> is referenced obliquely within a broader category of 'diversity'.
> (Khan et al. 2013, 1)

The use of 'diversity' as a catch-all phrase reinforces political ambivalence about the need to support multicultural arts practice and signals a retreat from particular consideration for it. The history of the arts in a multicultural Australia has a pattern of advocacy, progress, retreat and repeat.

Traversing the History of AMA

Those wanting to encourage arts practices that engage with Australia's multicultural society seek articulate and influential leadership. The Australia Council has, at times, expressed fierce internal resistance to the idea that migrants, ethnics or NESB artists (depending on the terms of the day) need 'special treatment' (Blonski 1992; Hawkins 1993; Bowen 1997; Sammers 1999). The history of AMA policies appears as either an abrasive or a lubricated continuum, often generated by the associated absence or presence of 'trust'. This ebb and flow of trust can lead to frictions in various areas: for example, in the engagement with federal government policies on multiculturalism; in the levels of arts funding by government; among the various and dynamic migrant constituencies; in the different ways in which complex identities can be creatively presented; in producing arts organisations' knowledge about the range of multicultural arts practices; and in the creative perceptions of, and by, NESB artists.

Cultural researchers (Blonski 1992, 1994; Hawkins 1993; Rowse 1985; Gunew and Rizvi 1994) and government sources (Gardiner-Garden 1994) have documented the historical signposts of AMA up to the mid-1990s. Blonski's chronology elucidates the development of 'multicultural arts' policy and is prefaced with an account of its historical value. Blonski (1992, 3, emphasis added) interprets these hard-won and -lost debates and negotiations as:

> A far more complex and difficult process of redefining culture within the bureaucratic context of at least one cultural agency in terms of interconnectedness rather than exclusion or oppositions. This suggests that the administrative processes and the debates within Council have to go *well beyond the instrumental.*

Ideally, the shifts in attitude required of the Australia Council could be more than just 'grafted on' programs that have the potential to go 'beyond the instrumental' (Blonski 1992, 3). Arguably, there is a need for transformational and relational leadership styles. To go beyond quantitative statistical 'access and equity' monitoring requires systematic and systemic change to understand the broader qualitative effect of multicultural artistic production and its subsequent potential to alter Australia's cultural landscape.

It is difficult to assess any broad impacts of AMA policy initiatives across and beyond the arts. The Australia Council has been criticised for endorsing policy programs that are neither measurable nor accountable in terms of outcomes (Keating, Bertone and Leahy n.d., 3). One way to identify effectiveness may be to analyse whether the AMA's policy outcomes have gone 'beyond the instrumental' to generate longer-term change across the arts sector. The following discussion of the intentions, results and issues of the 2000 and 2006 AMA policies identifies productive moments within a set of fractured narratives, locating the multicultural arts discourse within the broader project of 'redefining the culture' (Gunew 1994, 1). Issues of leadership in navigating this complex context are paramount and generally tend to rely on charismatic approaches; however, the capacity for relational leadership skills may be seen to produce a durational effect that can slide over into the next phase of policy or strategy development.

The AMA Context

The role of the Australia Council is to support and fund contemporary art practices in Australia, including multicultural arts. This remit highlights the paradox whereby the vast majority of funds and, subsequently, institutional reverence are directed towards major performing arts companies that produce and present what are frequently termed 'heritage' arts (Blonski 1994; Eltham 2015; Pledger 2017). There is still a view that multicultural arts practices are lacking in contemporaneity because they are pigeonholed within community arts and cultural development (CACD) (Khan et al. 2017, 19). The view that CACD is not contemporary may stem from its association with 'cultural maintenance' and its claims of producing 'social cohesion', suggesting that the role of community arts is to lubricate and cohere, rather than be shaped by equally critical sparks of creativity.

The Australia Council struggles to demonstrate its claims regarding the centrality of difference in its funding decisions for multicultural arts organisations (see Table 4). Ahmed (2012, 29) describes this experience as the 'gap between symbolic commitments to diversity and the experience of those who embody diversity'. The symbolic commitments tend to be limited to statements on webpages or paragraphs in annual reports. It is the NESB artist who experiences the gap in resources. Institutional staff can also embody diversity as 'diversity workers' (Ahmed 2012, 25). The unsettling nature of doing 'diversity work', either within or upon an institution, requires enormous persistence—particularly in uncovering those habits that are 'not named or made explicit' (Ahmed 2012, 25). The institution is irritated by the necessity to unpick and unpack the habituated status quo against diversity because, while 'habits save trouble, diversity work creates trouble' (Ahmed 2012, 27). This troublemaking is noticeable when considering multicultural arts policies and practices. Deciding what kind of trouble to make and how to make it forms the modus operandi for those developing multicultural arts policy. Most people doing 'diversity work', therefore, have an almost impossible task: to decipher the hidden intricacies of the institutional machinations. These can be likened to a 'black box' phenomena, whereby habitual processes are so ingrained they occur with limited awareness from the 'actor' (Latour 1987). The 'diversity worker' must be able to identify those habits that inhibit institutional diversity and find leaders who will attempt to address them through the policy statements and initiatives that the institution agrees to adopt.

The Origins and Development of Multicultural Arts Policy, 1973–99

Historical accounts of the first few decades of the development of federal cultural policy in Australia (Rowse 1985; Macdonnell 1992; Johanson and Rentschler 2002; Craik 2007) refer to 'ethnic' or 'multicultural' arts but, other than Blonski (1992, 1994) and Hawkins (1993), rarely examine multicultural arts policies in any depth. Appendix B outlines a chronology of multicultural arts policy at the Australia Council until the present time. Craik (2007) proposes a timeline that captures the phases of Australian cultural policy development:

- pre-1900 settler culture emphasising nostalgia and a new beginning
- 1900–39 state cultural entrepreneurship
- 1940–54 the era of national cultural organisations
- 1955–67 organisational patronage (government funded specialist bodies)
- 1967–74 policies of growth and facilitation
- 1975–90 access and equity and community cultural development
- 1991–95 diversity, excellence, cultural policy and cultural industries
- 1996–[2007] the review cycle and a return to neo-patronage.

Craik identifies multicultural arts content appearing as part of the developing national cultural narrative from 1975 onwards. It is worth noting the exceptions to this, such as the establishment of the Musica Viva national chamber music organisation by Romanian/Austrian immigrant Richard Goldner in 1945 (Musica Viva 2018). As a cultured migrant who generated creative experiences in his new post-WWII home, Goldner represents the 'potential' rather than the 'problem' version of the migrant and the arts.

Ethnic 'communities' are positioned as a problem from the naissance of the Australia Council. The first executive officer, Jean Battersby, appointed in 1973, acknowledged the existence of, what was then termed, 'ethnic minorities' and, in step with the times, their right to uphold their 'traditions'. Their place was firmly 'other'. According to Rowse (1985, 52), Battersby saw ethnic minorities as a barrier to expanding connections to the arts alongside distance, complex bureaucracies and 'indifferent attitudes to the arts'. He argues that, for Battersby:

> Ethnic difference appears as part of a list of obstacles to be dealt with in the Arts' reach out to the community. The term 'community' in her book embraces a great variety of policy issues. Collapsing 'difference' into 'distance' helped to preserve this misunderstanding. (Rowse 1985, 52–53)

These early dilemmas of where and how best to deal with 'ethnic minorities' reinforces their characterisation primarily as a 'problem', as opposed to a creative 'potential' within the newly formed federal arts agency (Blonski 1992, 3). The early and predominant structure of the Australia Council consisted of a governing board mostly made up of chairs from each of the artform boards that, in turn, were made up of expert peers. All members were appointed by government. Ethnic or multicultural arts did not have a separate section or board, but did have an advisory committee made up of NESB members usually from each of those artform boards.

Blonski (1994), in her aptly titled essay 'Persistent Encounters: The Australia Council and Multiculturalism', identified three durational phases in the development and retraction of the arts in a multicultural Australia between 1973 and 1994. The first phase (1973–82) identified ethnic artists through extensive fieldwork by an ethnic arts officer. Council dealt with the need for access through the establishment of a community arts committee as part of its structure (Hawkins 1993). However, it was widely considered, even by critics, that the small amount of funding allocated to community arts was insufficient. In 1975 community arts included some version of an 'ethnic arts' dialogue within its purview (Blonski 1992, 15). Despite persistent internal advocacy by Community Arts Director Rosalie Bower, and the brief appointments of an Ethnic Arts Committee and a Multicultural Arts Committee, there was no subsequent development of policy because it was 'regarded as a low priority' (Blonski 1994, 199). In 1978 the report commissioned by the federal government, *Post-Arrival Programs and Services to Migrants* (also known as the Galbally

Report), recommended that the Australia Council initiate more active engagement with, and support for, ethnic communities and artists. The evaluation in 1982 by the Australian Institute of Multicultural Affairs was highly critical of the Australia Council, which was subsequently goaded into action (Blonski 1994, 200).

The second phase (1982–86) saw a rapid change in multicultural arts policy. A council-wide policy resulted in major structural reform with dedicated staff to oversee the suite of changes. The internal changes specified lines of reporting and monitoring, use of incentive funds to be matched by artform budgets, and staff awareness of, and research into, multicultural arts policy development. Communication strategies included definitions of multicultural projects and ethnic artists, promotional publications and artist conferences. The results were increased staff confidence, clarity of roles and remits, increased recognition across all artforms for multicultural artists and a tripling of funding towards multicultural arts, even though it was a small fraction (3.1 per cent) of the Australia Council's annual expenditure (Blonski 1994, 201).

The third phase (1987–89) was one of hiatus and pushback by internal powerbrokers regarding multicultural arts. This was a period in which heated debate 'raged' about the Australia Council's grant funding criteria of 'professionalism, excellence and creativity'. The artform boards resisted calls to develop multicultural arts projects and advice on how to allocate funds, and instead successfully argued that council should abandon their centralised multicultural incentive funds. A recommendation from the Department of Immigration and Ethnic Affairs that the Australia Council increase its efforts to support multicultural arts did not occur due to funding cuts and a management review. However, attention to multicultural arts continued, and the term 'Arts for a Multicultural Australia' was first adopted at the end of 1989. This new branding was based on the view that the term 'multicultural arts was problematic and even meaningless' (Blonski 1994, 201–02), since 'multicultural arts' could refer to all arts practices, and not all NESB artists wished to be viewed as 'multicultural'.

A fourth phase can be distinguished between 1990 and 1996. This phase is characterised by rebranding, deeper institutional embedding and demonstrated relational leadership through closer working relationships with the states' arts agencies (Blonski 1994, 202). The AMA 1993–96 policy is distinguished by a period of national research and report writing, conferencing and the publication of what remains a definitive text, *Culture, Difference and the Arts* (Gunew and Rizvi 1994).

Blonski's retelling identifies lengthy periods of internal and external friction across many levels within the Australia Council, beginning with disagreements in the 1970s when each artform board was expected to specify their role in assisting migrant artists. Historically, these periods of friction have led to short productive phases of traction and change. Those phases have been characterised by trusting working relationships between program managers, Australia Council Multicultural Advisory Committee (ACMAC) chairs and the directors of either the community arts section or policy and planning section, depending on the location of the AMA policy work in the organisation. The supportive influence of the council chair and the CEO are essential. Key productive moments are associated with articulate and politically astute ACMAC leadership, members and staff who recognise the importance of artist involvement, and critical debate about multicultural issues within the arts.

The 1970–90s have been characterised by the Australia Council as decades of steady, increased inclusion, and there is little to suggest in the council's annual reports that this inclusion was a result of any external pressure. However, it is more realistic to portray these decades as a series of frictions caused, in part, by a lack of mutual trust. Mutual trust is multi-directional and needs to be reciprocated (Weltecke 2008). Therefore, trust needs to be evident between the council and the 'ethnic', 'migrant', 'multicultural' or NESB artist. When trust is evident between these parties, the increase in adequate traction can improve the multicultural arts milieu because a supportive environment should lead to more creative production.

Persistent Frictions

From the outset, a consistent friction was demonstrated by the ongoing structural issue as to whether 'ethnic arts' should reside solely in community arts (itself a cause of friction) or be integrated throughout the artform sections, and whether there should be special programs of support. The Australia Council has been described as a 'territory marked by competing cultural discourses' (Blonski 1992, 3) generated in debates between artform silos and institutional priorities, elite practice and community engagement, and the general public's and politician's awareness of the arts. This structural quandary underlined a lack of trust in the art produced by the so-called ethnic artist. Providing access was often interpreted as a barrier to achieving excellence because it opened the way for amateur artists to have access to limited resources. The 'ethnic artist' role had been designated as upholding traditional arts and crafts, which in turn raised questions about their capacity to be artists with contemporary practices (Hawkins 1993, 120). These early days saw tensions established around issues of trust and leadership of ethnic arts both in terms of eligible creative endeavours and questionable aesthetic assumptions on the part of the institution.

The location of multicultural arts policy work within the Australia Council was also a cause for friction. Throughout the decades between 1975 and 1999, responsibility for AMA shifted back and forth between the community arts section and the more centralised policy section (when such a section existed). Historically, both sections had an agreed understanding of debates leading to policies for inclusion (Hawkins 1993, 87–88). When AMA was located in the Community Arts Board— or the Community Cultural Development Unit as it was variously known—it had strong advocacy at the council table through the chair, but limited influence across the entirety of the council. When AMA was positioned centrally within the strategy and policy division, it had greater leverage through access to the council chair and as a central area of internal structural influence. Throughout the 1990s, a semblance of stable structural positioning had been achieved for AMA through the role being positioned in the strategy section, even though this was seen by some as a rupture from the 'supportive environment of community arts' (Sammers 1999).

The annual reports of most government institutions present public narratives of 'achievements' without airing internal debates. Former Australia Council chair Hilary McPhee (1995) provided this account:

> By 1982 a Multicultural Policy was adopted, a fund set up and the position Multicultural Arts Officer created. In 1988–9 this overall expenditure on multicultural arts was 3.7% of the Council Budget. In 1993–4 it was 11.6% and has all the hallmarks of being one of the most successful policy initiatives implemented by the Australia Council.

The Australia Council's policies incorporated the government's approach of disseminating multilingual communications about their programs, appointing NESB assessors and advisers as part of the institutional workings and presenting staff awareness programs (Hawkins 1993, 87). Appointing NESB peer assessors and staff champions remains the main strategy of the Australia Council today. Internal statistics demonstrate their commitment towards institutional inclusion. The 1990s saw first (NESB1) and second (NESB2) generation NESB artists at levels of 16–18 per cent as grant assessors and 26–29 per cent of staff. Grants approved to artists and communities appear to have settled at the earlier target, which saw an increase from 3 per cent in 1986 to 'a peak of 14 per cent in the mid-90s' and 8–9 per cent in 1999 (Sammers 1999). However, these steps of progress were not adequate for multicultural arts to become 'embedded' across institutional practices. Significant downward trends occur in times of institutional stress, usually caused by reduced funding appropriations from government. When government appropriation is reduced, multicultural arts falls off the agenda (Blonski 1994).

AMA 1993 articulated the results of crucial debates about who determines 'excellence' and how best to encourage greater access to services and deliver equity of resources. It challenged prevalent notions by rejecting 'narrow definitions of excellence, culture and artistic practice' (Australia Council 1993, 3). This statement was made prior to the release of *Culture Difference and the Arts* (Gunew and Rizvi 1994) and can be seen as a reflection of the emphatic concern of consecutive ACMAC chairs Sneja Gunew and Fazal Rizvi. Gunew was one of the authors of *Access to Excellence: A Review of Issues Affecting Artists from Non-English Speaking Backgrounds* (Papastergiadis, Gunew and Blonski 1994). AMA 1993 considered issues such as the impact on mainstream arts companies, communication, access and equity, and highlighted the relationship between Indigenous and NESB artists (Australia Council 1993, 2). Discourses about 'excellence' and the creative potential arising from collaborations between Indigenous and NESB artists continued into the 2000 and 2006 AMA policies.

The 1993 policy also articulated the scope of characteristics of the NESB artist and what constitutes a multicultural arts project. These definitions are reproduced here in full, as they remain the most current definitions and attest to the array of options that could attract funds to art projects:

- by first generation artists—Australian artists born in a non-English speaking country and whose first language is not English;
- by second generation artists—Australian artists born in Australia of overseas-born parents from a non-English speaking background;

- that involve a majority of immigrant artists of non-English speaking background or second-generation artists;
- are ethno-specific arts projects of an ethno-specific group;
- are conducted by a multicultural arts organisation;
- are from non-arts ethnic or multicultural organisations whose primary objective is specific work on the multicultural nature of Australian society; and
- whose main objective is to promote cross-cultural awareness;
- target ethno-specific communities in general;
- whose content relates to the multicultural nature of Australia and where the art production involves a majority of artists or groups of non-English speaking background;
- that explore and enhance cultural links between Australia and other countries or regions, in particular the Asia-Pacific region. (Australia Council 1993, 7–8)

Another persistent issue has been the capacity to evaluate policy. Former director of the community arts section Christine Sammers (1999) criticised the lack of mechanisms to 'coerce' decision-makers as well as the accompanying lack of evaluation and accountability:

> There is therefore little knowledge of the impacts of programs, targets, peer representation and other mechanisms on NESB artists employed, changing content of artworks audience access or other key objectives.

This lack of knowledge highlights debates over what works as a multicultural arts strategy and how best to make improvements. It also explains the sense of deja vu (Grint 2005, 15) experienced by so many NESB artists and cultural practitioners.

AMA 2000

The most recent Australia Council multicultural policies are those of 2000 (Australia Council 2000) and 2006 (Australia Council 2006a). AMA 2000 brought together tradition and innovation and profiled individual artists' practices as well as their roles in the community. By taking this focus, the policy attempted to alter perceptions of multicultural artists as only being relevant in a community setting with its attendant low status in the arts world.

AMA 2000 coincided with Prime Minister John Howard's tenure between 1996 and 2007. Howard was known for his lack of investment in multicultural issues, epitomised by his lack of use of the 'm' word of 'multiculturalism'. The arts portfolio received limited attention under Senator Richard Alston; however, any budget cuts to the arts were foreshadowed and were in alignment with most other portfolios. Philip Ruddock was the minister for immigration and multicultural affairs between 1996 and 2003, during which time he oversaw the development of offshore refugee detention centres and had limited engagement with the cultural side of his portfolio. This period also saw the rise of Pauline Hanson and her One Nation Party, built on a platform that claimed that Australians feared and mistrusted Asians (Marr 2017).

Despite this federal government's retreat from the earlier pluralist version of multiculturalism, this was nevertheless an extremely active period for AMA policy. Actor Lex Marinos completed his term as deputy chair of the Australia Council and chair of the Community Cultural Development Board (CCDB) and ACMAC, which, in 1998, led to the newly elected Coalition Government's appointment of television scriptwriter Deborah Klika as chair of CCDB; she subsequently also chaired ACMAC and Youth Arts.

The Structural Prominence of ACMAC

For over a decade since its establishment in 1989, the role and composition of ACMAC had been stable. The committee's role was to develop and monitor the implementation of the AMA policy:

> To make recommendations to Council on any issue which may affect the full expression of cultural diversity in the work of the Australia Council. This long-standing Advisory Committee is made up of members from each artform Board as well as three members appointed by Council who are external to the workings of Council. The Chair of the Committee is a Council member. (Australia Council 2002, 12)

Between 1998 and 2002, ACMAC consisted of 25 retiring and newly appointed members, which demonstrates the awareness of NESB artists by both the federal government (which appointed them to artform boards) and the Australia Council (which invited them onto ACMAC). It is also a salient reminder that the source of influence and leadership of ACMAC was due to its composition and focus, whereby peers from each artform section came together to discuss AMA policy issues, both broadly and in reference to their areas of expertise. ACMAC minutes from 1999 record the intention to, in their words, 're-vision' the AMA policy to give it a more strategic focus, and to improve the relationship with NESB artists, having identified the 'strong need to re-establish trust with the sector and Council leadership on AMA' (ACMAC n.d.-a).

In 1999 the development phase of AMA 2000 saw NESB artists being asked what their expectations were from an AMA policy. There had been some fragmentation of the sector caused by the CCDB's removal of funding for multicultural arts officer positions in local councils and the NSW multicultural arts organisation, Multicultural Arts Alliance, in 1998. This had resulted in a sharp decline in NESB artists' level of trust in the Australia Council's interest and ability to include them as part of the arts in Australia (Positive Solutions n.d.). Policy development, therefore, occurred through a range of communication channels including national consultation in the form of surveys, forums and face-to-face interviews with artists and cultural practitioners engaged in multicultural activities across a range of artforms.

Arts consulting firm Positive Solutions was engaged in 1999 to better understand the professional development needs of NESB artists. The responses included the view that the development of the arts in a multicultural Australia should be taken up widely across all arts sectors (Positive Solutions n.d., 17). Issues about leadership were also expressed, ranging from state government agencies that saw multicultural arts as 'too disparate', to individual artists who did not agree that there was a 'multicultural arts sector' (Positive Solutions n.d., 27). Several issues resonated with NESB artists who articulated the need for networking opportunities along with the recognition of prior experience and broader arts participation:

> I want professional development opportunities and am pretty clear about what I want and need. I would like it very much if someone took it upon themselves to provide opportunities which are not bogged down in 'community arts' models or targeting 'beginners'.
> (quoted in Positive Solutions n.d., 17)

Such comments highlight NESB artists' sense of disenfranchisement and reflect the lack of inclusion and recognition of their abilities. They also show that NESB artists expect professional development opportunities that take into account the complexities and changes in their working environment, which may otherwise be overlooked by large bodies such as the Australia Council.

A survey circulated to Australian artists requested feedback about the proposed aims and strategies under consideration before AMA 2000 was finalised. ACMAC members must have felt somewhat beleaguered at times, as their November 1999 minutes record that they were encouraged by the openness of the respondents who expressed surprise that council would even be interested in their comments. The themes articulated by artists went beyond the usual issues of funding to include such matters as communication, relationships and critical discussion:

- a desire and need for direct human contact with the Council
- a desire for information and material from the Council about AMA
- strong support for greater liaison with the state and territory arts agencies
- the need to promote, fund and encourage work
- the need to promote critical discourse with all parts of the sector including major organisations. (ACMAC n.d.-a)

The research for AMA 2000 focused on NESB artists and the broader arts sector. It was developed over two years through consultations internally with ACMAC members and staff, and externally with artists and arts organisations. In 2005 the Australia Council engaged consultants from Effective Change and Victoria University to undertake a national evaluation of the policy. This full policy cycle from consultation to strategy to implementation and evaluation is one of the intense periods of focus that reinvigorated the AMA policy.

Policy Intentions and Their Results

Eighteen months of research, consultation and strategic planning by ACMAC, as well as regular reports to the Australia Council and executive staff, resulted in a commitment of AU$2.08 million between the financial years 1998–99 and 2003–04 to deliver the policy objectives. As ACMAC chair, Klika had successfully navigated the process for improvements in activities, communication and trust between the multicultural arts sectors and the Australia Council, demonstrating relational, charismatic and transactional leadership to influence and negotiate this outcome.

My challenge was to deliver the raft of strategies with one other full-time staff member and the cooperation of other areas across the Australia Council. As Gunew (1994, 1) notes, the 'uneven' implementation of multicultural arts policy often frustrates the 'arts bureaucrats and artists themselves'. In this context, having two full-time staff members enabled time for the relational model of leadership to develop excellent relationships with the arts sector, especially those committed to multicultural arts who were essential for generating the momentum needed to implement the suite of initiatives. It also demonstrated distributed leadership by injecting funds into the multicultural sector to deliver the range of initiatives.

AMA 2000 developed a framework approach to deliver long-term strategies through skilling, promoting and engagement that could operate across the Australia Council's objectives. While the term 'multicultural arts milieu' was not used at this time, those three areas—skilling, promoting and engagement—aimed to positively influence the environment in which NESB artists worked.

The Multicultural Arts Professional Development (MAPD) program, managed by the Australian Multicultural Foundation and Kape Communications, partnered with RMIT University to deliver the 'skills' platform, which began in 2002 and ran until 2011. The executive program delivered an annual, national, accredited and creatively focused program on modest funding ($86,476 in its first year) from the Australia Council (Australia Council 2002, 113). The scope of MAPD has yet to be matched in its content and approach to multicultural leadership. Those attracted to the program included:

> Cultural managers, arts marketers, community arts specialists, producers, curators and artists who desired to build their skills in utilising cultural diversity for audience development, community partnerships, marketing and targeted communications: project development and international collaborations. (Kape Communications 2011)

Skilling and promotion were enabled by initiatives to produce and present high-quality and well-profiled artistic practice and content through Cultural Diversity Clusters (CDC) with Flinders University and kultour (a touring network formed by state-based multicultural arts organisations). ACMAC only ever ventured directly into the creative space once through the CDC. Making creative opportunities was a priority of the committee, but much harder to negotiate with senior arts development management, as it was seen as a form of creative 'interference'. ACMAC's approach was, therefore, to infiltrate the edges of creative production, and to form alliances that would inevitably engage in hybrid artforms through the acceptance of multicultural arts practices. The aim was to bring a number of NESB professional artists from different disciplines together to have their collaboration facilitated by experts with access to production infrastructure. The intention was to move beyond an approach of one-off projects, and to generate relationships that would lead to ongoing platforms:

> The aim of the Clusters concept was to stimulate relationships between well-resourced organisations to form partnerships for creative research and development which would lead to 'flagship' works which are multicultural in content. (Keating, Bertone and Leahy n.d., 32)

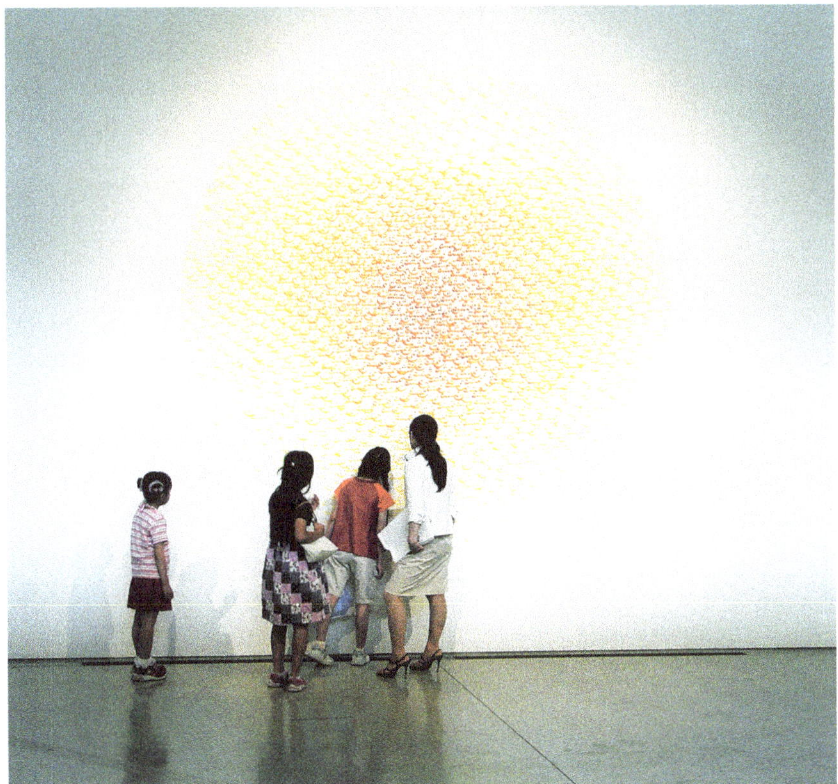

Image 4: Hossein Valamanesh, *Practice*, 2006

Saffron on paper, 20 parts 375 x 375 cm overall
Collection: National Gallery of Australia, Canberra
Photographer: H. Valamanesh

A partnership with the Australian Performance Laboratory at Flinders University Drama Centre was supported over several years, partly because of the potential to influence curriculum in tertiary education about devising multicultural content. Nine established artists mentored a group of emerging artists and worked with a team of researchers considered experts on 'intercultural and intracultural arts practice' (Australia Council 2005, 55). United by the theme of 'death', the artists worked intensively on their individual and combined arts practice. The artists included comic Hung Le, set designer Mary Moore, digital puppeteer Wojciech Pisarek, media artist Rea, dancer Yumi Umiumare, sculptor Hossein Valamanesh (see Image 4), photographer William Yang and performer Anna Yen (Australia Council 2005, 55).

I recall that some artform managers at the Australia Council worried that the CDC project would fail because it was stimulated by ACMAC and did not come from artists' expressed desires; however, given that ACMAC was itself made up of artists, this was a curious concern. The artists invited to CDC were challenged to collaborate across unfamiliar art disciplines. The result was that each made a separate contribution that flowed together as a visual and performance work, *Undiscovered Country*, which premiered at the inaugural OzAsia Festival. The piece did not aim to 'invoke a disparate display of multicultural art practices, but a resonance with the universality of feelings and memories invoked by death' (Adelaide Festival Centre 2007, 16). Working in 'laboratory' mode is now a reasonably common approach for artistic collaborative processes, and working directly with better-resourced arts organisations has since been taken up by NESB artists and groups as a successful model.

To improve engagement with NESB artists, forums were held in conjunction with other Australia Council or arts sector events, and regular electronic AMA *Bulletins* were issued. Within broader arts institutions, engagement also took the form of invited presentation events. One such event was held in November 2004: all CEOs and chairs of major performing and visual arts companies were invited to a presentation by Richard Kurin, director of the Smithsonian Institute, Boston (Kape Communications n.d.). Kurin, who also presented public lectures across Australia as part of the broader MAPD program, introduced the term 'cultural broker' to NESB artists and multicultural arts practitioners. In so doing, he effectively gave a name to the complex work undertaken by NESB artists, locating and endorsing it within a broader, international context of parallel activity.

In partnership with arts organisations and universities, ACMAC funded two significant conferences. The first was held in 2001 and was entitled Globalisation, Art + Cultural Difference—On the Edge of Change. The second conference, held in 2004, Empires, Ruins and Networks: Art in Realtime Culture, built on the momentum of the first. Both resulted in publications that were supported by ACMAC: *Complex Entanglements: Art, Globalisation and Cultural Difference* (Papastergiadis 2003) and *Empires, Ruins + Network: The Transcultural Agenda in Art* (McQuire and Papastergiadis 2005). These remain not only the most recent, but also the most substantial Australian publications dedicated to multicultural diversity and the arts.

An evaluation of the 2000 AMA policy, begun in late 2004 and completed in May 2005, found that the conferences were the most recognised initiative, followed by kultour. The level of recognition achieved by the two 'boutique' conferences reflected the cutting-edge focus of the field, concepts, presenters, and opportunities presented for discussion and networking. These conferences differed greatly from the type of conference events usually supported by the Australia Council (e.g. annual marketing summits). The benefits for artists included rare international and national networking opportunities and the possibilities of increased peer support that flow from these. Both conferences sought to open up perceptions of multicultural arts practices and to support such understandings with critical publications.

Issues Arising from the Policy Review

The challenge of how to measure cultural change was foremost in the consultants' evaluation (Keating, Bertone and Leahy n.d.). The 2005 evaluation of AMA 2000 used triangulated research via a survey that was sent to 1,000 members of the arts sector drawn from every third grant applicant over a certain period, 200 interviews conducted nationally, and analysis of Australian Bureau of Statistics (ABS) and confidential Australia Council data. The degree of equitable distribution of resources is one measure of a policy whose aim is to increase cultural production. At the Australia Council, in the 1990s and during AMA 2000, the grants to NESB artists and multicultural arts organisations hovered at 8 per cent, matching the nominal target set for a few years in the early 1990s (Sammers 1999; Keating, Bertone and Leahy n.d.).

A continuation of the AMA policy was strongly endorsed by 73 per cent of respondents. The relevance and need for the policy was supported by 41 per cent of respondents who thought the arts more '[adequately] reflected multicultural Australia' than five years prior. However, 31 per cent thought there was still 'a long way to go' (Keating, Bertone and Leahy n.d., 23):

> There is strong support for an AMA policy from artists, arts organisations and policy makers. The support is 'altruistic' and across the board. Beneficiaries and non-beneficiaries alike agree on this issue. (Keating, Bertone and Leahy n.d., 6)

AMA 2000 was considered by some to be groundbreaking because it:

> Represented a shift in how the arts in multicultural communities were viewed. It has long been recognised that the arts play a significant role in promoting social cohesion, social policy goals, economic growth, and shaping a nation's sense of identity. However, prior to the introduction of this policy, multicultural arts were typically seen as involving cultural retentive activities which had their roots in expressions of migrant cultural traditions. The introduction of the policy heralded the beginning of an era in which culturally and linguistically diverse (CaLD) Australians were seen as integral to the fabric of the Australian arts sector. (Rentschler, Le and Osborne 2008, iv)

These comments position the 2000 policy as an attempt to go 'beyond the instrumental' and to articulate the complex, cultural perspectives often associated with NESB artists.

Despite this positive commentary, the evaluation concluded that the AMA policy appeared to be 'tinkering at the edges'. The authors argued that NESB artists were not accommodated outside the grant process of the artform boards: there was no specific multicultural arts board, no targets for artform boards to meet and no expectation that they develop specific AMA initiatives (Keating, Bertone and Leahy n.d.). The review identified a distinct perception of the need for, and value of, multicultural arts awareness across the arts:

> The contention was that not only should there be an AMA policy, but that the policy should be 'the umbrella policy', acting as a central base from which policy and strategy formulation occurs. There was a strong concern that the policy had been marginalised over the years and that this trend, from the Australia Council, was continuing.

> In contrast, the only forum at which the value or relevance of the policy was questioned was the focus group held with a selection of Australia Council members, managers and artform board representatives. A minority of participants were critical of the on-going need to pursue the policy, displaying what Professor Andrew Jakubowicz described as 'a bored air of frustration' in reference to film industry 'heavy hitters" resistance to arts and multicultural policies. (Keating, Bertone and Leahy n.d., 30)

Crucially, and paradoxically, according to the consultants, the NESB artist was not found to be central in the AMA 2000 policy initiatives:

> One of the gaps found in the policy and its implementation is the lack of a broad brush approach to support the greater participation of artists. The evaluation repeatedly heard stories of NESB artists frustrated by their lack of success in securing Australia Council funding. The demographic analysis highlights that NESB artists, particularly first generation NESB artists, are under-represented in the group of grant recipients. The data is complex and indicates some variations in the experience of first and second generation NESB artists and variations across the artform boards. Taken together, the results highlight that there are some structural barriers to accessing funds. (Keating, Bertone and Leahy n.d., 4)

Using ABS data from 2001, the consultants found that:

> NESB artists were adequately represented in only two of the artistic occupations, viz. designers and illustrators, and visual artists and craft professionals. Authors and media presenters had the lowest NESB representation, at just over half the per centages expected. NESB musicians, who fared better, were still under-represented. (Keating, Bertone and Leahy n.d., 26)

Table 2 compares expected and actual levels of representation of NESB artists in 2005.

The gap between the expected and actual levels of representation of NESB artists is significant in light of the points made in Chapter 2 regarding the lower levels of professional representation across professions that are language-based as well as the impact on arts-related incomes.

Table 2: Expected and actual levels of representation of NESB artists in 2005

Category	Expected level of representation %	Actual level of representation %
Designers and illustrators	14.0	15.0
Visual artists and craft professionals	14.0	14.6
Photographers	14.0	11.7
Artists and related professionals n.f.d	14.0	10.9
Film, TV, radio and stage directors	14.0	9.4
Musicians and related professionals	14.0	9.2
Actors, dancers and related professionals	14.0	8.8
Journalists and related professionals	14.0	8.5
Media presenters	14.0	7.5
Authors and related professionals	14.0	7.5

n.f.d (not further defined)

Source: Keating, Bertone and Leahy (n.d., 26).

Alongside issues of income and representation, one of the controversial recommendations made by the evaluators was to decouple innovation from multicultural arts practice. While acknowledging that 'cultural diversity is seen as a driver for innovation in the arts field', they characterised the responsibility to innovate as an additional hurdle and burden for NESB artists to bear (Keating, Bertone and Leahy n.d., 6). In their view, the low levels of funding and arts workforce participation attested to the need to go back to 'core principles' of how NESB artists could be accepted into the arts in Australia.

Communication had improved between artists, multicultural arts groups and the Australia Council; however, many artists expressed concern that any criticism of the policy would be misunderstood and lead to its demise. Possibly because of this, few artists are directly quoted in the report, but their comments are analysed:

> The experience of difficulties accessing funding [and] the difficulty of articulating culturally specific or exploratory work continues to be a hurdle for NESB artists. If the notion of innovation is rested on the shoulders of a group of artists already experiencing structural disadvantage, the policy will continue to struggle to be understood, implemented or enshrined. (Keating, Bertone and Leahy n.d., 14)

State-based and funded multicultural arts advocacy and presenting organisations, such as NEXUS Arts (n.d.) in South Australia and Multicultural Arts Victoria (2018), which program and present performances or exhibit visual art, and which, in 2005, were still to be found in each state and territory, were noted as important access points into the arts sector for many NESB artists. They provided 'a vital focal point for multicultural arts across the country'; however, as Keating, Bertone and Leahy (n.d., 4) observed, such 'organisations are too often balancing on the financial brink for their potential to be reached'. This precarious environment for NESB artistic engagement has changed little over the years.

AMA 2000 Policy Evaluation Conclusions

The consultants who reviewed AMA 2000 found that, while it had overwhelming support 'across the board', it lacked an operational context; therefore, justification for the policy was assumed. This criticism was levelled at other policy statements released by the Australia Council as well (Keating, Bertone and Leahy n.d., 4). Successful gains had been made through the two conferences, subsequent publications and the touring initiative. Further:

> Despite the complicated framework of the AMA policy, one of its greatest strengths is the policy development cycle which was followed through—including research base; the consultative development process and its suite of multifaceted strategies. (Keating, Bertone and Leahy n.d., 6)

The consultants identified lower participation rates and incomes for NESB professional artists as being a serious problem. Danger also existed in the expectations placed on NESB artists in regard to innovation. A total of 94 recommendations were distilled down to a handful during the 2005–06 restructure of the Australia Council, and the council chose not to publish the evaluation report. The AMA policy was renewed in 2006, but the recommendation to strengthen the work and its position within the Australia Council was not supported.

AMA 2006

John Howard remained prime minister until the end of 2007, when Kevin Rudd was elected. The Australian Labor Party retained power for a further term when Julia Gillard was elected prime minister from 2010 to 2013. The ministers for the arts and sport during Howard's tenure were Senator Rod Kemp followed by Senator George Brandis, who remained in the post until 2007. Musician and environmentalist Peter Garrett was appointed Labor's minister for the arts and environment from 2007 to 2010. When the Liberal-National Coalition was elected in 2010 with Tony Abbott as prime minister, Senator George Brandis was re-appointed to the arts portfolio. The Gillard government's *Creative Australia* policy disappeared when Abbott came to power, in effect leaving AMA 2006 as the most recent, formal government statement on multiculturalism and the arts. In 2015, when Malcolm Turnbull took over the prime ministership, he promoted Senator Brandis to attorney-general and appointed Senator Mitch Fifield as arts minister to dampen the 'enthusiasm' Brandis had demonstrated for greater control over the arts budget (Eltham 2015, 2016).

Multiculturalism remained in ambiguous, bipartisan political favour during the post-Howard years. There was commitment to the policy but little attention was paid to it. Post-2014 saw the resurrection of the One Nation Party with four Senate seats. Leader Pauline Hanson claimed: 'I am back but this time I am not alone' (Marr 2017). From time to time, her party, which held the balance of power, was feted by the Australian Labor Party and the Coalition, neither of which spoke out against her anti-Muslim ideology, and some politicians claimed that One Nation had become 'sophisticated' (Marr 2017).

During 2005, the Australia Council and some of its artform boards were in turmoil as a result of an internal restructure begun in 2004. This upheaval included an unsuccessful attempt to end both the Community Cultural Development program and New Media Arts, and saw the dismantling of the policy, communication and planning section into a much smaller section of strategy (Australia Council 2006b, 13). Within this context, the council had to decide whether to endorse the next iteration of the AMA policy and accept the recommendations of the evaluation. My recollection is that, although soon to complete their appointments, then Australian Council Chair, lawyer, UNSW Chancellor and philanthropist David

Gonski, and CEO Jennifer Bott, both understood the importance of multicultural arts practices and both had ties to ethnic heritages that were important to them. It is also the case that the Australia Council's work as part of AMA 2000 had been acknowledged by international arts councils.

In the midst of this volatility within the agency and the arts sector, ACMAC Chair and music teacher Christine Pulvirenti steered the results of the evaluation through an 'unpredictable' Australia Council (Usher 2005). There was much negotiation over multiple drafts, recommendations and levels of expected expenditure. The need for such high-level, persistent fine-tuning with the council's executive, chair and deputy chair, and within the context of organisational upheaval, demonstrates that the policy had yet to become part of council's 'business as usual'. Ahmed (2012, 29) describes the work of 'diversity practitioners' as developing techniques to embed diversity or make diversity 'a given'; this requires 'institutional recognition of the value of diversity', which 'requires time, energy and labour'. Enormous amounts of time, energy and labour were expended by the Australia Council's 'diversity practitioners', with staff and the ACMAC chair working to ensure that AMA 2006 was endorsed, that financial commitments were made for the continuation of ACMAC, MAPD and kultour, and that an allocation of $600,000 over three years was made to boost the scope of three multicultural arts organisations.

Businessman James Strong was appointed chair of the Australia Council in 2006 and Kathy Keele, previously from Telstra and Qantas, was appointed CEO in 2007. On completion of Pulvirenti's term as ACMAC chair, former BBC broadcaster and active regional arts advocate Nicola Downer AM was appointed. By June 2007, the short-lived strategy section had been absorbed into a governance section and my role (which now had to demonstrate more responsibility across AMA, arts and health, regional and other areas) was moved into the newly formed community partnerships section, developed from the politically strategic CACD sector response to the 2005 restructures. The AMA's role had come full circle back to a more expanded community section of the Australia Council and, by 2008, along with other 'social' policy areas, would become one of several areas folded under the umbrella of the Cultural Engagement Framework (CEF) (Australia Council 2016b).

The Structural Position of ACMAC

The evaluators of AMA 2000 identified challenges faced by ACMAC regarding the recruitment of members, compliance of artform boards and the capacity of board peers to represent AMA issues, and recommended that:

> No case was found for disbanding the Committee. On the contrary, it was felt that the role of ACMAC should be strengthened, drawing in more Council members and external advisers. (Keating, Bertone and Leahy n.d., 4)

Appearing to focus on only one component of the recommendation, the senior executive team removed ACMAC's networked peer base through the artform boards and adopted a new structure that drew only from external experts. In spite of the successful funding of ACMAC (and MAPD and kultour) for another three years, this can be seen as the event that led to ACMAC's eventual dismantling at the end of 2007 (Australia Council 2009, 48–49). It can also be seen as a precursor of other things: another institutional shift dismantled the artform boards in 2013.

Even though the external experts appointed to the artform boards were knowledgeable and articulate experts for the arts in a multicultural Australia, removing the NESB connection to each of the artform boards significantly reduced ACMAC's influence. The members in 2006–07 were theatre director Teresa Crea (SA), international cultural facilitator Professor Amareswar Galla (ACT and Queensland), state multicultural officer Walter Gomes (WA), arts centre director Kon Gouriotis (NSW), academic Professor Andrew Jakubowicz (NSW), multicultural arts consultant Fotis Kapetopoulos (Victoria) and local council officer Tiffany Lee-Shoy (NSW). Not all were experts in the area of grant assessments and the machinery of the Australia Council, and they were not given the opportunity to meet with other peers or Australia Council staff on a regular basis. Their power was diminished because they were not appointed by the government and their traction within the systems of the Australia Council was curtailed. The membership of ACMAC was now only by direct invitation from the Australia Council. This compared unfavourably to previous government appointments to artform boards. The final reference to ACMAC in the 2009 Australia Council Annual Report barely acknowledged the committee's role over four decades:

> The committee comprised experts in areas of multiculturalism and the arts in Australia and internationally. In April 2008, the Council adopted a cultural engagement framework, of which the arts in a multicultural Australia policy is a part. As part of the framework, the Council agreed to convene advisory groups to assist in the development of initiatives and strategies as required. (Australia Council 2009, 48–49)

The Australia Council decided when, and under what circumstances, advice would be requested.

Policy Intentions and Their Results

The Australia Council's vision in 2006 reflected the view that 'Australia's dynamic cultural life and practices are embraced, celebrated and created by the diversity of our cultures' (Australia Council 2006a). Its stated commitment was to support and promote 'a strong arts sector that effectively reflects Australia's cultural diversity, by integrating the objectives of its Arts in a Multicultural Australia (AMA) policy through the delivery of its activities' (Australia Council 2006a).

AMA 2006 highlighted the council's vision of 'the diversity of our cultures' through the areas of leadership, participation and creative production, including between Indigenous and NESB artists. The first objective was to increase culturally inclusive leadership by ensuring governance as a culturally inclusive process, integrating multicultural aims into each of the council's activity areas, and increasing culturally diverse representation across the arts. The second objective enabled all Australians to participate in the arts by delivering specific audience and market development strategies, increasing awareness of, and access, to the council's programs, and brokering and engaging in partnerships. The third objective supported the development of creative content that reflected a multicultural Australia by encouraging cultural inclusiveness, supporting multicultural arts industry infrastructure and content development, and encouraging creativity that spanned the spectrum of tradition and innovation. The fourth objective encouraged creative interfaces between Indigenous and NESB artists by facilitating cultural exchanges (Australia Council 2006a).

A major focus of ACMAC was to demonstrate its national advocacy role and to broker partnerships to support infrastructure for multicultural arts. ACMAC had a clear link beyond the Australia Council to power and influence. Chair Nicola Downer's personal influence and positional leadership enabled a day-long event, Multicultural Arts: Cultural Citizenship for the 21st Century, to be held at Parliament House, Canberra, in November 2007 (Australia Council 2007). The arts symposium featured heads of state arts agencies, cultural theorists and artists, and included live performances by a range of artists. The event received an unprecedented amount of political attention and was attended by a number of high-profile politicians including Assistant Minister for Immigration and Citizenship Teresa Gambaro, Arts Minister Senator Brandis, and former minister for foreign affairs Alexander Downer. To date, no other arts event has received this level of political attention. This strategic event publicly associated AMA with something highly valued by the Australia Council—political influence:

> Organisations can be considered as modes of attention: what is attended to can be thought of as what is valued; attention is how some things come into view (and other things do not). Diversity work involves the effort of putting diversity into places that are already valued so that diversity can come into view. (Ahmed 2012, 29)

Ahmed describes how influential positioning can smooth the path to increase the profile of an issue. The word 'effort' is crucial here because it signals that the attention is unusual and not an everyday transaction. The location of the event and the access to influential parliamentarians such as Downer attracted high-calibre artists, arts bureaucrats, academics and commentators. Facilitated roundtables reinforced nationally relevant themes and concerns across the arts sector, including:

- ensuring the centrality of multicultural arts policy within the creative landscape
- improving the diversity of the governance of major cultural institutions
- increasing the capacity of the small to medium sector to build the creative capacities of diverse communities
- identifying the needs and trends in national multicultural arts research programs
- creating highly visible pathways across the spectrum of multicultural arts
- including NESB artists in cultural dialogue and decision-making
- developing strategic partnerships
- ensuring access to adequate funding (Australia Council 2007).

These objectives expanded upon and more clearly articulated those in the 2006 AMA policy. The language (active and specific) benefited from the focused consultation that relational leadership modes can provide. This process highlights the value of consulting members of the Australian arts community, academics and politicians when determining future AMA directions. Wide consultation was considered a strength of AMA 2000 and it also applies to the 2006 policy. In 2018 these objectives from 2007 remained on the Australia Council website as the only reference to the arts in a multicultural Australia.

Issues Arising from the Policy

Verifiable data assist in identifying trends in the policy landscape. An annual internal AMA report produced from the 1980s to around 2006 by senior policy staff at the Australia Council included successes and challenges as well as statistics on success rates from each section of the council. Internal debates about 'coding' (i.e. capturing data about grant applicants) to differentiate projects made entirely by NESB artists, or by more than 50 per cent of NESB artists, are present throughout these reports. The reports had multiple uses: they facilitated staff and board member engagement with AMA matters; they provided opportunities for institutional leaders at a range of staffing levels to display relational leadership capabilities with colleagues, artists and multicultural organisations; and they resulted in the enhanced coding of grant applications, to which I contributed as a staff member, through a new dashboard with streamlined coding processes for program staff who were able to generate the reports after each grant assessment meeting. However, as at 2018, no AMA reports have been made public by the Australia Council. The only longitudinal public data on NESB artists are contained in the Macquarie University Economics Department's research into individual artist's incomes undertaken every five years (Throsby and Hollister 2003; Throsby and Zednick 2010; Throsby and Petetskaya 2017). Those results corroborate the evaluation results of AMA 2000, telling a stark story of low participation rates and low arts-related incomes for NESB artists.

The diminution of the Australia Council's support for AMA continued with the 2006 shift in the make-up of ACMAC and its subsequent disbanding in 2007. The rationale given by CEO Kathy Keele was that ad hoc consultations could be held on an as-needed basis (Australia Council 2009, 48). From 2007, the AMA's navigational and advocacy leadership roles at the Australia Council declined sharply. The Australia Council's lack of institutional commitment was signalled when the long-term structural prominence of ACMAC was reduced.

The Australia Council did not provide funds to support critical discourse within AMA 2006. In the absence of an updated policy that would have been expected around 2011, a useful comparison point for how NESB artists perceive their situation in the arts 'scene' generally can be seen in *Artlink's Multicultural Arts* (1991) and *Diaspora* (2011) special issues. The titles suggest a move away from the term 'multicultural' and can be seen as an attempt by the magazine and guest editors to re-position the discussion. The 2011 issue includes six articles that feature NESB artists and their art practices; the majority of the articles have an Indigenous or international art focus or align with geographically specific art projects (such as Minto in south-west Sydney).

The language is generally apolitical; however, articles in the 2011 edition nevertheless emphasise the importance of multicultural influences in various artists' works. For example, artist, curator and former director of the 4A Centre for Contemporary Art Aaron Seeto (2011, 25) highlights the continuing paradox of cultural difference within artistic production in a multicultural Australia, regardless of the incredible levels of activity:

> To a large extent, experiences of cultural difference are either over-determined or entirely absent from contemporary Australian art discourse. Australian culture has yet to understand the impact that intercultural experiences have had on its evolution, and how the anxiety of locality—how we perceive, articulate and imagine the cultural histories which result from specific geography and history of this continent—impacts how we understand our art history and imagine its future.

Here Seeto is echoing the 25-year-old call by Blonski (1992, 3) for the arts in Australia to go 'beyond the instrumental'. Seeto suggests that policies have been ineffective, as they have not had any broad impact on the main art galleries aside from a narrow interpretation of what might be accepted. He implies that questions of multiculturalism, identity and naming are unfashionable in the contemporary arts scene:

> In more recent times, marked by fluidity, ease of cross border movements, communication and globalisation, when the terminology of multiculturalism arises, there's always a faint groan. Recently a young critic said to me that the term Asian-Australian was past its usefulness. (Seeto 2011, 28)

The idea that terms and phrases associated with multiculturalism are 'past [their] usefulness' is likely to be a prevalent perception, having accompanied discussions about multicultural arts policies since their development. While recognising that this is difficult policy terrain for young artists to navigate, Seeto (2011, 28) observes that the conditions that give rise to the need for such policies have not been erased:

> It is not as if the issues of xenophobia and political parity have
> been addressed, or that cultural difference is well understood by
> the institutions that frame contemporary art in Australia.

This suggests that deeper engagement to address the ignorance of contemporary institutions is required. As is often the case, it is the artist who provides this deeper engagement, as the policies of institutions offer little beyond rhetoric or a narrow view of the politics of multiculturalism. Seeto (2011, 31) is critical of the strictures of policy formation around cultural difference and yet, more importantly in many ways, he suspects that 'art world structures in Australia are inadequate to interrogate and conceptualise art practice that arises from its own history of diaspora and migration'.

Other artists in the 2011 *Artlink* issue describe their fluid identities and mixed practices without addressing policy. In discussing the influence of cultural diversity, performance artist Brian Fuata describes his collaborative working mode with other artists. In becoming adept in this mode, which works across cultural understandings and iconographies, artists have become less constrained in how they interact with each other's practices, demonstrating their agency in the creative cycle. As Fuata (2011, 23) explains: 'In relation to a notion of identity and the cultural diversity thereof, such a project reflects a contemporary arts society that is inherently diversified and acknowledging of that'. This artist engages with one artist at a time, and generates his own peer support network in the process of his practice. The value of professional creative networks is consistently raised as an important need for NESB artists (Positive Solutions n.d.; Keating, Bertone and Leahy n.d.; Stevenson et al. 2017).

For others, the themes of freedom of expression and 'displacement and exile' continue to be present, as in the work of Iranian-Australian migrant artists Nasim Nasr and Siamak Fallah. Relinquishing her practice from her place of origin, Nasr makes:

> Art from the unseen; from my memories. Living in Australia feels like I am in exile, this is something I cannot do inside my country. Now I've got my freedom I am happy, but there is a displacement between my past and my present. I am not really free from these things—they are always with me like a shadow. (quoted in Harms 2011, 46)

Melbourne-based theatre director and former Theatre Board and ACMAC member Bagryana Popov continues to draw on the relevance of storytelling as the mode for one of her works—an adaptation of the novel *Café Scheherazade* by Australian author Arnold Zable:

> What makes it urgent? Melbourne is an extraordinarily diverse city, there are so many different ethnicities, histories, faiths, in our society. Yet there are still sometimes—bewildering to me— questions raised about the value of multiculturalism and diversity. The urgency is to celebrate the people and to listen—to the stories from different lands—and how they are integral to our experience of Melbourne. (quoted in Andrew 2011)

Christos Tsiolkas, one of Australia's most well-known and commercially successful 'migrant' writers, openly claims his cultural heritage and discusses his sense of responsibility as a 'migrant' (Tsiolkas 2013). It is this awareness of responsibility that carries forward the aesthetic and social leadership of the NESB artist.

AMA 2006 Conclusion

During the implementation stage of AMA 2006, the Australia Council concluded its sustained engagement and historical relationship with NESB artists as artform board appointments and expert policy advisers. Regardless of how fraught the relationship had been, ACMAC had been a mainstay of the Australia Council's work, enabling a space for complex creative discourse. As a conduit to the sector, ACMAC had contributed to the multicultural arts milieu. The last ACMAC chair Nicola Downer used her 'charismatic' and 'positional' leadership to host the highest profile event for both ACMAC and the Australia Council at Parliament House, Canberra. In 2018, the aims for multicultural arts policy developed at that event, but no other references to AMA, can be found on the Australia Council website.

Conclusion

The periods in which traction around the AMA policy are demonstrated are few and short-lived. Blonski (1994) suggests that any increased attention to access and equity issues regarding multicultural Australia as a result of government directives to the Australia Council is undermined when government reduces its allocation to the arts. The hypothesis is that the Australia Council's interest in multicultural policy waxes and wanes in line with the federal government's interest in multiculturalism (Sammers 1999). However, this is not necessarily borne out, as one of the most productive periods for the AMA (1998–2005) was under the Howard government. An alternate argument is that, when times are financially robust, multiculturalism in the arts may benefit, but when times are financially constrained, it falls off the agenda. This suggests that creative practice and infrastructure for multicultural arts are not considered 'core business'. To limit support for an ideal to times when there are 'surplus' funds is not leading, it is opportunism at the expense of long-term change. It also indicates that the Australia Council has yet to move 'beyond the instrumental' (Blonski 1992, 3) in relation to its NESB constituents. Effective leadership in this arena has been evident when the sources of friction are managed so that adequate levels of trust facilitate the subsequent traction for change.

The AMA 2000 and 2006 policies (and, to a large extent, those preceding them) have similar overall objectives to promote, support, engage with and develop arts sector capacity for the arts in a multicultural Australia. The sector, when consulted, has similar objectives (as seen in the roundtable outcomes from the Multicultural Arts: Cultural Citizenship for the 21st Century event). These issues have been in circulation since the 1970s. And there is little evidence to suggest that the withdrawal of support for the AMA policy under the guise of 'mainstreaming' has been either timely or of use.

This returns us to the issue of leadership. Directing policy processes within the Australia Council requires astute attention to the politics of policy formation. A wide range of leadership attributes are required and these need to combine charismatic, adaptive and relational modes. The skills of 'attunement'—listening and responding to signals—are an important element of leadership within an institutional framework. These are not necessarily standard leadership repertoire, but when applied to the policy development processes of an agency, they have the potential to become a potent force that can cut through institutional lethargy.

There is a startling difference between support (from the Australia Council and the multicultural arts sector) for the genuine attempts to implement the ambitious wide-ranging strategies of AMA 2000, and the winding down of these continuing strategies that was overseen by executive staff at the Australia Council throughout AMA 2006. The removal of the structural significance and prominence of ACMAC signalled a slow and grinding diminution of any legacy for multicultural arts at the Australia Council.

Two more distinct phases can be now identified for the arts in a multicultural Australia that build on those discussed above. Significant investment in a raft of strategies that aimed to improve the conditions and capacity of multicultural arts between 2000 and 2005 can be described as a fifth phase. The sixth phase, which began with the release of the 2006 AMA policy, has an indeterminate end, but could be placed at 2007 with the dissolution of ACMAC, or at 2008 with the introduction of the CEF. In addition to the winding down of ACMAC, the sixth and final phase has witnessed the gradual diminution of structural influence and the end of major initiatives such as AMA conferences, MAPD and kultour.

The leadership for arts in a multicultural Australia has now shifted away from the Australia Council and into the arts sector. None of the AMA policies remain on the Australia Council website. The sole reference to multicultural arts that remains is to the 2007 event held at Parliament House. Consequently, artists and creative leaders who have taken on the mantle of leadership for creative multicultural diversity have had to develop other strategies to ensure creative production and longevity and to widen the sphere of partners and supporters beyond the Australia Council.

4

Creative Leadership: The Agency of the NESB Artist

Australia's multicultural society is yet to be adequately reflected through its art. Although many artists may be ambivalent about labels such as 'multicultural' or 'NESB' or 'CALD', it is they who contribute significantly to an arts scene that engages with the diversity of Australia's population, which in turn generates the space and provenance for further possibilities of a supportive multicultural arts milieu. As the previous chapters demonstrate, the extent of the challenges and barriers faced by non–English speaking background (NESB) artists in Australia means that there is a limited multicultural arts milieu here. In this and the following two chapters, I argue that consistent, creative and organisational leadership in culturally diverse arts production and presentation will produce a flourishing milieu. The artists who show distributed, transformative and charismatic leadership enable the milieu to creatively expand. Creative leaders are individual practitioners who push artistic boundaries and, by doing so, provide inspiration and opportunities for other artists.

Ideally, a multicultural arts milieu is one in which artists are located in, and examine, the 'shifting and entangled diversities' (Ang 2011, 788) and 'practices of exchange' that 'facilitate the continuation of intercultural relations' (Noble 2009, 51). Such a milieu expands the notion of the 'diasporic spaces within which much of the contemporary arts were produced by the so-called NESB artists' (Rizvi 2003, 231). My use of the idea of a multicultural arts milieu aims to capture and convey the creative, intellectual, social and multicultural context within which mainly NESB artists produce their work. Ideally, it nourishes and sustains the continuation and development of their practice. The role of creative leadership is essential to forging a supportive milieu and, vice versa, the milieu is essential to fostering effective leadership.

This chapter discusses the claim that new modes of creative leadership develop despite, or perhaps in part from, systemic constraints that respond to 'cultural diversity as an inescapable interactive context' (Mar and Ang 2015, 8). Those artists who respond to the opportunities of cultural diversity show creative leadership that builds a multicultural arts milieu. The issues and opportunities that impact upon their practices in that process include trust, visibility and equitable power in an environment in which, for many, little has changed despite the presence of multicultural policies. Their challenges do not align with research that claims that NESB artists perceive more advantage than disadvantage arising from their backgrounds (Throsby and Petetskaya 2017, 145). The artists I interviewed for this study were most forthcoming about their experiences. The characteristics of creative leadership that emerged include creative and cultural persistence, cross-cultural and intercultural competence, brokering skills, self-starting motivation, and political and social awareness.

The inconsistent attention paid to the arts in multicultural policies—which, at times, has been directly informed by NESB artists—has been more often eroded by periods of institutional disregard. The barriers to change include a lack of comprehension and recognition by mainstream arts institutions, inconsistent levels of critical engagement by the arts media and the small pool of NESB artists. Despite this pattern of systemic instability, the 11 artists I interviewed successfully produce work even though the majority experience tensions arising from their ethnic identities. Rather than see this solely as a burden, they use it as a creative spur to make creativity from friction, establish trust through legitimacy, and develop support and networks. The theme of creativity from friction captures the constraints of being typecast or limited by one's background, issues of creative and cultural autonomy, and intercultural practice. Establishing trust works to address constraints around opportunities for progression, such as critical appraisal and funding. Developing support and networks addresses family matters and combats cultural and geographic isolation—all of which contribute to developing a more sustaining multicultural arts milieu.

The artists in this study view their creative production as having the potential to reconfigure the symbols within society. Such ambition shows creative leadership. I describe the intercultural performances of Annalouise Paul to amplify the challenges and persistence of the artist. While this may seem to be overstating the effect of a (usually) small art project often relegated to the sidelines, such incremental contributions reflect the possibility of a more significant transformation.

Creativity from Friction

The theme of friction and its role in generating creativity emerged through accounts of the constraints interviewees experienced, including the lack of change in the arts sector exemplified by the typecasting of artists in terms of their background. The processes of intercultural practice and negotiation for creative and cultural autonomy reflect how artists respond to those constraints. As discussed earlier, in writing of 'contingent encounters', Tsing (2005, 4–5) suggests how cultures can change through 'new arrangements of culture and power'.

Many NESB artists pursue and negotiate 'new arrangements of culture and power' against the odds. The creative openness of unpredictability (the contingent) is used to generate possibilities of exchange whereby artists take the responsibility to increase the level of culturally diverse creative production, making meaning from the 'friction' they experience when navigating the contestations of multicultural Australia. As Gunew (2017b, 37) comments, they are 'dwelling on the small negotiations of everyday sociality' to germinate and develop creative benefits. Those small negotiations form part of the artist's ability to create opportunities despite their experience of low levels of change in the arts world.

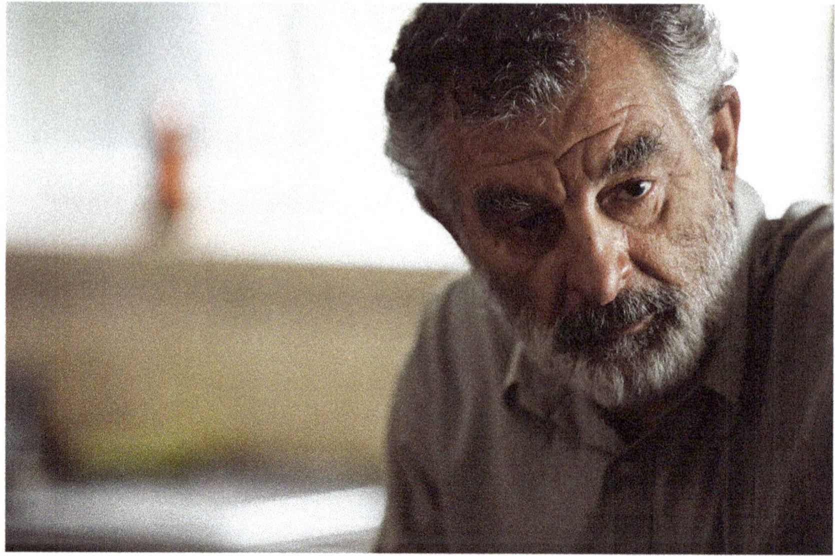

Image 5: Lex Marinos, *The Slap*, 2011
Photographer: Ben King
Courtesy: Matchbox Pictures

Stasis

The paradoxes of inclusion in multicultural Australia may stifle aspects of a dynamic cultural life, as Australia's creative potential is yet to match the 'richness of intercultural encounters in contemporary suburban settings' (Noble 2009, 48). There appears to be major obstacles across the arts sectors specific to NESB artists; however, change can and has occurred elsewhere in other areas of 'diversity' in the arts. Film director Rachel Perkins, for example, sees that Indigenous film and arts have achieved parity in Australia, but she sees little change for NESB artists, in particular for Asian-Australian artists (Radio National 2017). Lex Marinos, the most experienced research participant in this study, is a performer, presenter, writer and director for screen, stage and radio (Marinos 2014) (see Image 5). Referring to the stagnancy of multicultural arts over the past 45 years, Marinos (2015, interview) observes that:

> I thought as a nation we probably had matured to be much more reflective of the society we have. And it's not so. You don't see it on our main stages, and you certainly don't see it on our TV and film.

According to Marinos, the arts' ability to reflect multicultural society is still in its infancy and society is the poorer for it. A more mature arts industry, he suggests, would be able to express the richness of cultural diversity and would learn from a historical perspective to enable change. Annette Shun Wah, the director of the Contemporary Asian Australian Performance (CAAP) group, interprets the prevalent history of typecasting as being in stasis:

> When I look back now and compare [to the 1980s], it's still the case that people of Asian background don't get roles on television or the stage, or are limited to very few specific stereotypical roles. (A. Shun Wah 2015, interview)

Both Marinos and Shun Wah express frustration and a lack of 'satisfaction' with their respective careers based on visibility. Marinos, who has made these points a number of times, finds the lack of change exasperating. But he does not 'want to be that whingeing wog'; he worries that his complaints would be too irritating and a cause for discomfort by the mainstream art world. The 'whingeing wog' or the 'irritant' experiences the problem repeatedly and experiences also the friction characterised by banging one's head against a 'brick wall'. As the complainant, Marinos steadily grinds against the status quo, needing more persistence as institutional resistance increases (Ahmed 2012, 26). The lack of change over so many decades in the performing arts suggests avoidance of difference has become institutionalised. Marinos embodies the way the creative leader continues to articulate the issues of representation because diversity can only be considered as part of the status quo 'when it ceases to cause trouble' (Ahmed 2012, 27). However, a multicultural arts milieu characterised by the persistent call for change may not want to cease causing trouble. The inquisitive and diverse art practices that could emerge from the dynamic nature of migration patterns to Australia may see both welcome and challenging opportunities for creative disruption.

One of the issues for the arts in a multicultural Australia is the need to recognise it as an ongoing project that responds to the issues and opportunities of the day. It is not something to be solved at a single point in time. Gunew (1994, 1) makes a different point about 'trouble' and the politics of attitudinal change, whereby 'politicians cannot afford to be too out of step with public opinion, whereas artists cannot afford not to be'. The role of the artist, therefore, is to continually question and shift the status quo where possible.

Typecast: 'Send Us an Asian, a Greek or Something'

Typecasting and stereotyping, often based on appearance, exemplify the lack of change. Being typecast, stereotyped, cast in minority roles or not cast at all is a longstanding issue for NESB actors in theatre and screen in Australia (Bertone, Keating and Mullaly 1998, xi). The 1998 SBS documentary series *A Change of Face* dealt with 'the conspicuous absence of diversity on Australian screens' and was acclaimed for critiquing how people from 'non-Anglo Celtic backgrounds were ignored, stereotyped and miscast' (Ang, Hawkins and Dabboussy 2008, 164–65). To counter the lack of diversity seen on television, SBS produces contemporary drama narratives with 'migrants and their stories at the centre of the action' (Ang, Hawkins and Dabboussy 2008, 138). Nevertheless, a lack of opportunity remains the common experience for many NESB actors (Screen Australia 2017). Lewis (2007, 41) likens the frequency (or lack thereof) of NESB actors cast in minority roles to the 'spatial marginalisation of ethnic groups in cities'. Linking these two forms of cultural and spatial ghettos crystallises the sense of being barely visible. The slow pace of change regarding representation is a 'glacial' friction that steadily grinds away to eventually alter the landscape. The outer edges (or margins) at times move more quickly and generate greater heat to change the landscape, while the centre (or the mainstream) moves far more slowly. The pertinent simile, whether as an artist or a spokesperson, is that the margins 'melt' (burnout) more readily but also are more dynamically productive than the static centre. Marinos, an artist with a successful career, is aware of the need for more open, creative opportunities. In over 40 years of performing, he has only ever been cast 'as a wog', and he (unreasonably) blames himself:

> If I had been a better actor, perhaps I could have surmounted the systemic impediments. Yet, I do find it curious that every 10–15 years there is a call for more colour-blind casting and more diverse artists. (L. Marinos 2015, interview)

The repetitive nature of the calls for greater inclusion both indicate the lack of change and affirm the role of the arts in representing the diversity of Australians. Marinos (2015, interview) questions whether decision-makers with the power to program are best equipped to deliver arts programs that capture Australia's diversity:

> I wasn't prepared for the fact that it would be as difficult as it was and still is, as a NESB artist. When I was starting out, there were also two other young actors from Greek backgrounds. I would get called George or Nick, who were the other two guys, and they would get called Lex. It suddenly occurred to me that as far as casting directors went, we were interchangeable. We were wogs.

Marinos's experience in 1970 echoes that of Annalouise Paul in 2015. Paul is a dancer, choreographer and actor who has been practising internationally for over 30 years, uncovering her cultural heritage of 'two strains of Jewish' through her Sephardic father and Ashkenazy mother. Paul recalls her early experiences with actors' agents saying 'well, you're only ever going to get cast as an ethnic', and not knowing what that meant. In London, she was cast as Indian and in Los Angeles as Indian, Italian and Filipino. Back in Australia, being typecast remains an issue:

> As an actor, it's pretty much the same as it was 30 years ago. Two weeks ago [May 2015] an agent sent through a casting brief which was—can you send us 'an Asian, a Greek or something, not Caucasian' [laughs]. (A. Paul 2015, interview)

Actors such as Marinos and Paul experience a form of invisibility in a career based on visibility. They are not recognised as their individual selves by agents and, therefore, are not valued as individual performers. Within a 'star'-focused industry, this lack of valuing raises questions as to whether the arts system is able to open up sufficiently to support them.

Paul's experience highlights questions about who decides what diversity on screen looks like and how it should be represented. A casting agent saying 'send us an Asian, Greek or something' expresses disinterest and implies a very crude understanding of cultural heritages. To be compliant with calls for diversity involves meeting 'minimal requirements', whereas fulfilling the requirements moves beyond compliance (Ahmed 2012, 106). Compliance can lead to tokenism—'just ticking the box'—a disengaged response that is frequently identified with multiculturalism in the arts. Australia does not have 'quotas' for diverse casting or content, so there are no boxes to tick (apart from those that gather data for grant statistics).

Despite this, the 'box' continues to be seen as a 'potent contested symbol', as it represents a range of responses to calls for change in the arts industry. It is seen by some as diminishing the creative work of NESB artists and by others as an appropriate tool for affirmative action, and is commonly used by those who lack an understanding as to how the work 'fits into the larger artistic landscape' (Castagna 2017). When it diminishes the creative output or is not understood, 'ticking the box' produces a constraining friction. By contrast, when it is seen as useful to affirm diversity, the 'tick' can generate a productive form of friction. As with successful targets for gender equity, the litmus test would be whether an affirmative quota would contribute to a supportive multicultural arts milieu.

The industry claims a lack of professional actors as the reason for the lack of diversity. Such claims are often followed by calls for more training (Castagna 2017). Marinos (2015, interview) trains acting students from diverse ethnic backgrounds whose experience, he says:

> Is pretty brutal because they find it difficult to get an agent, and when they do, they're told that there's nothing for them. Or they might get rung up to play a greengrocer or a taxi driver or a terrorist or something. But they won't play the doctor or the lawyer or the boy next door.

This resistance from industry means NESB actors require persistence and self-confidence to proactively erode some of the small cracks and demonstrate creative leadership to make a change for themselves and for others. Ahmed (2012, 199) analyses the brick wall of resistance as an 'institutional limit' that is invisible until encountered. Artists are aware of the imposed limits often expressed as the wall or a 'closed door'. Writer and radio broadcaster Sunil Badami (2017) urges NESB artists to 'make a new door' because, for him, persistent attempts to break through existing doors are no longer worth the effort. Making a new door in this sense invokes the agency and creative leadership of the individual practitioner to forge new pathways for themselves and, importantly, for others. The value in the networking forums at which Badami speaks is that the solutions, regardless of their apparent simplicity, are shared among the artists present, validating their individual experiences and leveraging positive group responses. This is a form of relational leadership that builds from a set of relations and expands to influence others to achieve the aims of the group.

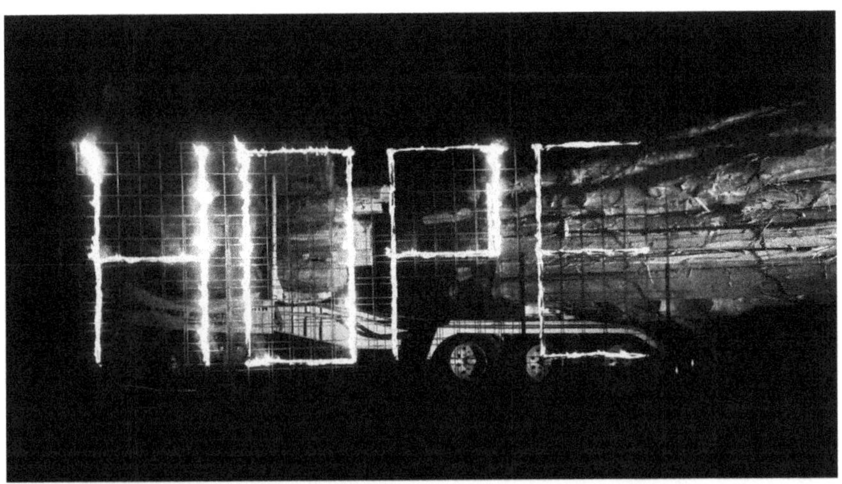

Image 6: Konstantin Koukias, *Sea Chant. Settlers, Ships and Saw-Horses*, 2001

Photographer: Lucia Rossi
Courtesy: Ten Days on the Island Festival

A Crack in the Doorway

Not all doors are firmly closed. Konstantin Koukias, a 'Greek-Tasmanian composer', trained at the Tasmanian and Sydney conservatoriums for music. He is the artistic director of an innovative small opera company, IHOS Opera (see Image 6), now based in Amsterdam. He accepted the advice of mentors as to the creative opportunities afforded by his Greek background:

> Peter Sculthorpe said to me: 'Konstantin if you want to become
> a composer you should use your Greek heritage to give yourself a
> point of difference'. So I started to study Byzantine church music.
> (K. Koukias 2015, interview)

Sculthorpe, an Australian composer, positioned Koukias within his ethnic minority—a move akin to typecasting. He also elevated this minority, seeing it as one with unique creative potential—a 'reified category of ethnicity' (Noble 2011, 830). The potential of ethnic artistic heritage to act as a creative 'point of difference' gives rise to a form of creative cosmopolitanism through a bicultural practice that hybridises, in this example, the traditional Byzantine with contemporary composition. In Koukias's case, the work appears purposefully reified and elite. At the same time, it is also accessible to the public, which accommodates the broader cultural processes of 'people-mixing' that contribute to an 'everyday cosmopolitanism' (Noble 2011). This capacity for an artistic 'avant-garde' (at the forefront of new processes) to be relevant to culturally diverse audiences brings the work into an everyday dialogue that contributes to a vibrant multicultural arts milieu. Koukias is recognised by his peers for his contribution but it remains to be seen whether his work will enter the Australian artistic vernacular.

Koukias was able to turn his cultural background to creative advantage and has had a 'supportive and positive experience' as an artist. However, he has also experienced conflicting expectations as to how he should position himself within the multicultural arts context by fellow Greeks. He describes the reception of his 'breakthrough piece' (Westwood 2017), *Days and Nights with Christ* (1990), which is based on his brother's experience with schizophrenia:

> That's what launched the company. IHOS is Greek for 'sound'. People were coming up to me, mainly Greek people, saying 'how come you're in a mainstream festival? You should be in a multicultural festival'. (K. Koukias 2015, interview)

These conflicting expectations constitute a form of 'friction': one pushes into notoriety in the mainstream and the other pushes against the low profile of the multicultural tributary. These frictions may also characterise the career of the NESB artist. Koukias manages to keep them in balance, his heritage and family history joining unusual or unfamiliar forms in contemporary classical repertoire. This form of bicultural hybridity is fairly well established now, but in 1990 it was experimental. The push–pull of who should 'own him'—the multicultural or the mainstream festival— suggests a sense of loss on the part of the multicultural programmer struggling to gain an audience and funding traction through the inclusion of contemporary, challenging work. Koukias, in extracting opportunities from creative tensions and establishing his own experimental opera company, demonstrates creative leadership.

Stereotypes from beyond Centre Stage

Opportunities for creative expression are further complicated when geographical location is intertwined with ethnicity. Forceful friction, which can be understood as striving against barriers in theatre and film, tries to break through the issue of whose voice is heard and which artists make the work. *The Finished People* (IMDb 2003), directed by Khoa Do, is an independent low-budget film about youth homelessness in the Western Sydney suburb of Cabramatta. It is often cited by people from the area as having its own 'voice' as distinct from being made by directors from 'places like the Eastern Suburbs or with a bit more money who would monopolise those stories and speak on behalf of us' (S. Ly 2015, interview). Vinh Nguyen, a 24-year-old freelance videographer who studied at University of Technology Sydney and whose parents came to Australia as Vietnamese refugees, wants more control over the narratives:

> I don't want to talk to my parents about the war, what was being a boat person like? I think that's degrading. It was a tough time, and we will never forget what happened in 1975. They've been here for 30 years, it's time to create new memories and experiences. (V. Nguyen 2015, interview)

Nguyen had been freelancing for five years, mainly on Western Sydney community arts projects, and, in 2015, received his first local government community arts grant of $4,000:

> I never thought of myself as multicultural. I identify very strongly with Western Sydney, and that equates with multicultural. It is such a mouthful to say: I am a multicultural artist from Western Sydney. I just say I am from Western Sydney. (V. Nguyen 2015, interview)

Nguyen expresses confusion and dismay at the array of labels that could be attached to him. Western Sydney has a high proportion of NESB artists (Hanna 2012, 5) and several arts centres that activate their culturally diverse artist populations (Knight 2013). The majority of artists who live in Western Sydney identify proudly with their location; they see it as a badge of honour (Stevenson et al. 2017, 15). Nguyen exemplifies how NESB artists often navigate their identity around labels to suit their situation. The belief that because he is ethnically different he is therefore 'multicultural' reinforces his experience of being 'other' when outside his home. Nevertheless, he navigates those borders, applying self-restraint to remain mute in the face of taunts about his Bankstown (an outer suburb of Western Sydney) home:

> Immediately it's jokes about getting shot, getting stabbed. You know, racism types. And it sucks but I'm forced to smile sometimes, just to keep any opportunity for jobs. Or make a slight in-joke about it. (V. Nguyen 2015, interview)

Nguyen's perception that he might be accepted if he represses a jarring retort to the racist slur is an example of a reverse form of 'tolerance' on the part of the 'tolerated', another familiar experience. As Hage (2000, 87) points out, the intention behind multicultural tolerance is a form of 'symbolic violence' whereby 'domination is presented as a form of egalitarianism'. The Sydneyites consider themselves to be in a position of power (the in-group) and assume that they can make jokes at Nguyen's expense. Further, they assume that there will be no retort, because Nguyen, who is trying to extend his career into Sydney, is not in a position of power. These exchanges can be viewed as friction—an unwritten, yet scripted, interaction of 'banter' to accommodate Nguyen.

Reading Nguyen's comments on networking as an example of 'everyday cosmopolitanism' positions them as 'situated and strategic practices of transaction in specific contexts' (Noble 2009, 46). The exchanges between Nguyen and his potential colleagues are strategic within a shared context of arts networking in the urban centre of Sydney. The banter tests the potential for relationships through a form of friction akin to slipping and rolling that generates momentum. Such exchanges also demonstrate the paradox of multicultural Australia, whereby those of diverse cultural backgrounds can experience inclusion and exclusion simultaneously (Ang, Brand and Noble 2006, 19–21).

Regardless, Nguyen's agency remains active, as he possesses aspects of the 'insider'. He knows when and where to attend freelance media networking events in Sydney and does not suggest that he is ignored. He displays traits of the 'creative aspirant' who requires an 'awareness of, and ability to play with, the symbolic codes around style and taste within youth-based, subcultural creative scenes to increase their chances of success in the creative industries' (Idriss 2018, 71). Nguyen networks as a self-employed media artist who experiences the socio-economic disadvantages associated with Western Sydney. He associates creative freedom as a benefit of living in Western Sydney in both 'aesthetic risk-taking and cultural difference' (Stevenson et al. 2017, 15). His aspirations are equivalent to many of the sole trader, creative entrepreneurs who have a pragmatic approach to generating income from their 'creative' enterprises, and who manoeuvre their careers to earn a 'decent' living rather than 'retain some romantic association with "arts for art's sake"' (Idriss 2018, 97).

Three generations of actors, Marinos, Shun Wah and Paul, share experiences of invisibility. Koukias and Nguyen are one generation apart and share similar class and isolated geographical backgrounds. They are, however, at different historical and creative places within the arts spectrum. Koukias successfully employs and promotes the cultural forms of his contemporary classical composition drawn from his Greek heritage, demonstrating experimental multicultural arts practice. Nguyen aspires to become a documentary filmmaker to give 'voice' to his ideas and those of the members of his local community. The more likely trajectory for him will be one of short-term employment contracts and volunteer video work. He seeks freelance work in Sydney and, having received a community arts grant, has not completely abandoned creative aspirations but will begin by taking a 'safer, less risky career path validated from within the ethnic communities' (Idriss 2018, 91). This validation comes from families and community groups and is linked to the capacity to generate income from media production, as distinct from pursuing a more financially uneven career in the arts. Nguyen has had to reconsider his artistic trajectory and is attempting to bridge the gap between Western Sydney and Sydney as a Vietnamese Australian media producer while judiciously navigating within the more familiar spaces of his ethnic community.

Intercultural Practice

In another part of the multicultural arts milieu is the independent professional artist who adopts an intercultural approach, as discussed in Chapter 1. For the NESB artist, intercultural can mean those who work across aesthetic codes and cultural codes of identity (Idriss 2018, 141). Hossein Valamanesh is an established Iranian-Australian sculptor and painter who exhibits regularly and whose work is included in many Australian visual arts collections (see Image 7). He graduated from Tehran's School of Fine Art Painting before migrating to Australia in 1973, where he completed a fine arts degree at the South Australian School of the Arts:

> Multicultural Australia meant that I was able to express certain ideas from that. Those works were very much to do with a different dwelling, different place. And then you bring that otherness to the view of the thing. (H. Valamanesh 2015, interview)

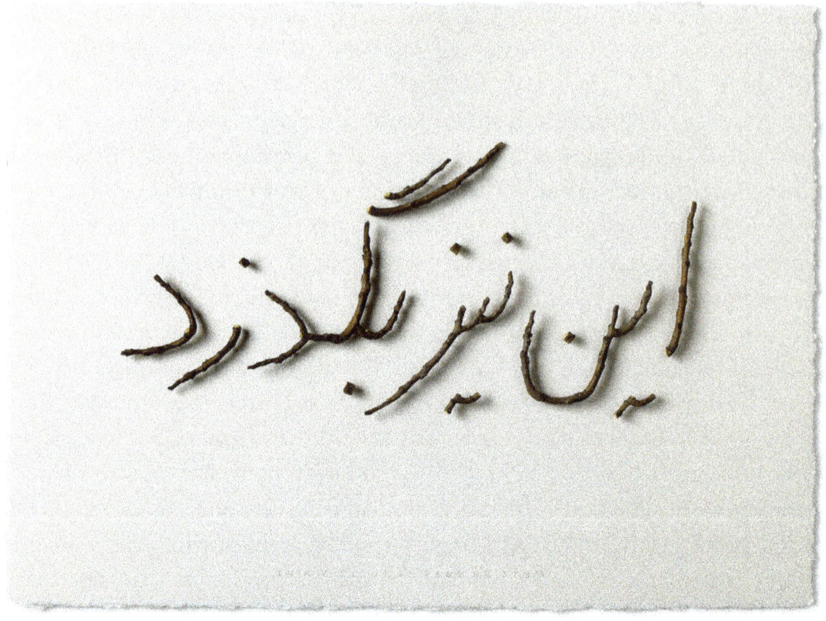

Image 7: Hossein Valamanesh, *This Will Also Pass*, 2007
Ailanthus branches on paper, 58 x 76 x 2 cm, edition of three
Private collection, Adelaide
Photographer: M. Kluvanek

Valamanesh carefully navigates away from being the 'other' while drawing on its creative potential. He does not see himself as 'other', yet he uses 'otherness' to make work. He has generated a different practice from his 'political art making in Iran' and now takes a calmer 'more personal approach, more to do with emotions and feelings and memory'.

Valamanesh echoes other artists who relocate themselves and their practice, wherein the importance of 'country, longing, belonging and inclusion' are linked with 'memory, history, lived experiences but also imagining the future' (Babacan 2011, 15). His approach draws on aesthetically recognisable forms associated with the Iran of his memory and is intercultural because of inflections relevant to his current context. Valamanesh views his work as having the 'flavour of what I am and where I come from', but he resists Iran as the only touchstone and hopes his ideas go 'beyond the idea of being from one place'. *The Lover Circles His Own Heart* (2003) (see Image 3), a contemporary sculpture based on the poem of the same name by the thirteenth-century poet Rumi, is an enlivened entanglement. The simple structure of the 'skirt' evokes the whirling dervish, yet, in the dimly lit gallery setting, its disembodied movement evokes a ghost-like and graceful reminiscence of the Iranian meditative sacred dance. Another reading of this work is as a futuristic metaphor for tradition and contemporary elisions that question whether the machine can adequately replace the mesmerising intention of the dervish.

Koukias's (2015, interview) intercultural work is also based on cultural symbols, in his case that of family musicology:

> I incorporated Byzantine chant in my early works, recording elderly Greek women, including my mother, singing thousands of years old folk songs. I mixed them within contemporary classical genre, incorporating pre-recorded tape and treatment of sounds, words and themes. Cultural, Greek themes.

Both Valamanesh and Koukias demonstrate innovation through enlivened entanglement by sensitively bringing one form of culturally specific traditional expression into dialogue with a new context. This process suggests a careful massaging in vision and sound as a form of cultural brokerage (Kurin 1997). Both Valamanesh and Koukias exemplify creative leadership: the individual practitioner through whom other artists may take succour and inspiration, because they push creative boundaries. As individual artists who have achieved recognition, Valamanesh and Koukias also evoke 'charismatic leadership' because they inspire, drive the project and demonstrate the benefits of creative risk-taking. They are the ones who take, or are given, prime credit, regardless of others who worked on the project. They exemplify creative leadership because they maintain their creative and cultural autonomy, as discussed in Chapter 2. Neither compromises their practice or becomes limited by others' cultural ignorance. Their niche artforms run the risk of staying niche, but their potential to influence art's history and contribute to a multicultural arts milieu outweighs that risk.

Koukias's and Valamanesh's ethnic and cultural heritages were the starting point for their creative practices and fed their success in mainstream arts. Both artists qualify their success; they feel that their careers cannot be too prominent—cannot have too much 'star-quality'—and that they must somehow sit back slightly. Koukias left Australia because he had to: without support from government arts agencies, his practice was stifled. Valamanesh (2015, interview) attributes his success, in part, to staying almost under the radar:

> I don't think my work was ever in the hot top ten or whatever. I never became too fast, too famous, too rich. I'm ambitious, but I just felt like things had to come to you as well.

Valamanesh's reflection demonstrates the quality of persistence and a quiet, yet striving, ambition that steadily edges along. It is possible to read his description as fitting the image of the 'ideal migrant' who contributes to, and 'integrates' into, society, making an advantage of the 'articulation of diverse cultural forms and use of the services of the state to assist him' (Hage 2000, 83–84).

Both artists can also be seen as mediating between 'cultures'. Mar and Ang (2015, 62) observe a shift in art processes towards mediation to generate 'understandings of difference and diversity'. Mediation is found in the role of an 'intermediary' (Totaro 1991, 12) or 'cultural broker' (Kurin 1997, 17) and assists in cultural translation. These modes of translation suggest a type of relational leadership or attunement capable of cultural interpretation that builds a flourishing milieu.

Knowledge of the sociopolitical as well as the creative context is essential to transact these relationships, the calibre of which, in this case, requires the artist to be adroit across several positions, not all of which are readily achievable. One is an ethical position about how to produce 'understandings of difference'. Another is the consideration of aesthetics as to what will be produced. Still another concerns the position of the NESB artist—how they will produce the work and where it will be presented to the public. Each of these positions engages in 'practices of cultural translation' (Ang 2003a, 33).

The constraints and opportunities presented through the issues of creative and cultural autonomy complicate the context and working processes of the artist. Trust is implicit yet must be earnt by the artist in the creative context of cultural translation. Trust resurfaces in public presentations of the artwork that involve a different set of structures in the art world.

Establishing Trust through Legitimacy

The issues of creative autonomy, translation, experimentation and typecasting discussed in the previous section raise issues around trust between the artist and their presenters and critics that inform considerations of legitimacy of the arts sector. Establishing trust will support creative risk-taking that increases the exposure of the artist and their work. Establishing trust encompasses the opportunities artists experience for creative career progression through the 'legitimate' processes of public presentation, published critical writing and funding. The discourse of creative practice typically positions NESB artists within community arts sectors (Hawkins 1993, 86–88; Blonski 1994, 199; Idriss 2018, 142) to the extent that multicultural arts have been equated with 'community arts' (Kalantzis and Cope 1994, 142). The result of this perception is that their art is not viewed as legitimate or validated as mainstream or traditional art. This perception persists even though NESB artists have low levels of employment in community arts (DARTS 2017; Throsby and Petetskaya 2017, 30).

There is minimal commentary about the relationship between NESB artists and those arbiters who present and profile artworks in major spaces and events. Within the context of creative leadership, gaining access to arts structures enhances the legitimacy of the artist's work and develops expertise and support for other artists. The roles of intermediaries and cultural brokers become even more important in this phase of the 'culture cycle', as they are the ones who generate pathways into the mainstream (or at least a large tributary) to attain recognition beyond an ethno-specific community audience that can limit creativity if only framed within 'normative communal terms' (Idriss 2018, 153). Being included in art networks that generate trusting creative relationships continues to be identified as an important need (Stevenson et al. 2017, 54). Demonstrating the skills and know-how to generate trust within funding and presenting agencies forms part of the leadership role of the NESB artist because of the public engagement with decision-makers and presenters.

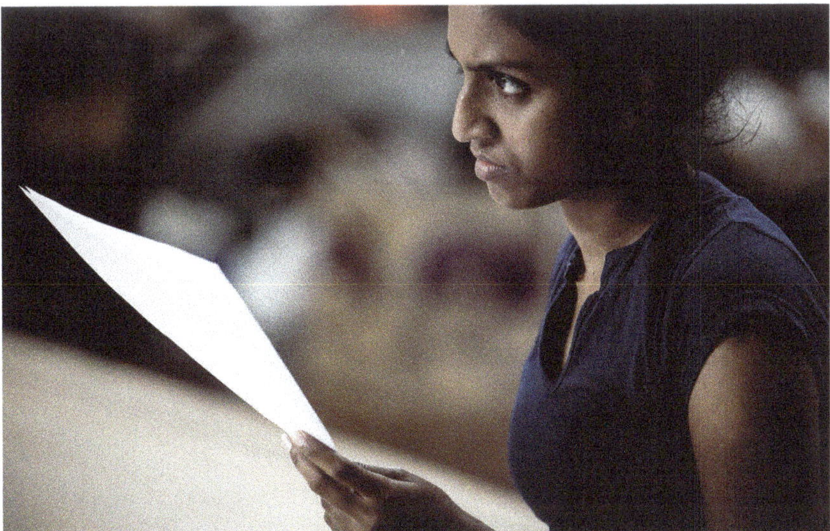

Image 8: *Counting and Cracking*, Belvoir Street Theatre, 2019
Photographer: © Brett Boardman

The Invisible Milieu

S. Shakthidharan is a writer, director, musician and composer based in Western Sydney (see Image 8). He was the inaugural executive and artistic director of CuriousWorks, established in 2006 to produce digital media within long-term community projects (CuriousWorks 2021a). CuriousWorks is known for its community engagement programs that utilise digital storytelling processes to evolve the everyday experiences of cultural diversity. Trimboli (2016, 14) describes their 'digital interventions [as] a mélange of new media and community-based art practices incorporating aspects of the conventional digital storytelling genre in a fluid fashion'. This 'mélange' led to the successful low-budget feature film *Riz*, which was programmed in the 2015 Sydney Film Festival and was well received (Morellini 2015). Shakthidharan (2015, interview) suggests that, alongside the visible indicators of stereotypes, there are less visible considerations such as the underlying challenges of the ethical and ethnic contexts for artists who work interculturally:

> The initiatives that intend to help artists from multicultural backgrounds never look at all at the surrounding things we have to do to ensure equitable power, to ensure that community respect and cultural understanding [is] done properly. And I feel like unless a policy tackles the full task, then it will always fall short.

The skills to accomplish the 'surrounding things' are rarely made explicit because the types of negotiation, care and responsibility within an ethno-specific or multicultural context are not necessarily part of the arts vocabulary or mindset and can, therefore, be 'invisible'. Artists are not taught how to develop trusting relationships as part of formal creative arts courses. NESB artists are perceived to acquire this capacity informally through their family, peers and, possibly, participation in ethnic community cultural activities. Idriss (2018, 142–43) argues that the challenges of creative self-expression (familial, class, geographic and creative isolation) are such that Arab-Australian artists retreat to community arts through 'capturing "authentic" stories as representatives or authority figures of the local community', and that this at least generates some control over the stories they produce. To work against these cultural blind spots is a point of tension and a marker of creative leadership, albeit often an invisible one, that requires respect and understanding, based in the development of trusting relationships.

'I Would Like a Culture in Which People Trusted Me More'

The linked issues of navigating intercultural constraints and understandings—issues that rarely appear on the mainstream radar—also provide creative opportunities. In Shakthidharan's case, this can be likened to the persistent erosion to widen creative cracks against near invisibility. Shakthidharan acknowledges and draws on his relationship with members of his community but aims to create his own door to a wider audience and have his work critiqued, 'as art is intended to be, in the public realm' (Idriss 2018, 142).

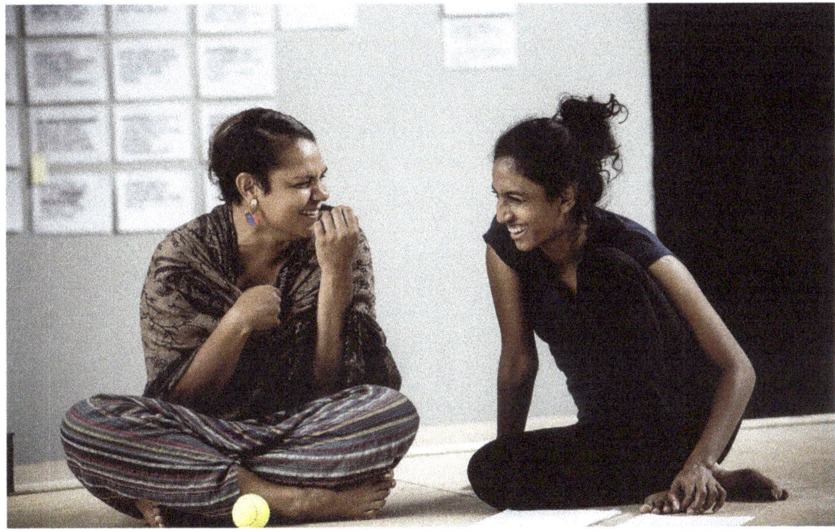

Image 9: *Counting and Cracking*, **Belvoir Street Theatre, 2019**
Photographer: © Brett Boardman

Shakthidharan's experience comes from pitching concepts to mainstream theatre companies and highlights issues he has faced as a contemporary artist (see Image 9). Despite having been awarded, and successfully delivered on, many grants, he perceives that he is still not trusted and therefore struggles to achieve his artistic vision:

> As an individual artist, I would like a culture in which people trusted me more. People keep telling me I'm ambitious and 'that's an amazing idea, but it's going to be difficult'. But what they're saying is—'your idea is different from my lived experience tand for me to understand it, is difficult. And it seems really ambitious'.
> (S. Shakthidharan 2015, interview)

This excerpt articulates the difficult relations with managers and directors of arts organisations and funding bodies that many NESB artists experience. The lack of trust congeals around the patronising turn of phrase that acknowledges Shakthidharan's 'amazing idea', yet, in the same breath, relegates it to the too hard basket. The issue may be one of ignorance on the part of mainstream directors. Regardless, Shakthidharan's concept is limited because they, the experts, 'know' what is achievable, and it would be too challenging to realise the project as he envisions it. Here, Shakthidharan describes a disconnect between his creative ambitions and the inability of mainstream theatre directors to adequately 'trust' his ideas. In this manner, Shakthidharan expands the context of cultural translation to include the ways he can translate himself into the broader theatre scene.

The 'disconnect' Shakthidharan experienced may also stem from the predominance of the Western canon and 'whiteness' in Australian theatre. When Lewis (2007) sparked controversy with her description of the lack of multicultural actors on Australian stages and screens, Meyrick (2007), a performing arts professor and experienced theatre academic, identified the issue as the source of content:

> The crucial omission is playwrights. It is unremarkable that white writers write plays about white characters that are cast with white actors. That's not cultural conspiracy, just life. Non-white writers, if there were more of them, would write other kinds of plays, and casting them would involve different choices.

Meyrick dismisses any systemic issues as an overreaction ('not a cultural conspiracy') yet fails to suggest why there are not more 'non-white writers'. His comments arguably demonstrate the dearth of understanding NESB artists experience because of ignorance on the part of influential directors in the performing arts sector. To a certain extent, Meyrick's response typifies the prevalent 'laissez-faire' attitude towards NESB participation in the arts. He identifies the issue of there not being enough 'non-white writers', but relies on the vague notion that, in the undefined future, more 'non-white writers' may somehow find their way into the theatre pantheon. His comment is another variation on the 'it will take time' trope.

There is a profound ignorance of different cultural forms that manifests as lack of understanding. Mainstage companies, masking their ignorance of different cultural forms, revert to the label of 'too ambitious' to avoid dealing with their lack of understanding—their inability to process ideas that are outside their scope of experience. Similarly, 'ambitious' is a double-edged term often used in conservative areas of the arts to invoke issues of creative (and, therefore, assumed, box office) risk. Curiously, 'ambitious' is rarely used in its leadership sense of going beyond the usual. Artistic ambition evokes a challenge between the artist and their artform; however, it evokes a different set of challenges when ambition shifts to the relationship between the artist and the gatekeepers of organisations, managers, funding bodies and presenters. For Shakthidharan, being told that his concept 'seems really ambitious' is an early warning about the uncertainty of 'untested' (or untrusted) culturally diverse art product; it suggests an amorphous yet tangible barrier to creative innovators who reference aspects of multicultural Australia.

In contrast, an exemplary relationship of creative trust can be found in Koukias's *Pentakostarion*, commissioned by Jonathon Mills for the 2010 Federation Festival of Melbourne. The piece, which toured to the Chicago Cultural Centre, draws on the ancient liturgical languages of Greek, Latin and Hebrew through ritual chant and instrumental effects—handcrafted bells, several played underwater during the performance. Koukias (2015, interview) describes it as a: 'Beautiful commission. Beautifully funded. Jonathon gave me open slather. When I asked for a set of 61 bells in quarter tones, Jonathon being Jonathon said, "Yes, why not"'. Jonathon's response makes explicit the trust inherent in enabling rigorous intercultural creative production. A vibrant multicultural arts milieu would expand the opportunities for ambitious creative risk-taking by NESB artists.

Critical Appraisal and Appreciation

Critical appraisal assists in generating trust in an artistic work; however, many critics find engaging with multicultural content challenging. Part of the issue stems from the lack of dedicated writing on multicultural artists. There are more, albeit intermittent, pieces published on the politics of multicultural arts than about work by NESB artists. A successful essayist, Peter Robb (2012, 103), for example, in writing about Greek-Australian actor Alex Dimitriadis, adopts the attitude that if the content has a multicultural aspect to it, it must be 'worthy': 'For a film that was earnestly multicultural and calculatingly mass market, *The Heartbreak Kid* was surprisingly good'.

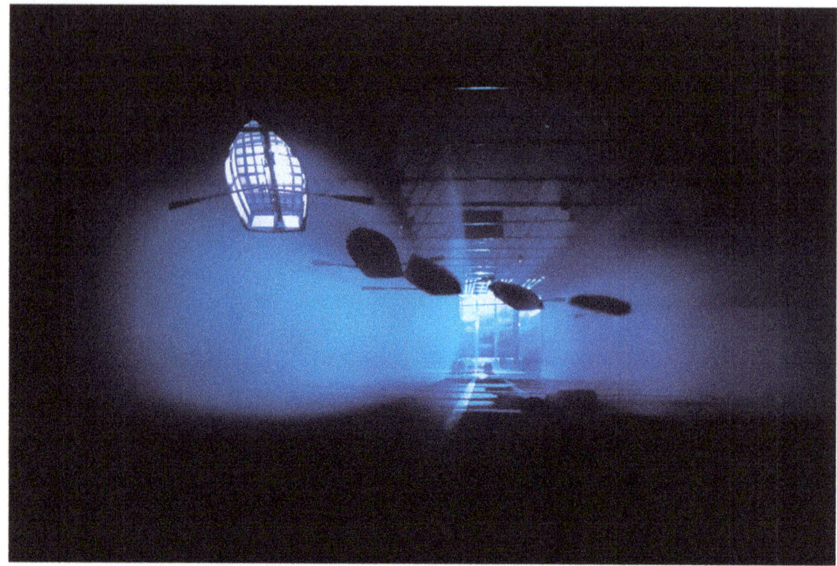

Image 10: Konstantin Koukias, *To Traverse Water*, 1995, Melbourne International Festival of the Arts

Photographer: Ann E. Wulff

The implication that a multicultural focus equates to being 'earnest' or politically correct and, therefore, not compelling or aesthetically valuable in its own right undermines public trust in the creative content. This approach to the critique of multicultural content applies across all artforms. For example, Koukias's *To Traverse Water* (1992) (see Image 10) was successfully received in Sydney and Melbourne, but the critics did not feel any need to do any research into the cultural milieu of the work: 'Deborah Jones wrote a wonderful review of it but said something like "it's all Greek to me"—which I found quite offensive' (K. Koukias 2015, interview).

A similarly dismissive comment in an otherwise supportive critique was made by a previous state gallery curator, Ian North, a 'trusted' commentator who expressed surprise at Valamanesh's early level of success:

> *Dwelling* [1980] is worth emphasising not only as, in effect, Valamanesh's first major public sculpture, but because of its oddity. It made no concession to ameliorate its out-of-placeness or its unabashed multiculturalism, a term then coming confusedly into Australian currency. Remarkably, Valamanesh has persuaded his audience over the last three decades to accept the appurtenances and signifiers of Iranian visual culture in his work as he established

his vision ever more firmly, operating not from ethnic ghettos but within the mainstream of Australian art. (North in Knights and North 2011, 7)

The view that Valamanesh would usually be considered as part of an 'ethnic ghetto' undermines his trusted status as an artist in the mainstream. Given North's influential position, his comments might have been more circumspect. Valamanesh questions whether there is 'such a closed shop? A closed community of so-called multicultural artists?' He reinforces the benefit artists receive from discussions around their work:

I've got enough good dialogue with people who look at my work, and people who write about or exhibit the work, that I feel like I'm not talking into the void. (H. Valamanesh 2015, interview)

This sense of connection to other artists and commentators is invaluable for the individual creative practitioner. I now turn to the ways in which creative leaders work with their personal supports to continue practising.

Support through Networks

Art as a 'tangible' career or work option is frequently discussed through an economic lens (Gerber 2017). However, the theme of support and networks identifies family matters, isolation, and access to sustainable and productive peer networks as constraints and enablers in the artists' experience.

Family Matters

Familial and cultural networks sometimes offer alternative relationships of leadership, trust and support beyond those purely within the arts sector. Two-thirds (66 per cent) of NESB artists place great importance on the support provided by their spouse or partner to assist their career; this is significantly higher than artists from English-speaking backgrounds (Throsby and Petetskaya 2017, 147). This suggests that there is a wide social and cultural context that the NESB artist must consider if they wish to develop and display creative leadership. The majority of the artists I interviewed had undertaken crucial negotiations with family members about entering the arts. Several postponed creative careers until they had completed family approved tertiary qualifications, usually in the fields of law, commerce or medicine. Permission from the family emerged as an important factor for second-generation NESB artists in their career path regardless of their ethnic background or class status; this mirrors the findings attributed to Arab-Australian male artists (Idriss 2018). NESB artists continue to seek and negotiate the conditional support of family:

> My folks agreed that I could have a year to see if I could make some kind of a living out of acting. And I'm happy to say 45 years later there's still a job on the horizon. (L. Marinos 2015, interview)

Twenty-four-year-old Sean Ly went from being an unemployed 'bedroom musician' to becoming assistant director on CuriousWorks' feature film *Riz* by volunteering as a youth arts organiser for Fairfield Council. He has since enrolled in a tertiary and further education course to gain a youth worker certificate. Ly (2015, interview) has an instrumental view of the arts as a 'vehicle for us to promote our side of things' (see Image 11), yet senses that members of the Cambodian community in Cabramatta would frown upon a creative career:

> Sections of my community would discourage me from arts. They don't see art as a true career. It's not a labour job, or it's not a desk job. It's not something tangible, but it's still a lot of work, and it tires you out. Like if that's what they see as proper work then the arts are definitely proper work.

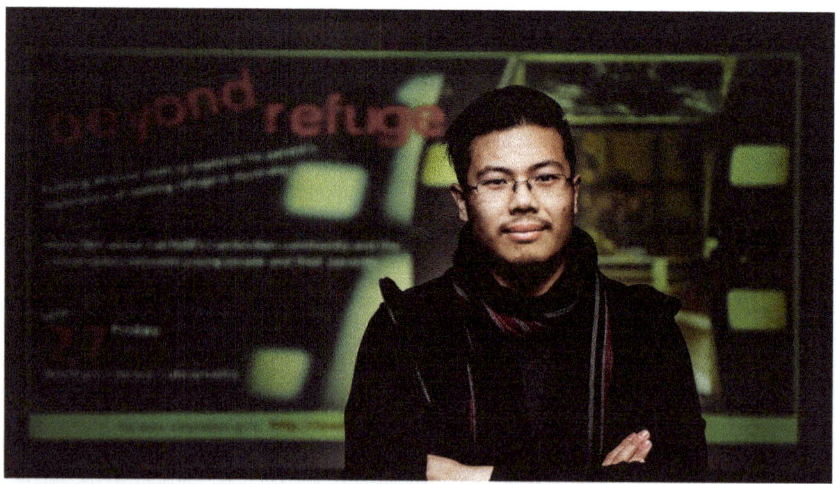

Image 11: Sean Ly (director and videographer), *Beyond Refuge: Flashbacks*, **2016**
Produced: CuriousWorks

As distinct from the perception (possibly) held by community members that artists live a free-floating 'bohemian' lifestyle, Ly appreciates the time and (often arduous) labour that artists invest in their work. This concept is not always considered by Arab-Australian artists from Western Sydney who see art as an income generating enterprise (Idriss 2018, 97). These findings can be applied to other ethnic groups as well. Ly was not encouraged to be an artist, and, having experienced 'long periods of unemployment', he will no longer pursue a full-time arts career. Instead, he prefers to be involved in the more acceptable community sector, because, as he explains, 'that's where I want to make a career to support myself in the future'. Working within a local council has its own challenges but carries the allure of employment that is more stable than the arts.

To facilitate arts projects as distinct from making them is a frequent route for practitioners and partly explains the low numbers of professional NESB artists. The low level of arts-related employment for NESB artists is also reflected in Ly's decision to become a council youth worker. This pragmatic response to the vagaries of a creative career is understandable and contributes to their low representation in the arts.

The issue of family support also cuts across class. Anna Lau struggled to gain permission from her mother to be a playwright. Lau is a young woman of Taiwanese-Malaysian parentage who arrived in Australia when she was one year old. She, like most of her friends, gained entry to study law or economics; however, she negotiated to study international relations because of the 'proximity to people's stories'. Ashamed of her Chinese background as a schoolgirl, Lau exemplifies Ang's (2001, 51) insight that 'if I am inescapably Chinese by descent, I am only sometimes Chinese by consent':

> I don't identify with migrant experiences because, having grown up here, that's never been my story. Asian arts tend to be suitcase stories rather than second-generation arts, so I feel like there's a lot of creative leadership needed to change arts relevance to me. (A. Lau 2015, interview)

'Suitcase stories' of unknown arrivals in a strange landscape were a feature of Australian representations of migrants in the 1980s. By differentiating herself from her parents and their 'suitcase story', Lau foregrounds the intergenerational friction of different cultural experiences. She persisted in an arts career after seeing inspirational theatre, even though it was not her milieu:

> It is hard to believe that Asian families would send their children to a specialist arts high school. I would have loved to continue Visual Arts and create a major work. I would have loved to attend a Performing Arts School. But, it would never have been my choice. Perhaps this has something to do with the lack of Asian-Australian artists on our national landscape. (Lau n.d.)

Linking the lack of family encouragement to the lack of Asian-Australian artists highlights two vicious cycles that reinforce the lack of cultural diversity on stage. The under-representation of Asian-Australian artists conveys the difficulty of a career in the arts and the low number of role models reinforces the low take-up. The arts are considered a poor career choice due to the lack of reliable income and low social standing. This, in turn, discourages the uptake of arts training, thereby perpetuating the low numbers. It is claimed that Chinese-American parents lack of support for 'risky' creative careers is not solely motivated by financial reasons, but because such careers:

> Involve subjective evaluation, thereby making their children vulnerable to bias. By contrast, careers in medicine, engineering, law or pharmacy require higher credentials which protect their children from the usual types of discrimination. (Lee 2014)

This subtle reason extends the value that migrants place on education to increase social mobility. The careers favoured by parents are seen to reduce the economic *and cultural* vulnerability of their children. This perception may alter with subsequent generations and as the benefits of the arts and creative thinking become increasingly recognised.

Shakthidharan's Tamil Sri Lankan background also instils self-reliance and economic responsibility (see Image 12). His mother is a performer and choreographer who did not want him to select the arts because she was keenly aware of their lack of stability:

> In my community, your own life is not what should come first. My uncle and anyone in my family thought it was stupid to get into the arts because it's a pretty dumb place if you're trying to look after a number of people financially. (S. Shakthidharan 2015, interview)

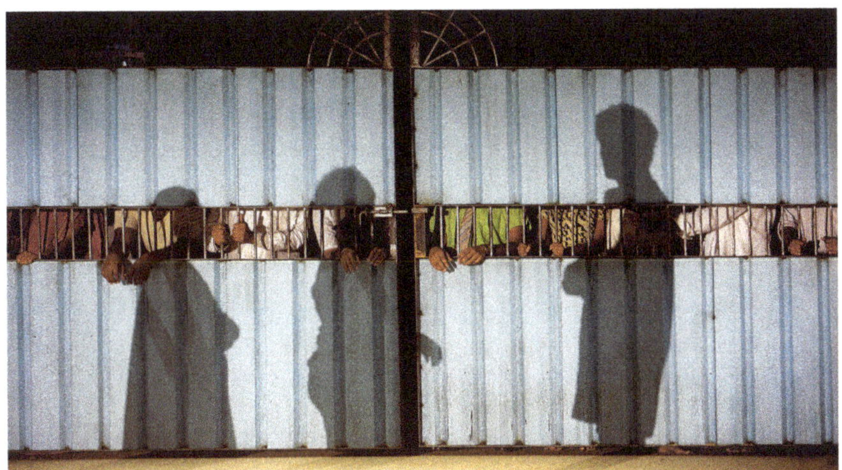

Image 12: *Counting and Cracking*, Belvoir Street Theatre, 2019
Photographer: © Brett Boardman

Shakthidharan managed these competing expectations by covertly enrolling in a university media degree as a first step on the path to realising his vision to get 'other' stories told. The financial constraints placed on him were ultimately beneficial, as CuriousWorks began with an independent (of government) income stream to deploy as the company saw fit.

To pursue an arts career in these situations hints at personal struggles that undermine or compromise family trust in some way. To undertake a family approved tertiary degree and/or find a degree that is personally (and creatively) satisfying is an early sign of the persistence required to work as an NESB artist. Such negotiations develop relational leadership skills through the management of negotiations, acknowledging the role of relationships beyond the drive for an individual artistic career.

Isolation: 'I Thought They Were Only My Issues'

Isolation was a topic raised frequently by the artists I interviewed. Likewise, 50 per cent of NESB artists from Western Sydney identified more opportunities to meet other artists as their most important need (Stevenson et al. 2017, 54). One creative leadership consequence of this is that those artists who recognise this need may draw on it to create networks with other artists for social and creative support. This may be one area that distinguishes NESB creative leaders, as it shows the ability to use friction creatively, changing adversity into an advantage. An isolated artist cannot share their concerns and, therefore, often internalises a sense of inadequacy:

> Looking back, I thought they were only my issues. I didn't realise it was systemic and what that means in terms of policy and infrastructure. It's very isolating. It diminishes your belief in what you think you can do. I think that's why I left [Australia]. I saw it as being very narrow visioned. And coming back I realised— something's really wrong here. How is it that it can still be this hard? Is it still me? (A. Paul 2015, interview)

These feelings are not easily expressed in public forums and, therefore, rarely get aired. Dancer, actor and choreographer Annalouise Paul is describing a milieu that does not support her. Having worked successfully overseas for many years, there is poignancy in her question—'is it still me?' This highlights the need for artists to adapt, adjust and create their own milieu. A productive milieu implies the existence of structures that enable risk-taking and supportive contexts to flourish (see Image 13).

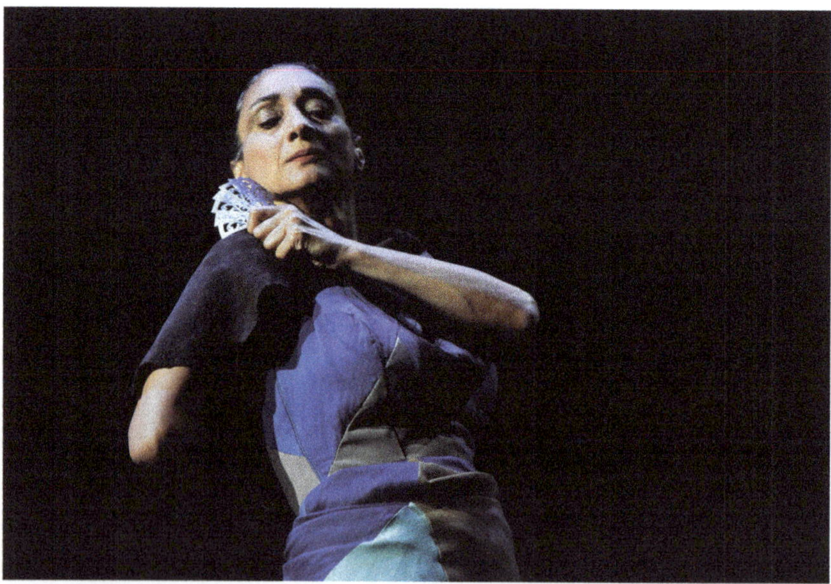

Image 13: Annalouise Paul, *Forge*, 2016
Photographer: Heidrun Lohr

Anna Lau experienced a different type of professional isolation when she finally began playwriting. Her creative endeavour became a point of difference between her and her Asian-Australian friends who all studied commerce, law or medicine and were not sure what playwriting was or why anyone would want to do it. Lau felt like 'a pioneer because I didn't know anyone who did it, except for me'. As an artist-in-residence at Shopfront Theatre, a youth co-op theatre in southern Sydney, she found the first stages of the creative process completely strange:

> I just felt like such a black sheep. Like the artistic director and the other artist-in-residence would just sit down and say 'For today's session I'm just going to play'. And I'm like—what is this concept of play? [laughs] I want to sit down and plan! (A. Lau 2015, interview)

Lau had not been exposed to artists. Until that point, her career path had been based on action plans, focus and deliverables. While these are also necessary for a career as an artist, they need to be balanced in proportion to the creative process. To Lau, the idea of 'play' was indulgent, but it was an indulgence with which the other resident was clearly familiar. Here Lau experiences conflicting emotions. She expresses pride and confidence as a 'pioneer' alongside rejection and isolation as a 'black sheep' in her first foray into the world of playwriting. The way an artist responds to these scenarios suggests the friction of 'breaking into', which paves the way for them to become creative leaders. Lau's isolation takes the form of 'cultural remoteness' (Idriss 2018, 71), whereby her upbringing and acculturation did not match the expected behaviours and styles of her new creative milieu. Role models may help to overcome such remoteness.

Role Models: 'They Get Proud by Association'

Exposure to role models instils confidence. This can happen within a small experimental arts scene, with super 8 film and tape loops, as media artist and cultural producer Panos Couros (2015, interview; 2017) explains:

> There was another Greek guy there who was the most articulate person I'd ever met. He became a role model because I thought— wow, how can someone from our cultural heritage be that lucid, articulate, and intellectually challenging.

Thirty years later, the same proud moment of recognition through ethnicity continues to occur. Valamanesh (2015, interview) recognises the importance of leading by showing:

> I go to high schools to talk where there's lots of young Iranian or Afghani. I can speak the language. They get really excited to hear that even someone from Iran has made it [as an artist] here. And they suddenly put their chest up, 'Oh he's from Iran. I'm from Iran'. They get proud by association.

Small moments such as these can be significant in the future choices of young people. Despite Valamanesh's claim that he has been included in the arts in Australia, he hints at the students' sense of isolation when he uses the word 'even', suggesting that it is rare for someone from Iran to 'make it' (see Image 14).

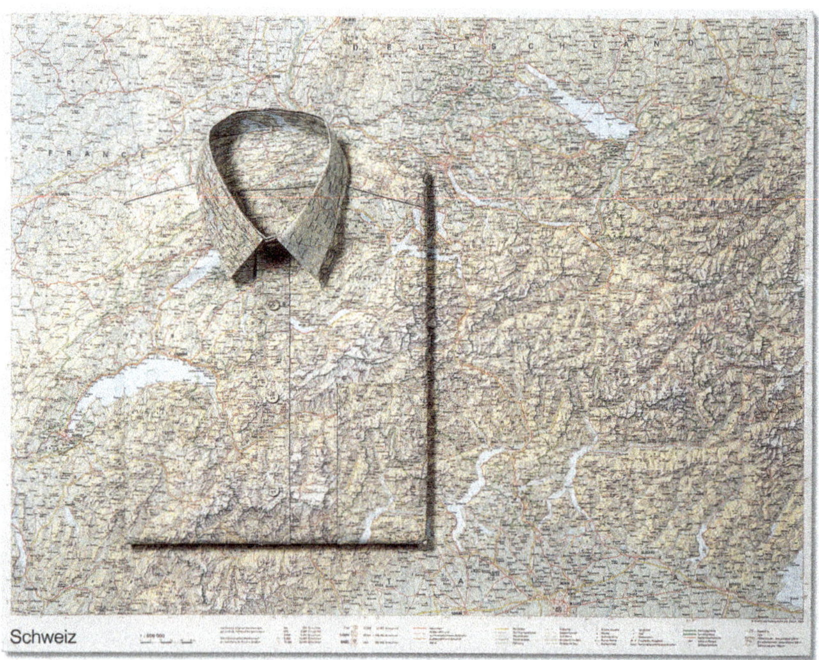

Image 14: Hossein Valamanesh, *Untitled Map*, 2002
Paper map on cotton, multiples of four, 62.3 x 77.5 x 7 cm
Private collection, Adelaide
Photographer: M. Kluvanek

All artists want exposure for their work, yet access to extended networks and avenues of support to facilitate that exposure can challenge the resolve of the artist. The more influential arts spheres, such as 'the big end of town' of the major performing arts companies and the funding bodies, can be difficult for NESB artists to access, making the forging of a trusted profile in the arts also difficult. Shakthidharan wants to be the one who is trusted with the financial resources to see his theatre work to fruition. NESB artists' experiences suggest an image of different planes of access that tend to operate independently and not readily engage with each other, but rather slide over one another. The mainstream is comfortable in its place in the central current and, to some extent, the NESB artist is comfortable in the tributary of the community arts worker. It is more likely to be the independent NESB artist who interrupts the current of the mainstream by their creative leadership, whether through recognition of their artistic work, developing networking capacities with other artists or negotiating productive working relationships across the arts sectors—all of which play into an improved multicultural arts milieu.

Productive Peers

The support of peers and networks is essential to the systems that independent artists create around themselves to shore up their precarious existence and art practice:

> Precarity is the condition of being vulnerable to others. Unpredictable encounters transform us; we are not in control, even of ourselves. Unable to rely on a stable structure of community, we are thrown into shifting assemblages, which remake us as well as our others. (Tsing 2015, 20)

Tsing elucidates precarity beyond unequal economic scenarios and emphasises the productive connections that can potentially occur between those who are different to us. The existence of networks that build trust across those interfaces contribute to successful multicultural art projects and milieu.

Lau is a confident young woman, but her experience of isolation extended through each stage of her forays into playwriting. Unlike the other artist-in-residence, she had no one to call on when it came to finding performers to read her script:

> All her friends were actors and all part of that industry. She just had
> to put it on Facebook to get like a hundred responses for actors.
> None of my friends are from that industry. I asked—do you have
> anyone left over that I could use? (A. Lau 2015, interview)

This tale indicates that Lau had neither the social, professional nor cultural contexts to activate her presence in the arts. Her determination to supersede these constraints is commendable. Shopfront is a workshop-based, performing arts organisation for young people in southern Sydney. It is considered an accessible route for young playwrights; however, it appears to have been unable to stretch enough to incorporate Lau adequately during her residency there 2014. In 2017 only two NESB artistic facilitators could be identified from the pool of 16 then on their books, limiting their ability to deliver on their rhetoric of access (Shopfront 2017). It was not until Lau attended programs developed by CAAP that she met artists with whom she could identify as mentors and peers. These examples identify a 'pushback' sensibility of the artist who, regardless of the nature of the gesture, contributes to a multicultural arts milieu. The artist must also push forward.

Persistent Creativity: *Mother Tongue*

Mother Tongue is a long-form choreographic work that presents an 'eloquent dance-poem on war, cultural tolerance and healing' (Paul 2018). After being initiated by Annalouise Paul in 2007, a 'pilot' was finally presented at Bangarra Theatre, Sydney, in 2014 (see Image 15). In 2020, the work still waits for its premiere. This process over many years exemplifies the persistence required of a creative leader through the iterations of creative investigation and logistics that should lead to a public presentation. The independent artist must be resilient; they must be able to reaffirm trust in themselves and their creative engagement with their work. The account that follows describes the trajectory of an intercultural work approximating an 'everyday' sense of the work involved. The use of 'everyday' needs qualification because the artistic result is not of the everyday; it may draw on the everyday through the proximity of diversity, but art is an abstracted and condensed expression of everyday encounters. *Mother Tongue* elicits how creative leadership responds to the barriers faced in that process.

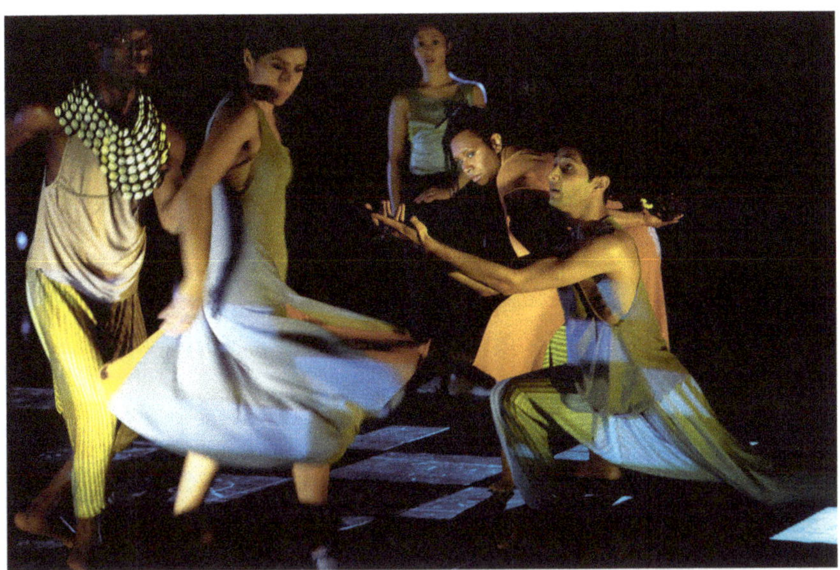

Image 15: Annalouise Paul, *Mother Tongue*, 2014

Photographer: Shane Rozario

I selected Paul as an exemplar because of the challenges she experienced at every turn to produce a major performance work as an independent practitioner with limited infrastructure support; because her extensive performing career includes acting, dancing and choreographing; and because her efforts demonstrate agency and creative leadership. Beyond her individual practice, her ambition is to establish the first Australian intercultural dance company, which would benefit other artists. Her experiences provide an opportunity to gauge the application in Australia of UNESCO's 'culture cycles', the value chain encompassing education through to distribution (Mar and Ang 2015, 7), and highlight potential interventions relevant to NESB artists.

Paul's intercultural practice began with her choreographing and performing a 'fusion' of contemporary and flamenco dance, and she continues to refine what it means to produce intercultural dance by working with other performers. *Mother Tongue* was the third part of a trilogy supported by Parramatta-based Western Sydney Dance Action (FORM Dance Projects n.d.-a). This dance organisation, now FORM Dance Projects, was part of the 'culture cycle' as it provided modest financial and administrative support in the crucial early stages of Paul's process. Their description downplays her challenges: 'Her enduring fascination with other cultures investigated questions of identity and intersections between cultures through cross-cultural dance/music relationships' (FORM Dance Projects n.d.-b, 9). This text points to the complexity of intercultural art through the use of floating signifiers—symbols or terms open to wide interpretation that rally people around a commonly understood issue. The term 'questions of identity', for example, rallies those who see themselves in the minority, while 'cross-cultural' elides the issue between crossing ethnic identity and cultural forms (e.g. contemporary and traditional music or dance). This collision of terms occurs within the arts because of confusion between ethnic identity as subject and the different cultural forms of art. Paul is positioned as a cosmopolitan art connoisseur whose source material 'fascinates'; her work is thus presented as a pleasurable representative of multicultural Australia. The risky result of her 'fascination' could be critiqued as part of the 'discourse of enrichment', whereby cultural engagements (in both senses of the word), including those of food and dance, take the form of a multicultural fair (Hage 2000, 119).

The various 'ethnic' stalls of the fair are perused by, and enrich, the 'real Australians, the bearers of the White nation' (Hage 2000, 118). Paul's position can be considered within the contemporary and changed version of the fair, whereby migrants (one assumes non-English migrants) also want to be enriched but are 'blocked' by the white multicultural fantasy that aims to maintain a central role in apportioning access (Hage 2000, 118). As we have seen, this controlling role produces a barrier for artists in terms of their access to bureaucratic and mainstream organisations. Hage's analysis falters when applied to artistic attempts to engage with cultural diversity, as he digs through layers of cultural mistrust. Art requires that mistakes are able to be made. Faltering also produces moments of vulnerability for the artist. In this faltering, the artist may demonstrate creative leadership. Such vulnerable processes suggest use of the sociological term 'quotidian transversality', in which opportunities from the everyday, or the quotidian, open up and reconfigure through interchange or the 'transverse' (Wise 2009, 23). Drawing on Cockburn and Yuval-Dais (1999), Wise (2009, 23) claims that the transverse provides an opening that goes beyond the hybridity of exchange, or assimilation of merging, and is therefore useful to the arts:

> [Transverse] highlights how cultural difference can be the basis for commensality and exchange: where identities are not left behind, but can be shifted and opened up in moments of non-hierarchical reciprocity, and are sometimes mutually reconfigured in the process.

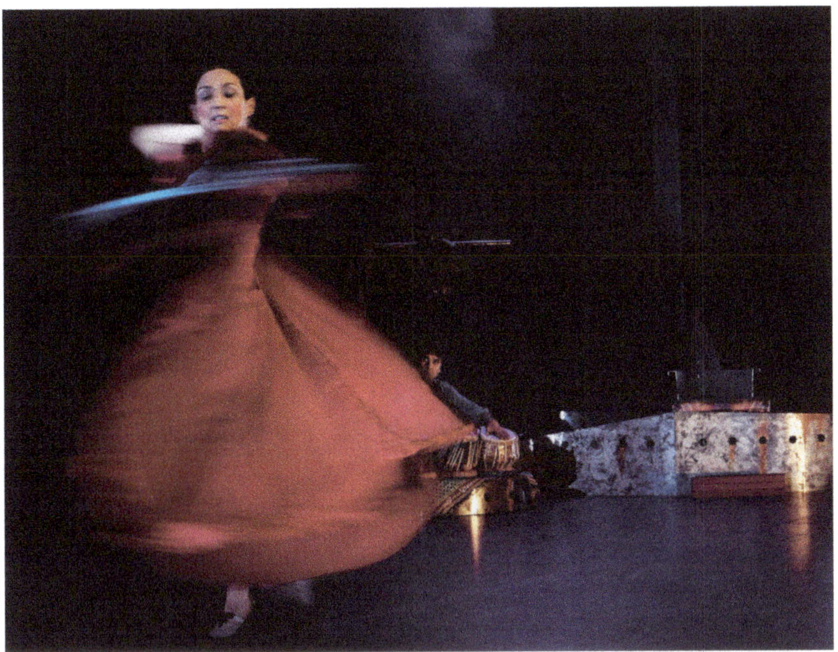

Image 16: Annalouise Paul, *Isabel*, 2008

Photographer: Shane Rozario

Such moments of reciprocity can become available in the tangible yet fleeting forms of performance. In the first of Paul's trilogy, *Isabel*, flamenco dance and tabla percussion explore Queen Isabel of Spain's notions of power and colonialism in 1492 (see Image 16). The second part, *Game On*, broadens the historical approach to produce a conversation between a tabla player and a contemporary dancer in which Paul questions 'how extreme cultures coming together can communicate'.

Everyday cosmopolitanism is evoked by a 'conversation' and is complicated when held between 'extreme cultures'. Paul articulates an inherent, almost abrasive, friction that she engages with on a creative level. Each artist challenges the other in both tradition (flamenco and tabla) and form (dance and percussion). In this example, the transverse shows that the interchange causes friction: it is not 'smooth' (Carmichael 2011, 65). Different creative knowledge sets come together to challenge the performers who take a risky path because the creative results are unknown. Even as choreographer, Paul cannot control the creative 'conversation'. The physicality of the performers highlights the dynamic interaction on stage and exemplifies the creative use of 'unpredictable interfaces' that arise from multicultural

Australia (Mar and Ang 2015, 8). *Game On* is bicultural and, therefore, more easily grasped by an audience. The interface through the individual forms of flamenco and tabla are reasonably familiar to Australians. The unpredictable aspect is that they are not usually in the same performance. As a bicultural performance (which, in fact, is what most 'multicultural arts' tend to be), *Game On* takes an incremental step towards establishing a multicultural arts milieu.

Paul approached the multicultural arts touring group kultour for touring support to widen the audience for *Game On*, only to discover that she was excluded because there was no NSW member. This realisation took her into the realm of arts politics. In 2011 she established Groundswell, a lobby group to generate support for the re-establishment of a NSW multicultural arts organisation (Paul 2010; Koubaroulis 2014). Over the next five years her arts practice continued, albeit at a much slower pace. This deviation is not uncommon among NESB artists who find they must be politically active to achieve structural change to improve their pathways.

Proceeds from a school's tour funded *Game On* at the Sydney Opera House. In 2011 Arts NSW and the Department of Foreign Affairs and Trade toured it to India whereupon it won two awards: Australian Arts in Asia and the Export Award. On the back of that success, Paul began work on *Mother Tongue*, a 'body percussion' piece with Bobby Singh, Miranda Wheen, Greg Sheehan, Albert David, Latai Taumoepeau, Lucky Lartey and Shruti Ghosh. The work is concerned with reconciliation and understanding between cultures. Paul (2015, interview) kept coming up against controversy and lack of appreciation or understanding of her intercultural style and the content:

> There was controversy about why I wanted to use six, seven, eight different cultures; why I was using Albert David, an Aboriginal artist and why body percussion. My answer was why not? The Australia Council wanted to see their familiar styles of contemporary dance, and couldn't imagine how it was going to look. A dance organisation said it was going to look like a variety show. At the other end of the spectrum, presenters were saying 'just put them all onstage together and jam'. There was a lot of extreme views about how culture should come together—so the smash-up idea of jamming and fusion: do whatever and then the elitist: 'is it going to look messy?', the aesthetic around it was in question.

The use of the adjective 'extreme' was personal this time, as it concerned Paul's aesthetic choices. This was her stepping towards a multicultural and intercultural (in both social and cultural meanings) work. She was offended by the presenters' suggestion to 'jam', a loose technique of turn-taking associated with non-classical music, because it devalued her skills as a choreographer. Such responses bring into sharp relief the lack of support for risk-taking. Luhmann's (2000, 94) definition of trust as a 'specific solution to risk achieved within a familiar world' applies here. The systems that fund development and presentation were not prepared to be part of Paul's solution. They did not trust her approach. She was not part of their milieu.

Mother Tongue fell prey to the 'yo-yo' funding of small grants. Frustrated that the project was not developing, the artistic team suffered a mini crisis, leaving Paul at a crossroad. She no longer knew 'whether it's meant to be a narrative or more abstract, and it went belly up for a little while'. A Bundanon residency provided the necessary creative space. Paul received some funds from Arts NSW and Bangarra provided a venue. Paul was proud that the dancers could be paid from box office sales, crowd funding and the bar. An exit survey and 'vox pop' with the culturally diverse audience members showed that most felt it could 'really go places' and 'it was ex-cell-ent' (Paul 2015).

Limited critical engagement by the mainstream media means that NESB artists often have to rely on niche funded arts magazines such as the now defunct *RealTime* for critical appraisal. In the case of *Mother Tongue*, the reviewer invoked a clumsy metaphor of a wildlife park:

> Kinetically, *Mother Tongue* is a sculpture park of rich, exotic forms coming from Torres Strait, Chile, Indonesia, West Africa, Brazil and India. Since Paul does not innovate from appropriation, strict fusion or exploding traditions, and maintains the integrity of colliding cultural forms, her seeking 'new choreographic futures' for intercultural dance proves an admirable challenge. There are moments in *Mother Tongue* when movement and gesture founded on the primordial geometries of collective motion and sound sublimely commune towards a unique horizon. (McNeilly 2014, 33)

To arrive at that sublime point took seven years work and relied on multiple sources of inspiration, resources and income. Touring is the next phase in the 'culture cycle'. kultour had ceased touring culturally diverse work by 2014. The mainstream organisations such as Performing

Lines and events such as the Australian Performing Arts Market that were expected to take on that role were guarded in their response to Paul's work. Paul was warned by the project director of the International Network for Contemporary Performing Arts, the Australia Council–funded network that matches the 'market development aspirations of Australian artists with opportunities and resources' (Australia Council n.d.-b), that:

> 'You're ahead of your time. Australia's never going to get it, get out'. And I just thought—I don't know if I'm ahead of my time or Australia's just way behind it. (A. Paul 2015, interview)

The project director's comments do not show leadership: they are another way of saying 'too ambitious'. Abrogating the responsibility to champion ambitious projects, the project director shut the door on Paul's aspirations with alacrity. *Mother Tongue* highlights the gaps in the full application of UNESCO's 'culture cycles' (Mar and Ang 2015, 8–15), notably the risk-averse nature of support for the arts by funding bodies in development, presentation and national and international marketing. Paul's project is multicultural in content and concept; it generated positive audience responses and delivered a professional outcome, mainly on a volunteer basis over several years. Its processes were only challenged when intersecting with the arts 'industry'. The diverse cultural and creative backgrounds of the artists underpinned *Mother Tongue*, enabling the performance to work 'across cultures' and develop 'cross-cultural partnerships' (see Image 17). The full spectrum of the 'culture cycles' was hindered by concerns expressed by sector gatekeepers who, confronted by the concept of *Mother Tongue*, signalled their reluctance to support and program the work. The symbolic role and reception of this performance are also part of the 'culture cycles'. The audience response to *Mother Tongue* reinforced its relevance, but only after surmounting the barriers presented by the funding agencies and dance experts to locate that audience.

As mentioned, Paul's ambitions go beyond her own practice. Demonstrating her support for a multicultural arts milieu and leadership role, she sought partners to establish the first national intercultural dance theatre company in Australia, similar to the Indigenous and internationally acclaimed Bangarra Dance Theatre:

> It will be multi-nation, here's that word—multicultural. Multiple cultural expressions. As a creative leader in that role, I would seek advice and support from those around me; it's about having multiple viewpoints that are working towards the one thing. (A. Paul 2015, interview)

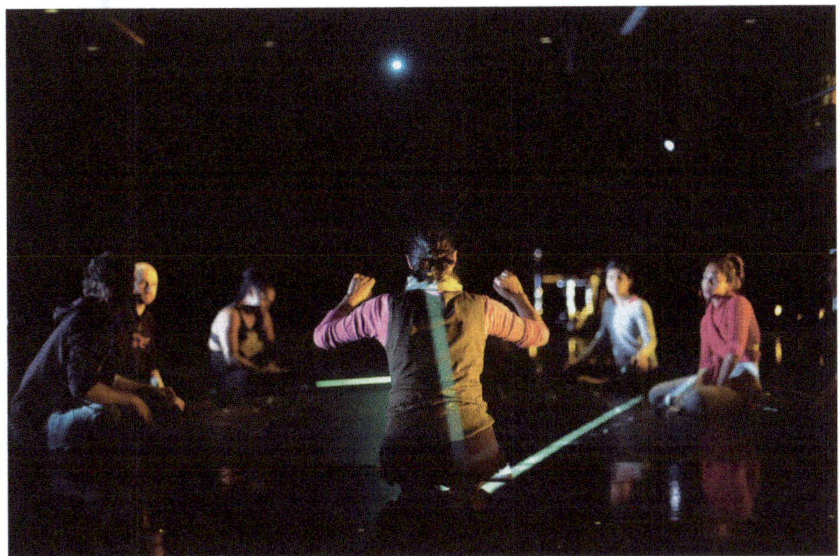

Image 17: Annalouise Paul, *Mother Tongue*, rehearsal, 2014
Photographer: Shane Rozario

Creative Leadership

Analysis of the paired themes of friction and creativity, trust and legitimacy, and support and networks demonstrates the constraints and opportunities that NESB artists can experience in pursuing a creative career. The artists in this study demonstrate the characteristics of creative leadership that inform and draw upon multicultural Australia, and articulate how best to creatively, politically, financially and pragmatically navigate, and intervene, in the arts system:

> Creative leadership now is about finding and working with individuals within the systems who have a mutual vision with you. Finding the resources to do that, because that's separate to project funding. (S. Shakthidharan 2015, interview)

Creative leadership is about producing and presenting work that is relevant or, as Lau (2015, interview) put it: 'Being able to create something that resonates with people. I haven't seen anything in Australian arts that resonates with me'. Lau was not alone. Only one interviewee identified a recent Australian artwork as satisfying, although many could provide an international example. Creative leadership for a younger, second NESB generation is based on a different set of experiences. A daughter of migrants, Lau rarely sees her generation presented on stage and screen, an exception being Benjamin Law's Chinese-Australian sitcom *The Family Law*, which screened on SBS television in 2016.

For Nguyen (2015, interview), creative leadership changes perceptions and enables a closer appreciation of people in new and contrasting situations:

> Recently Dad went to the Fringe Festival. I cannot imagine any other Asian parent in their sixties going to a Fringe Festival. That is a good story. That is about creating contrast and clashing of different cultures, and seeing the result.

Nguyen contemporises his father and is keen to articulate new narratives of someone who is open to a new life. He places his family inside an arts scene (which he considers unusual and potentially risqué) and views the creative potential as 'clashing' to produce unexpected outcomes:

> It's about taking risk. It's about speaking out. I'm an advocate as well as an artist, by just speaking out. It's about taking people with you and adding value to something that's already there. It's about pushing things beyond what's expected. (A. Paul 2015, interview)

This is a direct example of creative friction. For Paul, there is a political edge to leading creatively as well as going beyond the expected norms. Valamanesh and Koukias are among those artists who found their creative edge via their ethnicities in relation to the Australian context. Valamanesh creatively leads by doing 'to just show that it can be done, from my honest view as an artist'.

Conclusion

NESB artists navigate the friction between competing aspects of innovation and the maintenance of cultural heritage. Innovation is a synthesis of fresh ideas into new forms of production that resonate within contemporary society. Cultural heritage is a 'collective memory made tangible' that surfaces through forms of 'expression, maintenance, representation, recognition and renewal' (Anheier and Isar 2007, 30). These characteristics are frequently positioned as mutually exclusive binaries for multicultural arts practices. However, I have shown the ways in which NESB artists push this binary 'beyond what's expected'. By doing so, they demonstrate creative leadership through the persistence required in the face of stereotyping barriers. The artists in this study demonstrate the principles that promote diverse cultural expressions by producing work that comes from 'working across cultures' and being able to develop 'cross-cultural partnerships' (Mar and Ang 2015, 8–10).

The majority of the artists in this study faced challenges in the broader 'industry' aspects of success, particularly in relation to being programmed, presented and promoted. They all support and recognise the contribution of NESB artists' work to Australian society, despite the lower rates of financial support from state-sponsored arts programs. The income gap from their art practice is lessening; however, the number of professional NESB artists is half that of NESB employees in the overall workforce (Throsby and Petetskaya 2017, 142). The arts industry's resistance to include NESB artists as 'leaders', the paucity of resources for culturally diverse infrastructure and negative perceptions as to the value of an arts career in Australia are just some of the reasons for the glacial pace of change.

Nevertheless, some NESB artists have developed and maintained careers in the face of such odds, demonstrating creative leadership through their agency within the Australian arts sector. These artists possess the ability to cross between, and adapt to, different cultural spheres, including the possibility of communication across intergenerational changes; a practical understanding of the delicate tactics and strategies required to navigate their immediate cohort of friends and family, as well as the arts sector in its myriad aspects; being prepared to participate in the inevitable link between arts and politics that will confront them at some point, in particular issues of inclusion in the arts; and being prepared to push the boundaries of the canon and to creatively adapt aspects of their cultural heritage. These adaptive elements use relational, distributive and charismatic leadership modes.

5

Challenges of Institutional Leadership: Reluctance in the Australia Council

Policy development is a site where creative leadership can translate into institutional leadership—as is the case with artists from non–English speaking backgrounds (NESB) who have participated in the Australia Council Multicultural Advisory Committee (ACMAC) and as advocates for the arts in a multicultural Australia. In this chapter, I articulate how the creative leadership capacities of NESB artists can inform institutional leadership through participation in governance and policy development. Both staff in institutions and art practitioner peers can demonstrate institutional leadership for multicultural arts practices, and this is ideally shown when the strategic aims of the agency and those of multicultural arts policy align. However, NESB artists often face challenges and contradictions when they become affiliated with the apparatus of a government arts agency, in this case, the Australia Council. In particular, I explore the empirical data that underpin the central role of ACMAC in formulating the Arts for a Multicultural Australia 1996 and the Arts in a Multicultural Australia (AMA) 2000 and 2006 policies, and the implications for sector leadership caused by ACMAC's dissolution in 2007.

A multicultural arts milieu is most likely to flourish when there is active engagement and leadership by institutional funding bodies. This engagement includes options of governance, the ability for internal champions to progress change, the ways external expertise is accommodated on a regular basis and how advocates gain experience. Institutional leadership also refers to positional leadership and, in the context of the Australia Council, applies to the experience of two ACMAC chairs and several members who describe their combative experiences of governance. Relational and distributed styles of leadership were often displayed by ACMAC to manage these experiences, while transactional styles of leadership were more likely to be displayed by the executive. The Cultural Engagement Framework (CEF), which is the current mechanism adopted by the Australia Council, is promoted as delivering greater internal and external accountability across all diversity areas and, therefore, bears close critique in terms of delivering to the arts in a multicultural Australia. These institutional issues of leadership are explored through the friction arising from governance, the use of expertise to garner trust and the crucial role of networks to produce traction.

Adapting Friction into Governance

Consultative groups provide expert advice to confirm or adjust institutional aims and strategies. The political pressures that often underpin the need for a policy response can generate internal debates regarding strategy implementation and, in so doing, highlight the potential for friction in governance. One of the remits of diversity advisory committees such as ACMAC is to identify where adjustments (of whatever scale) need to be made. In hierarchical, rule-bound institutions, such adjustments (a result of friction in the first place) may also generate friction in response. The internal institutional development of a policy that, in the end, appears as a neat summation of intentions and actions often comes about through 'robust debate' and compromise. It can be a 'gritty' experience because policy development tests the boundaries of influence and power between advisers and the institution. As Tsing (2005, 6) points out 'difference can disrupt, causing everyday malfunctions as well as unexpected cataclysms. Friction refuses the lie that [global] power operates as a well-oiled machine'.

Policy statements in the arts are often presented to the public as the result of a smooth process of identifying issues and addressing gaps. However, internal processes are more likely to be charged with difficult debates. Challenges to the image of their smoothly running institution mean that institutional leaders may 'open the door' to discussing the challenge in question—in the case of the Australia Council, cultural diversity in the arts—or they may push back as a form of 'profound resistance' (Blonski 1994, 206). The engagement by those in Australia Council leadership roles towards issues of cultural difference in the arts appear to have generated a significant moment in each decade of its existence. These moments include:

- the establishment of an advisory committee in 1975
- the first multicultural policy proposals adopted by council in 1985
- ACMAC-led national discourse about multiculturalism in 1994
- significant resources invested across discourse, artistic and market development in 2000.

Each of these productive phases resulted from creative and institutional frictions that required energy to (re-)establish the AMA agenda and also generate the subsequent momentum for its ongoing delivery. This history suggests an institutional pattern that begins with disregard, prompts criticism from practitioners and subsequently catalyses the institution into developing a response and, sometimes, a process for change.

The Mirage of a Legacy

The chairs of ACMAC all held positional leadership roles. As government appointees, one of their main remits was to steer the issues raised by their committee to be approved at the level of the Australia Council Board, the highest level of internal governance and decision-making (a schematic organisational chart of this period is at Appendix C). ACMAC was usually chaired by the chair of the Community Cultural Development Board (CCDB). This was the case for two research participants: actor Lex Marinos and comedy scriptwriter Deborah Klika, whose stories provide rare insight into governance roles at the Australia Council. As government appointees, they can be described as 'political' chairs because this is 'the world of some art boards. They are a play between heroes, politics, power and personal crusade, where being visible and speaking out oscillate with invisibility and discretion' (Rentschler 2015, 106). Rentschler depicts the tension in arts governance leadership between public profile, government expectations and attending to a constituency. ACMAC chairs had to juggle these roles with other members of the Australia Council governing board, other members of ACMAC, and the complex and changing constituency in the 'multicultural arts' sector—and do so in relation to the government of the day.

Marinos established his creative leadership as an actor and multicultural advocate. This role merged with his institutional leadership during his roles at the Australia Council as deputy chair and chair, respectively, of the CCDB and ACMAC. The AMA policy area is also a site in which the creative leadership of NESB artists can merge with institutional leadership. In such contexts, their creative leadership is stimulated by social and political engagements that may inform their practice as well as develop advocacy capabilities. This process can also move them into the spotlight as candidates for institutional leaders in a governance role.

For example, Marinos's appointment as chair of ACMAC coincided with his position as director of NSW's Carnivale Multicultural Arts Festival. He viewed this dual role as:

> Invaluable, in so far as it meant I was dealing on a daily basis with NESB/CALD artists across all disciplines, and was constantly reminded how difficult it was for them to assert their own voice and how marginalised they were by funding bodies at every level. (L. Marinos 2020, email correspondence)

Being uncharacteristically circumspect, Marinos (2015, interview) describes his time as ACMAC chair from 1995 to 1999 as 'stimulating but very challenging and frustrating'. Klika, ACMAC chair from 1999 to 2002, more pointedly recalls the experience as one of a 'fight'. She was heartened in 2015 to find the 2000 policy still online:

> It's good that it had some staying power beyond my time, because a concern one has when one goes through such a process of fighting for such a policy, is that once you go, the policy disappears. But it was worth the effort. (D. Klika 2015, interview)

This comment is telling in a number of ways. The metaphor of a 'battle' is illustrative of the antagonistic process Klika experienced within the institution. It highlights the AMA policy as a site of struggle and implicitly positions the Australia Council's leadership in equally 'combative' roles. Her reference to 'such a policy' suggests that the battle had become an anticipated and ingrained process. Klika also voices the concern that the pressure brought to bear by a 'champion' may dissipate when they leave the institution, with staff in executive roles retreating from, rather than continuing to implement, changes across the institution. The institutional rhetoric of support for greater diversity often relies on the charismatic and committed individual to present the appearance of a committed institution, yet, without such champions, there may well be 'no commitment at all' (Ahmed 2012, 135). Ahmed (2012, 19) describes diversity champions as those appointed as 'diversity practitioners' who can also 'teach us about how we inhabit institutions'. That is, the champion needs first to be able understand the specifics of the internal 'institutional life'—a complex task that requires observation and relationship building before their role can become effective. The scope of the challenge for the 'diversity worker' is to manoeuvre through the institutional structures and cultures often built to resist change. My role as a senior policy researcher was, in part, to ensure that the transition between chairs and members maintained momentum for the policy.

According to Sirkin, Keenan and Jackson (2005), four elements contribute to effective institutional change: project duration, particularly time between project reviews; performance integrity, or the capabilities of project teams; the commitment of both senior executives and staff; and the additional effort that employees need to make to cope with change. The authors' key argument is that all four factors need to work in concert to deliver change. Yet, they are difficult to track because integrity, commitment and effort are all intangible and often need to be underpinned by consistent and effective leaders. While a chair appointed for a maximum of four years may be able to adjust institutional commitment for a limited period, they are reliant on subsequent leaders after they leave. Uneven support has dogged the history of the arts in a multicultural Australia. The Australia Council's leadership continues to appear reluctant to maintain its ambit (or commitment) of transforming the arts in Australia to better represent its multicultural society.

Therefore, transformational leadership, when challenged by complex issues, may prompt a return to the previous status quo. The inbuilt mechanism that requires fixed-term appointments to decision-making roles—including ACMAC, the governing members of the Australia Council and executive management—can also limit the momentum for change and meaningful legacy. Effective institutional leadership could exist in a productive relationship between transformational and positional leaders. Councillors need the leadership of the bureaucracy to be able to activate and negotiate change throughout the various staffing levels of the institution, while bureaucrats need the vision and influence of the councillors to maintain the relevance of the institution.

The ACMAC chair had to find respect at the council decision-making level, while also engaging with the staff of the institution. This positioned the ACMAC chair as a central, institution-wide, relational leader in a space to increase the likelihood of longer-term change. There was a brief time when this did occur within the Australia Council. During the development of AMA 2000, Klika was ACMAC chair and Dr Margaret Seares was executive chair (i.e. both the chair and the CEO of the institution). The combined positional leadership of these women in influential roles, as well as their relational skills, initiated changes that led to a decade of resources allocated to implement an effective AMA policy.

The era of joint support for AMA continued when Jennifer Bott was appointed CEO (1999–2006). Bott (2015, interview) described Klika as 'thoughtful, strong and pragmatic', and as someone who also acknowledged the 'fight':

> It was not sort of schlepped [passed] off as a kind of irritant or whatever. I respect Deborah for that. I think she had to fight for that. Then it filtered from the Council down in many ways. It made a lot of difference once AMA was taken very seriously at the governance table.

It was a significant challenge to have AMA taken 'seriously'—not as a slightly irritating friction that could easily be dismissed, but as a priority among competing priorities and contexts. Here Bott reinforces the hierarchy in the Australia Council, while also observing a change in the members of the governing body. Klika's use of both relational and transactional styles of leadership temporarily altered the status quo of governance. This change supports the experience of a battle, but also the attitudinal shift that enabled adequate resources to implement the AMA 2000 policy initiatives nationwide.

The Australia Council approved an unprecedented $2.08 million for AMA initiatives over six years, averaging $350,000 per annum (Keating, Bertone and Leahy n.d., 31). The per annum sum appears modest; however, the forward budget agreement-in-principle (conditional upon similar levels of funding from government) over six years is a commitment that is yet to be repeated. The Australia Council's recommendations to strengthen and commit long-term allocations to subsequent AMA policies were not endorsed.

The Reluctant Institution

The management of AMA within the institution is indicative of another way of, as Bott puts it, being 'taken very seriously'; this presents opportunities for positional and transactional forms of leadership. Each of the many (six or seven) institutional levels require positional leaders who comprehend the issues and support the momentum for AMA strategies for arts sector transformation. Long-time senior bureaucrat at the Australia Council, Executive Director of Arts Funding and Engagement Frank Panucci (2015, interview) observes that, while it is now easier to 'articulate the diversity conversation', environmental limits remain in place:

> Those famous two steps forward, one step back; you feel that a lot of times in that [multicultural] space. Part of it is about the arts and cultural space that, like a lot of these areas, are fundamentally determined by the general public and political discourse. While you think you have made the progress in a specific area, you can't remove it from the context within which you operate.

Awareness of context is an essential understanding required by any leader. Panucci is aware of the lack of traction, but deflects the reason for structural barriers in the arts onto society and government, which alleviates the Australia Council of any institutional responsibility. Klika, on the other hand, addressed the Australia Council's institutional responsibilities and achieved an unprecedented commitment to AMA during Prime Minister Howard's term, one characterised by a government that dismantled inclusive multicultural values and support structures (Ho 2013, 38).

Different approaches to change are expressed in the interviews with former ACMAC chairs, Marinos and Klika. These range from actively negotiating a positive impact where possible to taking a laissez-faire approach and leaving the outcome to 'market' or society. The motivations for Marinos and Klika to maintain their efforts stem from their respective leadership aims for change, but are articulated through different approaches. Their criticisms view policy intervention as being either inadequate or overbearing. Klika's (2015, interview) view of the role of arts policy is that it should not override creative intentions or be too prescriptive:

> What I hope policy does is shift people's ways of thinking to be relevant to today's society. But I also recognise that sometimes policy can go too far and we find it difficult to decide if it's good or bad art because it's been ticked off under a policy. That's my problem with policy; sometimes you can't tell whether it's the cart or the horse in front.

Marinos's view is that the policy levers are not direct enough. He argues that the Australia Council's lack of conviction for AMA shows through its unwillingness to ensure major companies address their consistently low levels of engagement with NESB artists:

> The AMA policy is given some regard, but not pursued with much conviction. It's as though having the policy in itself is enough, to say 'this is what we've done'. But it's rarely implemented. If they do audit the major organisations for instance, I'm unaware that they have conversations that say—your representation is very low and do you have any strategies to redress that? (L. Marinos 2015, interview)

The conundrum is that having a policy 'to point to' can alleviate the pressure on action because it takes the place of 'doing' (Ahmed 2012, 86). Whether policy outcomes should be tied to government funding is a perennial discussion that involves quotas, compliance and the use of taxpayers' money. It frustrates Marinos and others to see structural change avoided by major organisations, such as state theatre companies. Indeed, the issues of government funding, quotas and policy remain live topics (Gonsalves 2017).

As a performer, Marinos remains close to the issues and observes improvements in other contexts that fuel his thoughts regarding the lack of comprehensive change for the arts in multicultural Australia:

> Many companies have had an outstanding record with opportunities for Indigenous artists and I think that's a laudable thing. But it puzzles me, because it seems odd that the same thinking doesn't carry across to cultural diversity, in which areas they're lamentably woeful. (L. Marinos 2015, interview)

Marinos and Klika articulate a fundamental schism about implementation methods. Klika is tentative about over-prescribing to artists, while Marinos advocates prescribed outcomes to organisations. However divergent their views, both chafe against the lack of seriousness shown by the Australia Council in addressing the barriers experienced by NESB artists:

> Council was a bit reluctant to implement policies they claimed to believe in, but stopped short of implementing in any meaningful way. It was never a demand that was placed on companies in terms of employment. (L. Marinos 2015, interview)

The methods of policy implementation highlight the discord between intentions and the methods of delivering those intentions. Discord can inhibit change in a bureaucracy concerned about negative attention, particularly negative attention from politically influential chairs of major companies who are frequently affiliated with government in some way. However, there have also been small signs of change, with companies such as the Melbourne Theatre Company (MTC) and Belvoir Street advertising 'diversity' projects in 2018. In partnership with Multicultural Arts Victoria, the MTC Connect program aims to bring young people of culturally diverse backgrounds into the company as marketing and programming advisers (MTC 2014).

Klika (2015, interview) feels that institutional responsibility falls short in maintaining the steady momentum for change and advocating to government on behalf of NESB artists:

> The Australia Council has to keep doing that work for those seeds to flower 20, 30, 40 years on. I get depressed when they just maintain a status quo because that's easier, and they don't push the envelope with government.

Klika's comments conceptualise a succinct institutional leadership role for the Australia Council. The chances for this role to flourish, however, have diminished significantly since the disbanding of ACMAC. The impact of a void where once consistent advice was provided has affected the institution in several ways. It is difficult to keep abreast of developments in the multicultural arts sector because the structured opportunities for NESB artists to provide regular input across all artforms no longer exist. Subsequently, on the occasions when 'cultural diversity' may come onto the agenda, it is unlikely that all councillors (Australia Council board members) have had exposure across all the issues and artforms, or can speak with any confidence about the arts in a multicultural Australia. Executive staff members, therefore, become default advisers, most of whom are also unlikely to have in-depth knowledge of cultural diversity.

The embattled experiences of Marinos and Klika, as two ACMAC chairs appointed by different governing political parties, illustrate the Australia Council as a site of struggle regarding AMA. Disbanding the expert advisory function of ACMAC removed regular opportunities for the Australia Council's Board to engage with issues that affect NESB artists. Both chairs describe the unwillingness of institutional leaders within the Australia Council organisation to advocate to government on behalf of

NESB artists, or to require that any organisations with secure Australia Council funding demonstrate and address 'cultural diversity'. These are two ongoing and unresolved leadership issues within the institution regarding the degree and means of intervention required to increase multicultural arts activity in Australia.

The Fragility of Funding

The Australia Council's main responsibilities are to disburse government funds to the arts through a national process of grant application and peer assessment. A positive outcome of a successful grant application is where 'money is translated into cultural artefact' (Hawkins 1993, 133). The steps to take in making an application include being aware of funding guidelines; approaches to, and negotiations with, arts funding staff members; comprehending and applying the guidelines for a submission; and awaiting the final decision. Each of these steps produce pressure points in the interactions between applicant and institution including how to interpret the guidelines that have taken staff innumerable rounds of meetings to agree upon, what kind of questions to ask the staff members who are trained to deliver information in a particular way, the intensive work required to produce a completed application and the machinery of processes (software and human) that produce a final result.

As part of the application process, the Australia Council collects data about each applicant's background. For example, the *Australia Council Annual Report 2015–2016* indicates that 'disability' attracted $375,000 in dedicated funds, 21 per cent of grants were awarded to regional artists or organisations, and $9.9 million in funds were awarded to Aboriginal and Torres Strait Islander artists or organisations (Australia Council 2016a, 48, 61). However, the report makes no mention of dedicated funding for multicultural artists or organisations. Despite multiple requests to the Australia Council since commencing my research, specific data on grants awarded to NESB artists have not been provided. This suggests a lack of transparency around these data. I have instead had to extrapolate information from various published Australia Council reports to build a picture of Australia Council funding to NESB artists.

The Australia Council's 2016–20 corporate plan (Australia Council 2016b, 7) provides a statistic on support to NESB artists and organisations:

> Since inception, [1973] more than 14% of the grant funding allocated through our programs has gone to culturally and linguistically diverse groups. In 2015–2016, $3.1m was awarded to artists and arts organisations who identify as belonging to culturally and linguistically diverse groups.

Three possible data scenarios emerge when the figures from the *Annual Report 2015–2016* (Australia Council 2016a, 17) are intersected with those in the corporate plan (Australia Council 2016b, 10):

- If all grant funding is considered, including government initiatives and major performing arts (MPA) companies, NESB support equates to $3.1m/$173.8m or 1.8 per cent.

- If funding that includes government initiatives and excludes MPA companies is considered, NESB support equates to $3.1m/$66m or 4.6 per cent.

- If only Australia Council grant funding is considered (excluding government initiatives and MPA companies), NESB support equates to $3.1m/$50.6m or 6.1 per cent.

These calculations are inferred from the Australia Council's published statistics for 'CALD artists and organisations' and expenditure reporting, and present a raison d'être behind the announcement of a target of '14% of funding [to be] allocated through our grant programs to projects by people from culturally and linguistically diverse groups' (Australia Council 2016b, 8). This transactional aim does not provide details as to how a 14 per cent target will be achieved.

Navigating the System

One of the inhibiting factors for individual NESB artists may be the lack of familiarity with the bureaucratic processes of applying for funding. In the late 1990s, Arts Queensland demonstrated leadership by 'accompaniment' through a series of innovative grant writing workshops in an attempt to even out the playing field:

> They delivered a series of workshops where the multicultural artists would act as a funding panel to assess [anonymised] real grants. It honed in on the technique of writing a grant. Afterwards, there was a 70 per cent increase of grant applications from multicultural artists—that's huge. (P. Couros 2015, interview)

Reversing the hierarchy of expertise on excellence improved NESB artists' comprehension of how to prepare better grant applications. Increased numbers of grant applications illustrate the workshops' success; the workshops can also be seen as opportunities for artists to develop creative leadership. The value of any grant, beyond the money, is the recognition and level of trust it signals from peers.

Gaining that recognition is further complicated by the perceived hierarchy of genres within specific artforms. The aesthetic hierarchies perceived between innovation and cultural maintenance produce friction during grant assessment meetings. A Dance Board and ACMAC member observed:

> How an excessively marked interest in innovation undermines the possibility of funding other types of work dealing with cultural heritage. Cultural maintenance was viewed as both a matter of the group the applicant belonged to, and of the way the application was structured. (ACMAC n.d.-a)

This memory articulates the flawed perception that innovation and heritage are mutually exclusive, which AMA 2000 attempted to address by profiling the links between tradition and innovation (Australia Council 2000). This excerpt also highlights that the need to articulate such aesthetic connections applies mainly to NESB artists. This issue was raised again in 2017 by NESB artists. For example, dancer and choreographer Aruna Gandhi reflected that she felt that her lack of success in arts grants applications was because her Bharatanatyam practice was considered neither contemporary nor innovative (Castagna 2017).

When faced with a low level of funding and a lack of employment opportunities in the creative sector, some artists have taken the entrepreneurial response of establishing creative enterprises (Idriss 2018, 95–117). For example, CuriousWorks established a fee-for-service role, drawing on the media technology skills of those in the company. This income stream supported the company's other aims to deliver not-for-profit projects with community partners, because even secured grants were inadequate to deliver all the ambitions of a project:

> Your ideas are bigger than funding anyway, and so it has to be supported elsewhere. This is in the context of not being from a middle class where you only have to look after yourself. So you have to have a solid business model. (S. Shakthidharan 2015, interview)

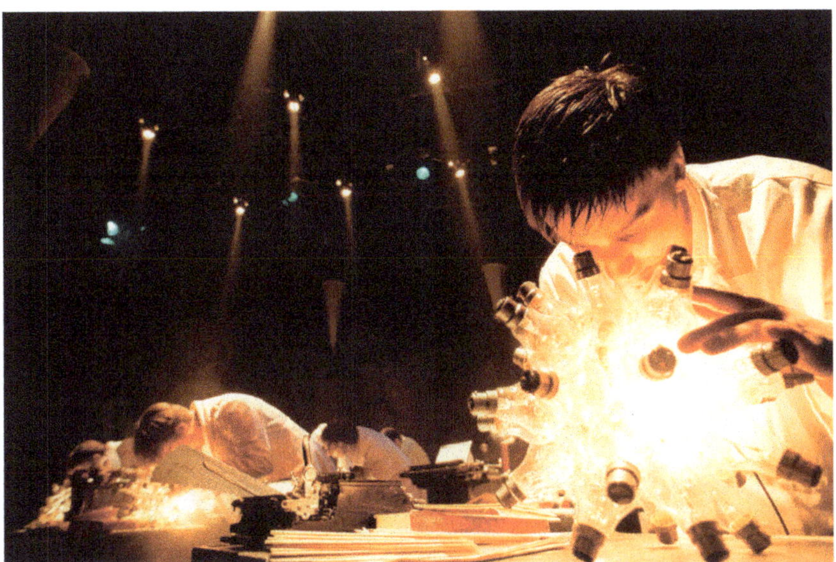

Image 18: Konstantin Koukias, *Tesla—Lightning in His Hand*, 2003
Photographer: Lucia Rossi

The issue of class raised in this quotation points to the uneven family support for creative pursuits experienced by NESB artists. Shakthidharan's solution to maintain a 'solid business model' exemplifies a pragmatic response to the friction caused around levels of funding, but also points to the strategies and efforts being made to maintain the business.

The fragility of funding to the small to medium (S2M) sector increases because the state art agencies and the Australia Council agree that if one agency stops funding a company the other will also 'defund' them. Koukias had kept his experimental opera company, IHOS, in production for 25 years on small amounts of organisational funding (see Image 18). Several years ago that persistence looked successful:

> We'd just opened a massive opera at MONA [Museum of Old and New Art] with seven sold-out performances and all on budget, when IHOS got de-funded. It was only a matter of time before the state would pull the plug and I couldn't keep begging from patrons. I had to rely on a lot of teaching to survive because I was only ever on a stipend of $10,000 a year. (K. Koukias 2015, interview)

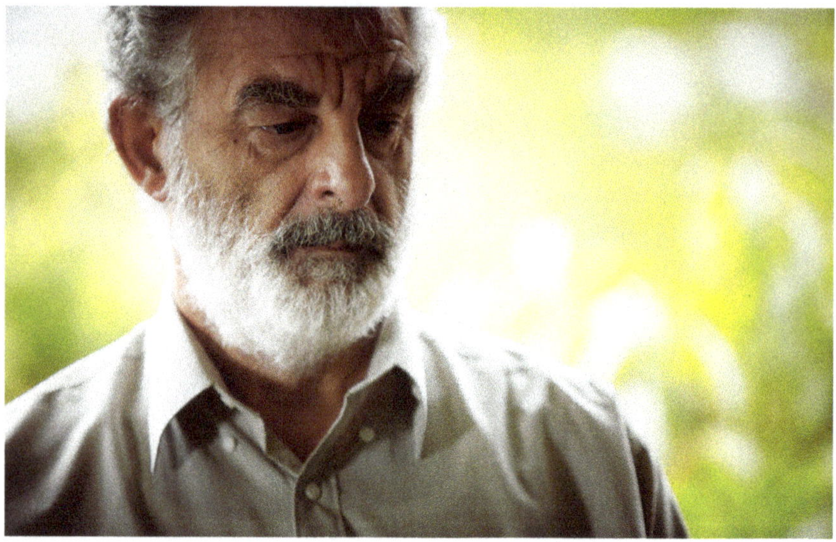

Image 19: Lex Marinos, *The Slap*, 2011
Photographer: Ben King
Courtesy: Matchbox Pictures

These two examples reveal the tenacity of the NESB artist to manoeuvre around low levels of institutional support. Both CuriousWorks and IHOS are companies that provide enormous creative opportunities for many NESB artists. Therefore, any reduced capacity through loss of funding impacts negatively in a ripple effect.

Support for the arts in Australia fractures along lines of historical privilege. Marinos (2015, interview) (see Image 19) is highly conscious of the inequity in funding and accountability that quarantines MPA companies from failure compared to the vagaries of funding experienced by creative risk-takers in S2M companies:

> The majors are the ones who've been able to parlay their position with sponsorship and [a] subscriber base and can most absorb any cuts. The money should go to those smaller independent companies who are trying to do new work and advance the evolution of the arts.

This highlights the tense struggle for funds, particularly in the S2M sector, where the creative risk-takers are often located (Stevenson et al. 2017, 12; Eltham 2016). A low-risk approach to questions of excellence reinforces this tension. A model put forward by Kalantzis and Cope proposes turning the current funding model on its head. They suggest that, because low-risk projects emphasises the known, organisations with proven track records should be provided with short-term funds, whereas high-risk artists with future potential should benefit from a 'long-term venture capital approach' (Kalantzis and Cope 1994, 31–32). Given that many NESB artists are perceived to be high-risk, this (albeit utopian) approach could reverse the trend of lower support for their work.

Fewer multicultural arts organisations are now federally funded. Since 2016, only seven of the 128 funded organisations (5 per cent) have a specific multicultural arts focus and these received $1.6 million of the allocated $28 million (6 per cent) (Australia Council n.d.-a). This shows that the Australia Council still struggles to communicate effectively or demonstrate relational leadership across the increasing diversity of Australia's population (ABS 2017). This is a leadership issue that will need to be transparently addressed if they are to increase their grant approvals to 14 per cent for NESB artists and groups (Australia Council 2016b).

For institutions like the Australia Council that are attempting to engage with such diversity, strategies of 'accompaniment' (Lynd and Lynd 2009, 93) or 'attunement' (Gibson 2005, 273) could be employed. Accompaniment respectfully shares skills while attunement adjusts for dissonance, tries to pick up less common signals, and sets up a feedback loop with the aim of developing trusted relationships. The frequency and manner in which the institution tunes in to the messages of artists and advocates indicates how 'seriously' an issue is taken. In the case of the arts in a multicultural Australia, the amount of influence the institution is prepared to exert upwards and outwards is another indication of its leadership intentions. The past decade has seen a paradoxical shift by the institution away from providing regular opportunities to meet with NESB artists, while simultaneously attempting to develop a cohesive approach to diversity issues through the CEF.

Cultural Engagement Framework: Between Aspiration and Implementation

Within the Australia Council, all 'social' diversity policy areas have come under the umbrella of the CEF since 2008. The CEF views diversity as a 'great cultural asset that leads to greater artistic vibrancy and innovation' (Australia Council n.d.-b), an approach that resonates with the instrumental productive diversity argument (Cope and Kalantzis 1997; Bertone 2002; Ho 2013, 37–38). The 2011 iteration of the CEF foregrounds legislative compliance. The Australia Council claims a transformational leadership role through the CEF's remit of integrating strategies for artistic excellence across the diversity of Australian society, encouraging participation and enjoyment of the arts, and ensuring council services are socially and culturally inclusive (Australia Council 2011).

The framework is not described as a 'policy' but as a 'mechanism' to engage with diversity and increase 'the relevance, dynamism and reflection of contemporary Australia through the arts'. 'Diversity' is specified by the Australia Council as encompassing 'first nations people, children and young people, older people, people with a disability and regional and remote Australia, and with a focus on disability' (Australia Council 2016a, 52). The focus on disability aligns with government legislation. The CEF principles incorporate diversity through:

- respect and interaction
- dialogue: through access to resources
- artistic excellence: to produce greater artistic vibrancy
- inclusiveness: to encourage mutual respect and harmony
- belonging: to generate a sense of identity
- community building: to strengthen communities (Australia Council n.d.-b).

The aims to foster artistic vibrancy and harmony are inspirational, if generic, values. The ideals appear achievable because actions such as dialogue, encouragement and interaction can be demonstrated by Australia Council staff, even though these are difficult to gauge. Whether the principles are sufficient to generate shifts in Australian cultural life is questionable, given that the crux of the CEF remains one of resource allocation and that, 10 years after its inception, the detail and timing to enliven the CEF is yet to be published.

The institutional responsibility for the CEF sat with Executive Director of Arts Funding and Engagement Frank Panucci (2015, interview), who views it as a 'breakthrough' in the maturation of the Australia Council:

> The CEF has put a way of structuring and talking about itself internally, in a different space than when we were doing the Arts in a Multicultural Australia policy. At times I think some parts of this organisation thought AMA was either an imposition or somewhere they could push stuff to. There's nowhere to push things anymore. If you don't address it in this place, then there'll be someone that will ask the question of why it wasn't addressed.

Here Panucci acknowledges the institutional shunting of responsibility for AMA identified since the 1970s. 'Pushing' articulates the energy expended to avoid engaging with AMA. The description to 'push stuff' captures the internal friction of institutional responsibility. However, the CEF notwithstanding, the current absence of dedicated institutional responsibility for AMA brings into question the capacity to generate traction. In reality, there may be little difference between the perception that AMA was an 'imposition' and the quasi-policing role of CEF champions to 'ask the question'.

The internal institutional focus of the CEF requires the ideal proposition of active endorsement by all staff, led by 'champion' advocates. Another intent of the CEF is to stimulate change in the arts sector; this is relevant to Marinos's question about how the major arts organisations are encouraged to perform. Panucci (2015, interview) claims that a productive shift has occurred within the 'open' grants programs:

> The alignment in the general programs to the needs of artists of cultural[ly] diverse backgrounds is better than it was 10 or 15 years ago. At times you still need specific interventions. But that becomes a resource question. So we have to be vigilant in monitoring the outcomes.

This statement is arguably inaccurate about the support to CALD artists on two fronts. The alignment to their needs has not improved because they remain underfunded. Panucci's statement also suggests that monitoring is the main mechanism to understand the experience of NESB artists in the absence of dedicated resources. The CEF is an institutional internal model and difficult to prise open, but those in a close outer circle can provide some perspective.

Executive Director of Carriageworks Arts Centre Lisa Havilah (2015, interview) suggests that those who claim a 'lack of resources as a rationale do not have diversity at their core'. Pino Migliorino, a specialist in multicultural business advancement, is the only consultant to have formally reviewed the CEF. He views the 2015 federal budget decision (to move significant funds from the Australia Council back to the Department of the Arts) as fatal to the CEF's implementation: 'I thought, that's [the CEF] off' (P. Migliorino 2015, interview). This raises questions about the centrality of the CEF. Migliorino found that the CEF had 'compartmentalised' each of the areas for attention and had become what he described as 'an internal mechanism' limited to human resources. The issue of internal resourcing also came to the fore:

> There are leaders in the executive, as well as project officers, who want to be employed fulltime to do this work, but can't because they have to do other jobs. The philosophy of creating this in terms of an 'on top of' approach doesn't work. (P. Migliorino 2015, interview)

The scope of 'cultural diversity' leadership for the CEF has, therefore, been limited within the institution. Panucci argues that 'CEF champions' will deliver its aims; however, Migliorino's (2015, interview) observation is that 'there's a policy void right now. And no one's championing it. I have not heard anyone talk about arts for a multicultural Australia'. Alongside the issue of resources (human and financial), relational leadership is required to identify and embed diversity principles in Australia Council work practices:

> Fundamental principles should be driving the organisation. What are the access principles? And in those access principles, the organisation will tend to deliver across what is fundamentally a very narrow band. So this becomes remedial. (P. Migliorino 2015, interview)

The term 'remedial' suggests both a 'back to basics' corrective action and the process of triage associated with an emergency to remedy a crisis or collapse. Both actions identify the severity and level of priority of the situation before treatment. 'Remedial' implies the institution is retro- rather than proactive: 'We know that non-English artists and audiences are not engaged yet. So they require quite specific tactics' (P. Migliorino 2015, interview). Attending to the needs of specific groups generates friction between competing priorities, but Migliorino further argues that the institutional support must meet the 'infrastructure needs and cultural competency in the existing services' of NESB artists.

Migliorino identifies two significant gaps that the institution needs to address for cultural diversity to thrive, gaps that fall between aspiration and reality:

> We must make do, enmeshing our desires in the compromise of practical action. The bridge we stepped off is not the bridge we stepped upon. Yet to cast away the memory of the first bridge

> denies desire. To pretend it is the same as the second bridge is the
> baldest lie of power. It is only in maintaining the friction between
> two subjectively experienced bridges, the friction between
> aspiration and practical achievement, that a critical analysis
> [of global connection] is possible. (Tsing 2005, 85)

NESB artists 'make do' with less funding and with fewer employment-based arts networks than their English-speaking background peers. The corporate history or memory of AMA initiatives resides in two or three remaining staff members who could be considered as those on Tsing's 'first bridge'. Those on the second bridge are arguably those staff 'champions' or intermediaries who are expected to understand, promote and monitor the CEF's aims. The CEF may be future oriented but monitoring alone will not generate future change. As with any policy area, a negotiated agreement requires leaders to establish the agenda and associated research, and provide vision, aptitude and internal political experience.

The manner in which the Australia Council profiles its support for cultural diversity contributes to a multicultural arts milieu and underpins the trust that NESB artists have in it as an institution that distributes funds. In the 10 years since the introduction of the CEF, the term 'multicultural' has all but disappeared from Australia Council documents to be replaced by 'cultural diversity'. In the council's 2016–20 corporate plan, the word 'multicultural' is completely absent, while 'cultural diversity' appears once. Further, from early 2018 onwards, AMA policies have disappeared from the Australia Council website. The Australia Council's inability to acknowledge its previous corporate role around AMA, failure to use the term 'multicultural' and lack of a cultural diversity action plan indicate institutional reluctance to engage with this sector of the arts. More broadly, this reluctance can be seen as a refusal by the current leadership of the Australia Council to proactively engage and take action on the issues affecting this sector.

Establishing Trust through Expertise

Regular engagement with advisory experts within the institution can test or generate trust in institutional processes and also develop trusting relationships between staff and peers. I argue that, were this to occur, a more permeable institution would be created that would maintain its relevance across the arts sector.

The ACMAC Member

The ACMAC model was central to maintaining momentum for AMA because it held a robust internal position with external links to advisers and experts. ACMAC members held increased status and legitimacy because they engaged in broader debates beyond the assessment of grant applications. The government appointed members for three-year terms to artform boards, and then NESB artists were invited onto ACMAC (Keating, Bertone and Leahy n.d., 49). ACMAC was the only committee with formal links to other artform board members. Despite being the only NESB artists at grant assessment meetings, their positional leadership was increased because they had access to two council chairs— their own artform board and ACMAC. Many recall the productive and convivial atmosphere of ACMAC meetings despite having, at times, tense policy debates.

ACMAC members were exposed to a rigorous, if informal, training ground, that increased their capacity to articulate expert knowledge about art practices in a multicultural Australia. It also increased their ability to discuss the issues and develop and critique the effectiveness of specific AMA strategies. Multicultural audience consultant Fotis Kapetopoulos (2016, email) describes the relational leadership within the 2006–08 committee as:

> Exceptional, as it was not ideologically bound, as much of this area can be, but rather had a vision to make diversity an essential creative and economic focus of the arts. There was a diversity of people, with divergent views who came together as experts.

Very few, if any, formal opportunities for this level of national professional development for advocates for the arts in a multicultural Australia that directly link to the Australia Council now exist.

The link to peers on other artform boards elevated the standing of NESB artists, even if they were initially uncertain or ambivalent about what it meant to be ACMAC members. Then theatre director Teresa Crea was an ACMAC member during the early 1990s, one of the more progressive eras for AMA policy implementation. She recalls the combined experience and knowledge of practitioners and academics as productive for the institution:

> The leadership was most effective when the committee was chaired by individuals with a deep philosophical understanding of the field with a mix of practising artists. Simply ticking [an] NESB box was not enough for leadership and guidance on this complex issue. The committee acted at times very much as a 'brains trust' identifying issues and potential strategies to support and articulate AMA policy. It was one of the few places where issues of policy and practice were discussed at a deeper level. (T. Crea 2016, email)

Crea articulates the value of the creative leadership of 'politicised' NESB artists and the institutional leadership of academics. Together, they broadened the conceptual thinking of ACMAC and, by extension, the artform boards. This relational leadership drew on the collective skills of the members. Academics contributed to institutional leadership through their capacity to analyse policy issues that could impact NESB artists' experiences. This knowledge base of practice, theory and policy enabled the committee to bring together a range of political, historical and practical perspectives critical for formulating long-term strategies. The comments by Kapetopoulos and Crea suggest that ACMAC demonstrated characteristics of distributed leadership (discussed in Chapter 2), which rotates and draws on the different skills of the members to lead as needed. When displaying distributed leadership, ACMAC can be seen as a highly functional network.

An alternative perspective suggests that ACMAC brought tokenistic legitimacy to the Australia Council, and was more like a 'paper tiger' (L. Marinos 2015, interview). Curator and 1990s ACMAC member Nikolas Tsoutas (2015, interview) agrees:

> It was a political excuse to have the Arts for a Multicultural Australia because it sounded right for both parties [Australia Council and multicultural advocates]. They were paying lip service to multiculturalism rather than addressing the need for change.

These multiple perspectives highlight the institutional and multifaceted 'tug of war' that is characteristic of AMA. ACMAC members demonstrated intellectual, cultural and artistic leadership across all artforms, something that was not achieved elsewhere in the carefully guarded artform silos. Yet, on the other hand, ACMAC was a place to 'push stuff' to. It was not given enough power or resources to actually effect the change it continually articulated. Regardless, the legacy of ACMAC resides in the numbers of artists who were exposed to ways to conceptualise and act on diversity in the broad scope of Australian arts. That legacy is significant because it built confidence in those members as creative leaders who could also learn about and attempt to influence the direction of an institution. In this manner, despite its apparent reluctance to deal effectively with some of the issues raised by ACMAC, the Australia Council demonstrated a level of institutional leadership through its support of ACMAC.

Tension at the Business End

In the context of the Australia Council, peers are discipline experts who are brought into the sphere of the institution to provide advice or assess funding applications. During this process, artist peers become trusted experts via their recommendations on the awarding of grants. There is overwhelming endorsement by the arts sector and the Australia Council for the principle of peer assessment and arm's length decision-making from government (Parliament of Australia 2015). My empirical research highlights the different ways in which trust is conferred or dismissed through institutional processes, many of which revolve around behaviour and discourse. As Bourdieu (1984, 461–62) notes:

> This crossing-point between experience and expression is where the professional producers of discourse come in; it is here that the relations are set up between the experts and the laymen, the signifiers and the signified. The dominant language discredits and destroys the spontaneous political discourse of the dominated.

The process of 'destroy[ing] the spontaneous … discourse' applies to the microcosm of an assessment meeting. It encapsulates committee members' experience of a muted discourse, if not silence, when outside the supportive environment of an ACMAC meeting. Within the arts grant assessment process, for example, all peers are nominally considered to be 'experts'; however, what Bourdieu calls the 'professional producers of discourse' invariably take the lead. Within the ACMAC framework, one NESB peer attended each assessment meeting. Regardless of their creative expertise, their vocabulary and expressions sometimes differed from those of other peers; in such cases, influencing funding choices away from the familiar was a challenging task. To be able to articulate an alternate discourse that challenges the dominant one in the context of a meeting is a precise skill beyond advocacy. It requires relational leadership to establish trust and respect with other peers.

Although writing of cultural taste, and not about government grant assessment processes, Bourdieu (1984, 6) succinctly captures their political dimensions:

> The science of taste and cultural consumption begins with a transgression that is in no way aesthetic: it has to abolish the sacred frontier which makes legitimate culture a separate universe, to discover intelligible relations which unite apparently incommensurable 'choices'.

To transgress is to cross into unfamiliar and often unacceptable territory. To assess an arts grant is a cultural–political–economic act in which discussions of aesthetic merits are subsumed beneath budgetary considerations. In the case of ACMAC and the roles of individual peers in grants assessment processes, their commentaries can be seen as transgressions that challenge the 'separate universe' (Bourdieu 1984, 23) of what is conceptualised as legitimate culture. Tensions build because, as the only NESB artist at grant assessments, there are assumptions (by everyone else in the meeting) of cross-disciplinary multicultural arts knowledge and expertise across the range of applications. The issue of whether the NESB artist and their knowledge is trusted by the other peers depends on the experience of those others peers and the ability of the group to unite 'apparently incommensurable choices' (Bourdieu 1984, 23)—which is usually achieved at some point in the meeting. The NESB artist's presence and the assessment group's final recommendations are then used to legitimise grant allocations by the Australia Council.

Persistent assertiveness is required to counter the conflicting pressures in the elite atmosphere of those meetings. ACMAC members noted that they felt like outsiders at such grant assessment meetings. This feeling was even acknowledged by those with extensive organisational experience and expertise, including Tsoutas, a previous director of several contemporary arts organisations. Tsoutas (2015, interview) recollects his experience in the 1990s:

> You were sort of stigmatised. You were there, not really to be able to engage and represent the whole oeuvre of the policymaking in the OzCo [Australia Council] or visual arts or whatever, because you were limited to talking about multiculturalism. The question of trust was ever present. The problem was that they couldn't easily dismiss me because my vocabulary exceeded the bounds of the cultural discourse.

As a practitioner expert in the area of multiculturalism and the arts, Tsoutas was well positioned to articulate issues of multiculturalism, art, policy and processes; this included an acute awareness of how he was perceived, both in meetings and in terms of the overall process. Tsoutas's experience reflects Bourdieu's (1984, 462) argument regarding the ways dominating discourse is adopted by the dominated. However, in this case, the expert whose knowledge 'exceeded the bounds of cultural discourse' (Tsoutas 2015, interview) was required to be more erudite than the other experts in the room. This is a rare skill in Australia, where the type of education that develops knowledge of multicultural issues is unlikely to be found in the arts academy or in the informal mechanisms of family life (Idriss 2018).

The Question of Targets

Complementing the requirements of setting directions and developing policy was the requirement of monitoring the progress of grant and initiative successes. For most of its existence, ACMAC reviewed an annual AMA report that included statistical data. This was even though, as Crea (2016, email) states:

> The struggle for and against 'quotas' and 'definitions' of NESB was a constant—difficult, but necessary. There were too few other avenues to help quantify what was happening in the field.

This requirement was established at the time of ACMAC's inception, with data circulating internally and only intermittently being made public. For example, former council chair Hilary McPhee (1995) reported growth in expenditure on AMA of 7.9 per cent between 1988–89 and 1993–94. Marinos, as chair of the CCDB, challenges whether levels of expenditure was across all artform boards. This query is also endorsed by Hawkins (1993, 118). According to Marinos (2015, interview), 'NESB artists were very strongly over-represented within our fund, and it managed to make the under-representation in the other funds look better than they were'.

The AMA targets could also be limiting, and not simply because they were much lower than Australia's demographics:

> Once you reached that quota, it was cut, so it was no longer about merit. If [an] NESB applicant was assessed later in the meeting, they were chopped because they were not in the milieu of [Australian arts]. Your name automatically, whether you're first

> or second [generation NESB], put you into that multicultural
> thing and they had Buckley's [no] chance of getting any funding.
> (N. Tsoutas 2015, interview)

Targets within the Australia Council's model were a point of compliance to limit a result to a maximum rather than minimum quota; this is described by Ahmed (2012, 106) as a 'minimalist cop-out phrase'. Compounding that minimalist ceiling is whether the target reflected the multicultural composition of Australia. In 2015 the Australia Council's view was that targets were too complicated because of the increasing complexity of Australian demographics:

> An agency would not be able to go down a target road unless they
> were in an environment where targets were considered to be an
> appropriate way of doing things. Wouldn't you be saying—targets
> [for] around that demographic of people who are within the first
> five years of their arrival in this country and the most difficult
> period of settlement? (F. Panucci 2015, interview)

Linking the issue of targets to an 'appropriate' environment allows the institution to evade the question of targets and appears to close it down as an option for consideration. Panucci, however, articulates some of the nuances that would need to be considered at a micro-policy level in order to engage with the increasing complexity of cultural diversity through migration and intergenerational change. Twelve months after my interview with Panucci, the Australia Council advised that it would aim for 14 per cent grant allocations to CALD artists and organisations by 2020 (Australia Council 2016b). This was an internal shift; it was not prompted by any political shift in the council's context. It implies an awareness of lagging performance and the need to show institutional leadership again for multicultural arts. Further, it brings into question the issue of trust between the Australia Council and its companies, because it incorporates a tacit acknowledgement that the arts sector is performing below par where multicultural arts are concerned. The institution shows transactional leadership, which appears to be an effective form for an arts funding agency with limited resources, enabling it to engage more broadly with the sector. For transactional leadership to be effective, however, specific transactions need to be articulated. The announcement of a 14 per cent target would be more convincing were it accompanied by transparent expectations of what the institution requires of its funded organisations. Arts Council England (ACE), for example, publishes results of company inclusion in programming and employment and their expectations for organisational cultural diversity, and also produces materials to assist organisations in achieving those expectations (ACE n.d.-a).

Post-ACMAC Peers

The evaluators of AMA 2000 identified challenges faced by ACMAC regarding the recruitment of members, compliance by artform boards and the capacity of board peers to represent issues regarding the arts in a multicultural Australia, and recommended that:

> No case was found for disbanding the Committee. On the contrary, it was felt that the role of ACMAC should be strengthened, drawing in more Council members and external advisers. (Keating, Bertone, Leahy n.d., 4)

The senior executive developed a new structure that drew only from external experts invited onto the committee. This 'relaxing' of committee appointments may have indicated the start of a shift to artists becoming 'ad hoc' advisers. Peers are now contracted on a rotating basis for several assessment meetings. Media artist and cultural producer Panos Couros, an ACMAC member during the development of the 2000 policy, was an invited peer in 2016. He participated in three assessment meetings and found negligible multicultural awareness:

> Because if it wasn't for me in that room—particularly for the literature round, some really outstanding writers from non-Anglo background would not have been considered. I had to put a case for them, saying: 'This is what makes the fabric of our society, to understand our own separate and combined mythologies and backgrounds. So this is really important work. Why aren't you even considering it?' All of a sudden we got four NESB artists up in the top six or something like that. (P. Couros 2015, interview)

The first issue raised by this recollection is that ACMAC was folded prematurely. One of the outcomes of ACMAC was the increased capacity of both novice and experienced NESB artists to assess and advocate for quality arts projects, particularly multicultural art projects. Another issue suggested is that Australia Council staff members are either inexperienced or inattentive to CEF issues within this new system of short-term peer appointments. This may explain why there were no briefings about CEF areas at the meetings Couros attended; this, in turn, would reinforce the lack of knowledge about CEF on the part of other assessment peers.

A third issue flagged is future professional development opportunities for novice advocates and assessors, both to develop the skills and abilities of advocacy and peer assessment and to critique the overarching values still evident in the arts. Couros demonstrated leadership in speaking up in support of work that he considered marginalised within the assessment process. His was a style that arguably developed through multicultural advocacy experience with Arts Queensland and his time with ACMAC.

ACMAC acted as an informal professional development opportunity for artists to hone their skills in advocacy and sector leadership. It was diluted when it was decoupled from the arts board model to an external expert-only panel, because the responsibilities held by ACMAC were positioned at a distance from the main business of grant assessment. This has resulted in reduced opportunities for novice multicultural advocates. The eventual disbanding of all artform boards and replacement with short-term peer appointments has not redressed this imbalance. The 19 per cent of CALD peers (Australia Council 2016a) cannot all be assumed to have adequate and informed experience about multicultural arts policy and discourse. The capability for multicultural advocacy relies on bold, knowledgeable, articulate and experienced peers who can advocate within the strictures of the institution. This range of capacities are found in transformational, transactional and relational leadership styles, all of which are needed at different times, even in the same grant assessment meeting.

Traction Afforded through Networks

ACMAC also facilitated bringing NESB artists and cultural practitioners into local and international dialogue through discourse and exchange. ACMAC initiatives have included conferences, publications and roundtables to enhance the traction for multicultural arts practices. ACMAC encouraged critical thinking because it placed multicultural discourse within the wider sphere of the arts.

Traction through Critical Discourse

During the 1990s, ACMAC members identified the need for critical discourse in Australia and proactively used their positions to stimulate discussion in the arts:

> One of the reasons [the Australia] Council was unable to make any informed decision was because there was limited literature generated from within Australia. ACMAC decided to fund a publication which was the first one that tried to define, or engage with the discourse. [*Culture, Difference and the Arts*] is a critical publication. (N. Tsoutas 2015, interview)

ACMAC remained proactive in this aspect of its role. Such initiatives enabled ACMAC members and other Australia Council staff to keep abreast of AMA issues and how the field (including practitioners, academics and bureaucrats) was addressing the arts in a multicultural Australia. The 2000 ACMAC body was able to broaden the scope of discussions in *Culture, Difference and the Arts* (Gunew and Rizvi 1994) by commissioning two international conferences: Globalisation, Art + Cultural Difference— On the Edge of Change held in Sydney in July 2001, and Empires, Ruins and Networks: Art in Realtime Culture held in Melbourne in April 2004 (Art in Society n.d.). The networks and positional leadership of Tsoutas at Artspace, a contemporary arts centre in New South Wales, Papastergiadis at the University of Melbourne and ACMAC working in concert enabled lively engagement with ideas of multiculturalism and creative difference in Australia.

The evaluation of AMA 2000 found that these were among the most recognised initiatives of ACMAC and the 'majority view was very positive' (Keating, Bertone and Leahy n.d., 39). The continuation of the conferences was seen as 'consistent with the leadership role of the Australia Council' (4). Both conferences aimed to develop 'intellectual and artistic frameworks for Australian multicultural arts within an international context' (32). The conferences generated traction for the artists when they saw themselves among their NESB peers, which, for many, was their first experience of this. Opportunities for NESB artists to come together nationally have since declined, but are well attended when they do occur. Crucially, the scale and scope of the 2002 and 2004 conferences are yet to be repeated.

After the second conference, ACMAC hosted a roundtable with the local and international conference presenters to generate additional strategic input into the AMA policy. An internal report summarised the first roundtable. Facilitated by Annette Shun Wah, the participants (a veritable who's who of cultural diversity practitioners and theorists) considered future prospects through two main discussion points. The first was to 'break down the dominant perspective which governs cultural industries' and the second was to 'deal with cultural difference beyond the categories of "multicultural" and "indigenous"' (ACMAC n.d.-b, 1).

The roundtable developed practical suggestions based on the conference debates to gain greater traction for the arts in a multicultural Australia through art practices and positioning 'cultural difference' as the site of change:

1. The aesthetic question of cultural difference needs to be fore-grounded. In promoting work dealing with cultural difference we need to look at the quality of the work rather than just ticking boxes, counting heads and filling quotas.

2. Cultural difference is the hub. Cultural difference is the cutting edge of history. (ACMAC n.d.-b, 2)

The first point places aesthetic developments that engage with cultural difference at the centre of the debate and outside the paradigm of the quota. American artist, advocate and an Empires, Ruins and Networks conference presenter Coco Fusco advised the group to orchestrate both narratives: the need for quotas (to generate grant income) and the disavowal of them (as cultural critique). The second point centralises cultural difference and positions cultural diversity as both the mainstream in Australia and a driver for change. During the roundtable, presenters expressed the view that a historical transformation was taking place catalysed by issues of cultural difference; however, this is a transformation that is yet to be found in Australian cultural institutions.

One ambitious proposal arising from the roundtable was to develop a workshop on Art + Cultural Difference + Global Collaboration aimed at maintaining a strong level of critical dialogue and at facilitating collaborative art projects within a national network of artists, academics, funding agencies and sponsors (see Appendix D). In effect, the workshop aimed to establish an Australian version of iniva (n.d.), a London-based research and exhibition centre for cultural diversity. The partnerships to be brought into the workshop were envisioned as community organisations, cultural producers, donors and sponsors, universities and art colleges, state and federal arts agencies, and public galleries and art institutions. The value of the proposed workshop model was that it could be scaled up or down and could be applied as a partnership model for culturally diverse small to medium enterprises. This process of discussing and developing the workshop project encouraged relational leadership between the participants to equitably share knowledge and ideas to reach beyond their own specific interests.

The Struggle for an Australian Multicultural Arts Company

Internationally recognised multicultural arts companies such as UK-based Akram Khan, iniva and Rich Mix serve as one measure of success of a multicultural society. However, all attempts to establish such a flagship in Australia have foundered.

The proposal of the Art + Cultural Difference + Global Collaboration workshop was not taken up by ACMAC. ACMAC considered that their existing AMA initiatives had adequate momentum to match the intentions of the roundtable. This was the first failed moment to establish an independent cross-disciplinary flagship for the arts in a multicultural Australia. One ACMAC member described the roundtable discussions thus:

> I could have been at an ACMAC meeting working on our policy. I found no major differences in the roundtable discussions. In fact, the discussion reinforced our direction, especially the incubator project we are working on, and many comments echoed responses to the current Planning for the Future [corporate plan] document. (ACMAC n.d.-b.)

Aside from resourcing issues, this comment points to a shortcoming in leadership by ACMAC. At the time, members believed that their committee's existence and position of influence within the institution was sufficient to generate change. From this perspective, the members lost sight of long-term and sustainable ways to generate traction. The potential offered by the workshop proposal did not gain traction, and the associated networks were not leveraged into action. It appeared there was a reluctance to be bold and ambitious within the Australia Council executive and ACMAC began to tailor its aims much more modestly, but not before delivering its highest profile political event.

The last chair of ACMAC, Nicola Downer, attempted to generate confluence for AMA with state and federal governments at a one-day symposium held at Parliament House, Canberra, in 2007: Multicultural

Arts: Cultural Citizenship for the 21st Century (Australia Council 2007). Downer arranged unprecedented access to federal arts, citizenship and foreign affairs ministers and many NESB artists performed at Parliament House for the first time. It had been decades since state and territory arts managers had come together in discussions with artists and cultural practitioners to spearhead strategic partnerships for multicultural arts. While it was not uncommon for those agencies to meet, it had been a long time since they had all come together to impress the benefit of multicultural arts practices.

The opportunity to meet federal parliamentarians drew the CEOs of state and territory government arts departments. The event increased the positional leadership role of the Australia Council among the multicultural sector and was claimed to have generated greater traction at each state's arts agency, which 'would look more closely at their existing multicultural policies and programs' (Australia Council 2007). At this time, aside from Arts Victoria (later Creative Victoria), most arts agencies did not have a multicultural policy. Alongside Creative Victoria, several other arts departments have since recognised the creative importance of multicultural diversity in their mission statements.

Downer used her political influence for the benefit of the AMA policy and demonstrated positional and charismatic leadership in doing so. It was to prove to be the last major event for ACMAC. Gouriotis, a former executive director of Casula Powerhouse Arts Centre, recalls being inspired by Downer's positive energy for ACMAC. Although an Australian Labor Party member and against prevailing perceptions, Gouriotis (2017, email), commenting on the appointments of Klika and Downer, claims that the 'Australian Liberal Party did more for ACMAC than the Australian Labour Party'. This acknowledges Klika and Downer as positional leaders (both had influential relations within the Australian Liberal Party) and relational leaders who advocated for AMA within in their own political environment, which was one openly challenged by governmental messages about multiculturalism.

While the aim for state arts agency partnerships did not eventuate, the idea of developing a national incubator—a centre for research or workshops—nevertheless persisted with subsequent ACMAC members and staff. As part of AMA 2006, staff commissioned a scoping study to determine the demand for a flagship or 'hub' event space to focus national and international attention and critical acclaim, and build on developments in artistic practices that explore multicultural Australia. An arts consultant with over 40 years experience, Justin Mcdonnell undertook this study. On this occasion, it was artists in the field who rejected the concept of a 'flagship' event or space on the grounds that it would take scarce resources away from already under-resourced artists:

> The practices are considered to be too diverse to be embraced within any one 'flagship' organisation. A multiplicity of hubs that might contribute, in time, to a national focus could be of value. Yet even there, the concept of 'hubs' was felt to be overly mechanistic. Process and pathway were preferred. (Macdonnell n.d., 1)

The respondents saw the 'flagship' approach as too interventionist on the part of the Australia Council and criticised the (assumed) redirection of scant resources that would come at the expense of grants to NESB artists.

Another attempt to cohere practice and theory around the arts in a multicultural Australia was with the reinvigorated Casula Powerhouse Arts Centre launched in early 2008. The opening exhibition, *Australian,* reimagined Casula as an international centre for cultural diversity in the arts:

> *Australian* projects an Australia that is beyond the horizon, an Australia that is shaped by multiple cultural identities, types of knowledge and the social conditions that are transacted at the moment of intersection within the common space of the public sphere. (Tsoutas 2010, 6)

This strong opening statement asked what it is be Australian and the implications of this within the multicultural context of the Liverpool region and beyond. Interestingly, in his scoping study of 2008 regarding the potential for a multicultural arts flagship, Macdonnell (n.d., 11) recommended that the Casula model be adequately resourced to deliver its vision as a 'centre of excellence':

> Uniquely at the moment in Australia, Casula Powerhouse seeks to value and contextualize the art within a cultural framework so that is sometimes celebrating art and artistic processes but at the same time wrestling with dilemmas of Australianity beyond the simplistic trope of 'one Australia' and through that seeking new interpretations of our culturally complex society.

The consultants who reviewed AMA 2000 and the consultant who scoped out options in 2008 for a multicultural flagship provided targeted recommendations, none of which were accepted by the executive leadership of the Australia Council. Casula is an example of a moment in which the Australia Council arguably held the potential traction to support a national flagship, only to flounder at the outset. In 2008 the Casula Powerhouse Board confirmed its new direction and accepted its name change to 'Casula, the International Centre for Contemporary Culture'. The remit of the revamped Casula was to bring local government, the Liverpool area's multicultural population and an international arts focus under the one roof (N. Tsoutas 2015, interview). But, despite Macdonnell's (n.d.) recommendation that the Australia Council support this expanded role that Casula wished to pursue, the proposal did not progress. Tsoutas (2015, interview) argues it was a 'missed opportunity to reinscribe the culture that we live in'.

Tsoutas's vision 'to reinscribe the culture that we live in' can lead to a productive result when cultures interact expressively. To 'reinscribe' means rewriting and re-presenting our cultural artefacts as:

> Diverse and syncretic. It takes multiple forms of expertise and brings them down to size. Individuals, including scientists [read artists], politicians, and activists, apply their eclectic perspectives in forming projects of nature [read art] making. We might begin by identifying distinctive confluences of knowledge, as well as the nodes of practice and discourse informed by these confluences. (Tsing 2005, 113)

In the process of locating and utilising 'confluences', leaders emerge who may have the capacity to generate traction for change.

International Policy Leadership Discourse

The last international event to profile the arts in a multicultural Australia was co-hosted by the Australian and British councils in March 2008. Making Creative Cities: The Value of Cultural Diversity in the Arts included presentations by Keith Khan, then head of culture for the London 2012 Olympic and Paralympic Games, Professor Marcia Langton and several former members of ACMAC (British Council 2008). ACMAC had been dismantled by this stage but the AMA policy was still in place. The British Council demonstrated its desire for transformational leadership regarding art and cultural difference in the Asia-Pacific region in its approach to the Australia Council on this issue. In turn, the Australia Council provided relational leadership by activating its networks of speakers and artists for the event.

The event brought together Australian and British artists whose work explores cultural difference and workshopped issues with artists, cultural practitioners and academics. Three themes were explored: ideas of different types of leadership, albeit undefined; support for creative production; and participation in creative cities. The theme of 'good leadership is not about one model' identified the need to move from a focus on individuals to the capacities of whole communities; to embed diverse groups and young people in decision-making processes rather than asking the occasional 'opinion'; to identify intercultural innovators; and to expand support beyond managerial leadership into 'intercultural, intellectual community, teaching and creative leadership' (British Council 2008, 7). Each of these criteria gesture towards the generic idea of leadership. However, as the arguments in this chapter show, different leadership is needed for different points of the policy cycle and the types of leadership depend on one's position in the arts sector.

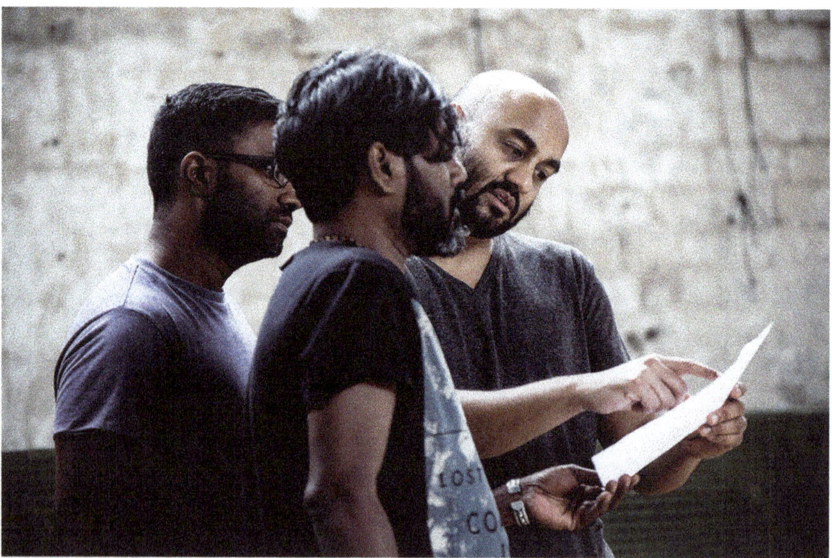

Image 20: *Counting and Cracking*, **Belvoir Street Theatre, 2019**
Photographer: © Brett Boardman

The Current Role of External Advisers

Opportunities for NESB artists to become 'embedded' at the Australia Council have since declined. Further, as I have argued, structured instances for professional development, such as developing the skills required for institutional leadership as external advisers, have also reduced in number. Artist, practitioner and CuriousWorks Director (until 2018) Shakthidharan (2015, interview) (see Image 20) notes that he is often asked to provide his 'opinion', but that he is often dissatisfied with the lack of results:

> We need to acknowledge corporate history, research what worked well in the past. Pay all the organisations who have been working from a lived experience at grassroots level for a long time to have an action-focused program. We get invited to where everyone talks about all their great ideas and nothing happens. It's like we're on this treadmill of issues that come up every two or three years. What are these things we talk at? And then the talks disappear, with no objective result. At a [recent Community Partnerships Key Producers] roundtable we asked Australia Council to come up with a concrete plan to match diversity on screen and stage within the next 10 years. Not how we'd 'like' to, but how we 'will', starting today. You say these things, but then it disappears.

This interview excerpt details the absence of traction by 'participating peers' in an arts funding institution that no longer seeks consistent advice from multicultural experts in the arts. It is a tactic to casualise expertise that gives the appearance of 'consultation'. The lack of traction stems from the inference that the issues are the responsibility of organisations previously known as 'Key Producers' that had four-year contracts with the Australia Council Community Partnerships Board.

By querying 'what are these things we talk at?', Shakthidharan identifies a lack of clarity regarding the role and direction of leadership. The Key Producers were expected to be leaders in the community arts sector but were not in a position to lead or effect systemic change within the Australia Council. The Australia Council did not provide them with sufficient resources or entry into the world of the major Australian art centres; nevertheless, it was expected that intransigent issues such as a lack of diversity across narrative and performance arts could be, if not solved, managed by financially vulnerable community arts organisations. The Australia Council demonstrates the appearance of interest by occasionally bringing arts sector positional leaders together, but appears slow to utilise their input or produce an accountable action plan, thereby reducing trust and the likelihood of traction.

Conclusion

ACMAC demonstrated positional and transformational leadership when it engaged with critical thinkers around issues of cultural difference. The committee demonstrated this in a number of directions: it led through its position at the Australia Council and through its direct engagement with critical discourse; it showed relational leadership for the arts sector and council staff by providing opportunities to network and engage in critical discussions of cultural difference; and it aimed for transformational leadership by utilising international expertise to unravel some of the complex issues the committee faced, including these results in recommendations to the Australia Council.

Institutional leadership for the arts in a multicultural Australia could be demonstrated by consolidating earlier policy achievements and continuing to identify current issues and the manner in which they will be addressed. I have shown the reluctance on the part of the Australia Council to refresh and develop their direction for the arts in a multicultural Australia, the importance of which is underlined by Klika (2015, interview), a former board member of two national institutions:

> The ABC [and] the Australia Council should show that leadership. Diversity is an evolving beast, and we should be encouraging the evolution, not encouraging the arrestment of multiculturalism. So yes, I think there's plenty of room for leadership at the institutional level.

Although leadership is a familiar term in the arts, it is often used without qualification, which lends it a rhetorical quality that verges on the meaningless. Hewison and Holden (2011) provide a road map of leadership styles that can be included in a 'tool kit' but do not approach the issues of leading for diversity in the arts. I have also elaborated on several types of leadership for the arts in a multicultural Australia as demonstrated through interactions within the institutional frame of the Australia Council.

Transformational leadership may be more appropriate for those who hold positional leadership at the executive and board level. This includes the more familiar type of personality-dependent, charismatic leadership found in the arts, but runs a high risk of delivering only short-term changes based on the leaders' length of tenure. Distributed leadership was demonstrated by ACMAC, as it enabled members' lead roles to be shared according to the skills of the group and to take into account its fluid cross-cultural and multi-artform membership. Relational leaders enable a vision and create trust in its delivery (Hewison and Holden 2011, 31). This chapter has highlighted the value of relational leadership that places the leader (e.g. previous chairs, some members of ACMAC and staff) in a more central position of developing the necessary relationships to enable others to take on the responsibility for change, thereby generating a longer legacy.

I argue that several leadership characteristics are present at the interface of the NESB artist and the institution. The NESB artist's role is one in which creative leadership capabilities become relevant for institutional leadership capacity. I have shown that the Australia Council's current model of drafting in expert peers on art and multiculturalism on an as-needed basis requires these peers to be experienced, articulate, knowledgeable and bold about supporting creative production and content by NESB artists. The decision to terminate ACMAC has left a knowledge and experience vacuum within Australia Council processes that is unlikely to be filled. Additionally, the current approach of short-term peer appointments appears inadequate as a 'training ground' for NESB artists to develop the range of characteristics needed to be effective multicultural arts advocates within institutional environments. This process does not develop longitudinal comprehension of the arts sector and, therefore, reduces the capacity within the arts sector for long-term informed policy input.

The advocacy work of Diversity Arts Australia (DARTS), the small organisation with a national diversity remit that replaced the kultour multicultural arts touring network, brings NESB artists together in different parts of Australia to stimulate a discourse of diversity that has been absent for several years. Regardless of the extent of external pressure that DARTS may exert on the Australia Council, it is unlikely to equal the internal traction of an institution-appointed advisory group, because DARTS cannot hold institutional positional influence.

The Australia Council published two statements in 2018 to address inequity in the arts. The first announced a target of 14 per cent grant expenditure on CALD; however, the council is yet to publish specific strategies on how it aims to achieve this goal. Broadly directed across areas of social diversity in the CEF, the second statement provides additional funds to the major performing companies to develop CEF-focused projects. Shakthidharan expressed disappointment that those funds would not flow to the S2M sector, which has practical experience of working with artists of diverse backgrounds and is able to extract high value from small budgets. These two initiatives may go some way to address immediate symptoms of inequitable use of resources, but may not be adequate to produce the systemic changes that the multicultural arts sector wants to see (Castagna 2017).

The issue of adequacy brings into question whether the 2018 version of CEF is an effective mechanism for generating change for the arts in a multicultural Australia. The Australia Council continues to demonstrate its reluctance. As Migliorino (2015, interview) observes, positional leaders within the Australia Council need to agree on the principles needed to focus the institution's long-term attention towards cultural difference. This level of vision and commitment is yet to become apparent, and is further hindered by a lack of internal 'diversity champions' (i.e. champions who represent each diversity area of the CEF) in dedicated roles. This internal staff role may be theoretically viable; however, if it is as an 'add-on' to substantive or prime staff roles, the potential for institutional leadership is dissipated.

One result of this institutional reluctance to engage with a multicultural society is that artistic activity continues to be produced in small, almost boutique scenarios. The next chapter turns to the leadership role of the NESB artist when partnering with major and mid-tier arts organisations on their own terms to show how multicultural creative practice pushes into greater circulation, thereby amplifying the current multicultural arts milieu.

6

Organisational Leadership: Expanding the Multicultural Arts Milieu

Organisational leadership refers to mainstream or small to medium (S2M) arts organisations that combine their influence and resources with those of non–English speaking background (NESB) artists or multicultural arts organisations to produce and present new work. Creative and organisational shifts occur in the arts environment when these partnerships become part of an organisation's regular program of activities. NESB artists are able to challenge the conventional art binaries of 'tradition' and 'contemporary' and disrupt the temporal trope that creative change 'will take time'. As Papastergiadis (2005, 40) observes of diasporic and Indigenous visual artists working in the mainstream: 'Their practice and status question the dominant assumption on the relationship between traditional authenticity and contemporary culture and test the limits of artistic agency and institutional structures'.

'Test[ing] the limits' is the basis of the creative process and can also challenge the capacities of arts organisations to manage difference. Artists confront issues of creative compromise and how to work within an unfamiliar structure. Organisations confront the challenges of new forms of production and content and how to engage with different audiences and expand existing audiences. I argue that the energy generated through these interactions and processes can lead to systemic change. I also argue that there are different modes of leadership and different approaches within those modes. In particular, relational, transformational and transactional leadership modes are all pertinent here. These leadership modes can manifest through various processes, including attunement, accompaniment and charisma. This chapter analyses how new forms of creative partnerships can change how NESB artists work with mainstream arts or their tributaries to produce and present their work. I argue that the arts sector generates a refreshed multicultural arts milieu when creative and organisational leadership are consistently combined. The milieu can re-form to accommodate creative leadership for multicultural arts practices as they exist and evolve.

This focus on arts organisations provides glimpses into the crucial infrastructure platform that enables the development and presentation of creative work. These glimpses reinforce that it is NESB artists themselves who must show creative leadership to 'make a new door' (Badami 2017) and work in concert with arts organisations that have the capability to produce their work. Artists navigate the void left by the significant redirection of federal and state funding away from multicultural arts organisations (see Table 4) and, also, the absence of a national creative hub for multicultural arts practices. Demonstrating both boldness and attunement, NESB artists work in conjunction with established arts organisations to expand creative opportunities and leadership skills for themselves and the wider artist community.

The confluence of productive, creative and organisational leadership can improve diverse art production and produce creative possibilities for NESB artists, along with the active dissemination of their work. The case studies in this chapter include the development of the relationship between independent artist Shakthidharan and Carriageworks and Belvoir Street Theatre Company, two major producers and presenters; the struggle by kultour for multicultural organisational independence, demonstrating the development of trust found in collaboration; and the joining of forces of a small company, Contemporary Asian Australia Performance (CAAP), with an arts industry organisation, Playwriting Australia (PWA). These examples explore how small, creative and organisational interventions can open up artistic practices to produce new and innovative artforms and different narratives about Australian society.

Turning Friction towards Sustained Interaction

Sustained and productive interaction between NESB artists, arts organisations and audiences generates creative opportunities that respond to the challenge of how to go 'beyond the instrumental' (Blonski 1992, 3). The issues of long-term change that gave rise to this challenge remain as valid today as ever, as Blonski (2017, email) comments:

> We felt that a deeper engagement was essential, but the concern also was how fragile this could be long-term. We were working within a period where there was a lot of writing and very interesting work being created. But we were all aware of how fragile this was. Building long-term support—financial, infrastructure, intellectual—was important but the question was, how to do it?

The skill to develop successful long-term support and relationships to be able to work in concert requires all parties to do the 'work' of diversity (Noble 2009, 51)—that is, to take the extra care and attention to produce a creative product or outcome that is more than a token presentation. Inclusion in a program can risk being tokenistic if the artist inhabits 'institutional spaces that do not give you residence' (Ahmed 2012, 176). A lack of residence can produce forms of tokenism in which cultural difference simply becomes a form of exotica to be savoured by the mainstream population as a form of 'cosmo-multiculturalism' (Hage 1997, 14). Hage (1997, 17) refers to the results of this as:

> Multiculturalism without migrants: a multicultural reality made of institutions that seem to exist without any migrant subjects to sustain it. In the process, it is somehow 'forgotten' that multiculturalism in Australia is, or at least *ought to be*, above all about migrant lives and inter-cultural interaction.

This forgetfulness is still to be found in many arts organisations today, and in their audiences. A more collaborative mode, by comparison, enables and presents art that enhances the work of NESB artists by placing it within the arts sector, not outside it. The artist and the organisations are active in producing creative 'intercultural interaction'. If consistently maintained, this method will generate artistic legacies that mobilise a more dynamic multicultural arts milieu and one that can be better linked to 'mainstream arts' as well as profile 'marginal arts'.

Making Multicultural Content Resident in Australian Art

The steps towards generating substantial accommodation for multicultural arts practices afforded by intercultural interactions could begin by identifying 'confluences of knowledge, as well as the nodes of practice and discourse informed by those confluences' (Tsing 2005, 113). To identify such nodes is to identify the places of creative communication and production that position and enable NESB artists to generate the creative and economic 'equitable power' that Shakthidharan (discussed below) wants to experience. Identifying how these 'nodes of practice' resonate with the range of practices NESB artists engage with, particularly those at the most precarious creative edges, brings the contemporary into dialogue with ethnic and migrant traditions. Smith (2006, 695–96) sees contemporary art not as 'persistent modernist formalism' but in the internal changes in the art of the 1960s and 1970s from a 'world reshaped by decolonisation and incipient globalisation'. An appropriate articulation of the 'contemporary' is exemplified by curator Okwui Enwezor's 2002 *Documenta 11*, an international exhibition held every five years. *Documenta 11* was based on ideas of 'transculturality and extraterritoriality' and was 'less a receptacle of commodity objects than a container for a plurality of voices, a material reflection on a series of disparate and interconnected actions and processes' (Enwezor 2002, 55).

The concept of 'accompaniment' is helpful here. Accompaniment joins individuals and groups with those with power and influence to generate new ways to achieve change. The crucial element is that accompaniment is an equal process in which skills and knowledge are equally valued. 'Attunement' presents another way to progress intercultural interactivity through close and adaptive listening. 'Confluences of knowledge', 'accompaniment' and 'attunement'—three concepts discussed earlier in this text—suggest that leadership can interact and contribute to an expanded multicultural arts milieu.

Enduring Enthusiasm: *Counting and Cracking*

Imagine a scenario in which an independent NESB artist is invited to make a work with a producing and presenting arts organisation. This opportunity raises issues of how to negotiate and present creative content that is outside the mainstream canon. For the organisation, this is a means to directly support the creation of work, expand their repertoire, be relevant in Australia and diversify their audience. The following case study looks at the initial collaboration of aspiring playwright Shakthidharan and Carriageworks, a major art centre and venue in the gentrified inner suburb of Redfern, New South Wales. Their project is an example of cultural innovation whereby 'the emphasis is on the creativity of the artist in the generation of innovative work to extend the focus of cultural expression' (Mar and Ang 2015, 6).

Extending that focus is enabled by at least two principles: first, by enhancing inclusive curatorial processes; second, by supporting a diversity of cultural expressions (Mar and Ang 2015, 7). In 2015 Carriageworks achieved both through its associate artist and resident company projects. Carriageworks and CoCurious wants the organisation to be inclusive and creatively relevant to its social and cultural environment. Therefore, she aims to:

> Support local artists to work more ambitiously around scale and audiences, and put their new work in the right contexts. And then place them within a program with international artists that might make pathways for them. (L. Havilah 2015, interview)

Havilah's programming is endorsed by the arts sector. The director of the Sydney Chamber Opera, a resident company at Carriageworks, commented: 'Carriageworks has come to be seen where contemporary art is at in all its manifestations' (Symonds quoted in Taylor 2017).

Havilah began her career by establishing an artist-run initiative at Wollongong, southern NSW, and she has held influential roles at the Casula Powerhouse Arts Centre, Liverpool, and at the Campbelltown Arts Centre. As Carriageworks CEO, at the time, Havilah introduced a number of initiatives that contribute to artists' professional development, including the establishment of the intermediary role of co-producer and providing associate artists with access to professional networks, mentoring, and time and space in which to develop a piece. Artist-in-residence programs offered by many organisations across all artforms provide space and time for artists to develop new projects; however, Carriageworks offers artists the space and opportunity to do a presentation at the end of their residency, even if their work is still in progress. Shakthidharan was selected as the inaugural associate artist from 2013 to 2015 because he seemed:

> Like an artist who would take advantage of a high level of support
> and mentorship. I was interested in what he would develop and
> what he represents regarding Western Sydney and how he works
> internationally. (L. Havilah 2015, interview)

Here Havilah supports Shakthidharan's creative ambitions, identifies
the relevance of Western Sydney for many NESB artists and values the
potential to expand international relationships. Themes of collaborating
with community, growing up in the digital revolution and working in
Western Sydney are the main influences on Shakthidharan's modes
of creative production. Of particular relevance here is how he bridged
his practice(s) into a professional career as a playwright. As an artistic
associate at Carriageworks, he gained access to mainstage organisations
through a combination of dedication, connections and opportunities.
His productive residency led to negotiations with mainstage company
Belvoir Street Theatre (Belvoir) for an epic, multigenerational play set
in Sri Lanka and Australia:

> Through their journey, we see a Sri Lanka riven by, but no means
> surrendering to, violent divisions—and an Australia transforming
> of, but also transformed by, the people that flee to its shores.
> (CuriousWorks n.d.)

Counting and Cracking has seen many iterations since its first development
grant in 2009, but Shakthidharan has stayed true to his original intention
to encompass four generations of a family's resettlement from Sri Lanka
to Australia. Maintaining the epic narrative format could be considered
a literary form of the 'vernacular cosmopolitan' (Gunew 2017b, 33–52),
acknowledged in creative terms as 'not an easy road' (Gunew et al. 2017,
596). The concept of the 'vernacular cosmopolitan' as proposed by Homi
Bhabha (Werbner quoted in Gunew 2017b, 33) is a '"cosmopolitan
community envisaged in marginality", a border zone'. The term can be
stretched to encompass the exchange of family and community-based
knowledge as a way of extending openness through artworks by NESB
artists. Even though Gunew et al.'s (2017, 595) focus is on cultural diversity
and literature across a range of diasporas, their observations translate to
playwriting about vernacular cosmopolitanism, particularly when they
describe literature by migrant writers as 'a palpitating absence, you feel it,
quivering and these absences are clamouring to be made visible'.

The evocation of clamour suggests a friction that demands attunement as well as accompaniment to publish more NESB writers. Making these absences visible is the intention of the collaborative processes described in this chapter that join creative aspirations with organisational support and know-how. Those stages leading to greater visibility can be tenuous for the NESB artist:

> Lisa [Ffrench, director of programs at Carriageworks] read the play, no one would read it because it's 190 pages long, and gave it to Chris Mead, artistic director of Playwriting Australia and [who at that time worked] in the [Carriageworks] building. Chris loved it, but he moved to MTC [Melbourne Theatre Company]. Meanwhile, Carriageworks supported a development of the play, and Eamon Flack, [director of Belvoir in Surry Hills, NSW] came to a reading both through my pestering Belvoir and Carriageworks' contacts. I didn't realise at the time, but he liked it. We also had a reading with Melbourne Theatre Company, but I think they thought it was one bridge too far. (S. Shakthidharan 2015, interview)

This comment highlights several aspects of development and production in theatre production. The decision-makers frequently move on and only occasionally bring projects of interest with them. This instability produces a stop–start scenario for artists seeking the right partners to see a project to completion. Keeping track of existing partners, and the need to find new ones, requires persistence and an ability to maintain a high level of enthusiasm for the project. It also demonstrates tenacity in staying true to the original impetus. Sustained effort is required to maintain momentum, which, for the NESB artist, as Ahmed (2012, 186) observes, 'might appear to others as stubbornness, willfulness or obstinacy'.

For Shakthidharan, leadership 'at our end of the spectrum'—that is, not the major performing arts (MPA) companies or the 'big end of town'—means being able to achieve a mutual vision despite setbacks and differences, and avoiding the creative danger of repeating the same style and type of project. His persistence aims to effect long-lasting change in the arts sector by establishing how to navigate difference in the arts:

> Success can be gauged by finding a mutual vision with people who are very different from you. Sometimes people in SMEs [small to medium enterprises] or groups of multicultural artists will band together, and they'll find solidarity with each other, but they're polarising. Sometimes you have to figure out the difficult way to work with people who are very different to you because that's the

> only way it will change. Otherwise, you end up accepting that
> is how it is, and that your only role in all of this is to complain.
> And I don't want to be that person. I want equitable power.
> (S. Shakthidharan 2015, interview)

Shakthidharan wants action. He eschews the essentialised role of the 'whingeing wog' (L. Marinos 2015, interview) and tries to work with people who are 'very different to you'. In this context, he speaks of working with people in very different organisational structures as well as different sociopolitical, cultural and creative perspectives. His analysis of what will make change draws on the 'permeable' quality of the relationship between organisations and people. He goes further in identifying what he feels will not work—in particular, that 'banding together' will not be enough to produce change. Although multicultural arts organisations do successfully 'band together' to support and find 'solidarity with each other', Shakthidharan thinks this is no longer enough. He feels it is important that those in leadership roles in multicultural arts organisations engage with those in positions of power to negotiate 'equitable power'. This constitutes a challenge that writer Olubas (quoted in Gunew et al. 2017, 588) describes an 'impossible negotiation'. The situation is one in which NESB artists are the only ones to make culturally diverse work, but, at the same time, the industry perception is that 'you don't need anything special, further time or attention because you already have it' (Gunew et al. 2017, 588). Attention is, however, required and includes economic, infrastructure and dramaturgical input around the aesthetic considerations of the work.

Shakthidharan observes that when a director is mounting a Shakespearean work, for example, the familiarity of the text means the director need only consider aesthetic and production values: 'They're like— aesthetically what am I trying to do here? That's all they need care about' (S. Shakthidharan 2015, interview). In a similar vein to Annalouise Paul's concerns (see Chapter 4), the aesthetics of intercultural work bring to the fore a range of new considerations that Shakthidharan (2015, interview) thinks must be treated carefully:

> My background is Tamil Sri Lankan and is influenced by classical
> Indian aesthetics and subcultures from south India, which is
> the Tamil connection. In Tamil classical aesthetics, there is an
> interrelationship between mood, humans and the environment.
> The question is how to subtly get the aesthetics of the cultures that
> are contributing to that work into our productions.

Shakthidharan touches on some of the areas to which he must be attentive. He acknowledges the challenge of using finesse to generate a classical mise en scène within a contemporary work. However, to subtly 'get' the subcultural aesthetic identifies a hierarchy of cultural artefacts that cannot be represented so subtly. In his description, subtlety appears as a type of friction in which aesthetic elements slide over one another, when, in fact, epic family narratives may require more bumps and circumnavigation to bring their dynamics to life. No reason is given for the need to be subtle, but it does suggest a tension around the question of *how much* ethnicity can be presented on the mainstage. This is similar to the criticism that the dominant culture will complain about 'too many' Asians/Moslems/Syrians (Hage 2000, 39). This aesthetic issue also resonates organisationally because, as the 'placement' NESB artist in a predominantly Anglo-Australia company, Shakthidharan may be challenged to 'fit in' and might not adequately 'bring in' his perspective if the performing arts environment he is working in 'rewards a focus on a dominant Anglo perspective' (Caprar 2018). Regardless of Shakthidharan's final choices and possible compromises, his point highlights how these details preoccupy the NESB artist when making a work they hope will become part of the Australian mainstream canon.

The cultural specificities of Shakthidharan's work require a translation across cultural modes that are unfamiliar to most audiences. The vehicle of four generations of a Sri Lankan (Tamil) Australian family suggests, at first, a bicultural piece that brings different dimensions of social, political, economic and cultural experiences into dialogue with each other. However, the potential for other layers to emerge through the matrix of 'mood, humans and the environment' (Shakthidharan, interview 2015) presents an opportunity for an aesthetic exploration that produces a hybrid outcome that goes beyond just an encounter between two cultures. To a large extent, Australian theatre has accepted the somewhat prescriptive vehicle of the first-generation migrant family 'suitcase' story (Kelly 1998). In the case of *Cracking and Counting*, the involvement of several generations alters that paradigm to complicate migration patterns and its impacts. It also has the potential to utilise the range of Tamil and Tamil-Australian aesthetic ethoses as a way to portray the experiences of migration to Australia.

Visual artist Tania Bruguera refreshes considerations of aesthetics to draw out the ethical dimensions of a cross-cultural or intercultural practice. Bruguera's (quoted in Donovan 2011) work concerns the 'role of the artist in society' in relation to organisational processes. She identifies a shift towards a greater ethical consideration as to how artists access the resources of major arts organisations. Issues of how ethics are taken into account in aesthetic decisions acknowledge the increased complexity for an artist like Shakthidharan when developing a new intercultural family epic. This is a type of relational leadership utilised by many NESB artists as they engage with their sources of inspiration and wield the infrastructure of an organisation unfamiliar with those sources.

The major organisations involved in the development of *Counting and Cracking* were Carriageworks (Carriageworks n.d.) and inner-city Sydney theatre company Belvoir (Belvoir n.d.). Shakthidharan and Belvoir matured Shakthidharan's aim for Tamil and Tamil-Australian aesthetic experience. This process contributes to a more robust multicultural arts milieu that alters how creative and organisational leadership becomes apparent. This approach is one way to provide 'meaningful, committed, resources, [in the] long-term process of shifting existing power dynamics' in Australian theatre (Canas 2017). As Shakthidharan (2015, interview) says, 'I want kids to be able to read my work as part of their curriculum. I had nothing like that growing up'.

The friction in the evolution of *Counting and Cracking* is one of subtle and steady sharing of experiences between a seasoned company director and an emerging playwright with a particular knowledge of cross-cultural media production. It is a friction that lends itself to crafting creative outcomes, rather like the slow and steady process of woodcarving. The play was slated for the 2019 Belvoir season. CuriousWorks profiled it thus:

> This is a stylised, epic drama about love, violence, silence and hope in families—all from the perspective of the insiders. In presenting the vastly different worlds of Sri Lanka in the mid– late 20th century and Australia in the early 21st century, *Counting and Cracking* ultimately shows how much we have in common— between generations, countries and ourselves—and the surprising consequences that flow from that. Writer/Co-Director: S. Shakthidharan; Director Eamon Flack. (CuriousWorks n.d.)

The use of 'surprising consequences' aims to generate curiosity and suggests there may be something beyond the safe trope of 'commonality'. The credit includes Shakthidharan as co-director—a triumph because co-directing formed part of his early negotiations with Belvoir. Unlike some playwrights, Shakthidharan would not simply hand his text over; instead, he wanted to co-direct to maintain cultural appropriateness and the 'spirit' of the work. His claim for equal power was a step in what he perceives as the right direction. Belvoir may consider what they need to do to have more works like his in the pipeline so that co-produced plays become 'business as usual' rather than the occasional burst of attention. The company may also reflect on how this project has impacted the organisation and what they may carry forward into future programming.

Exchanges of expertise need to consider both the artist and the company. Both parties are trading technical, cultural and ethical knowledge. Both parties are experiencing and overcoming small frictions and simultaneously learning from each other. Both parties are also learning how to trust in private and then trust creatively in public. Shakthidharan had to invest as much in training Belvoir in epic Tamil-Australian aesthetics as Belvoir had to invest in training Shakthidharan in the constraints that make a theatre production of that scale successful. This case demonstrates those 'unpredictable interfaces' (Mar and Ang 2015, 8) as an intercultural exchange that produces both creative and cultural outcomes. It also represents a public outcome in a traditional theatre space, which is another interface to be navigated in bringing new audiences to the theatre (Kapetopoulos 2004). These creative constraints shape the final work to increase audience and creative reach. At the same, they understand that:

> [To] recognise diversity requires that time, energy, and labor be given to diversity. Recognition is thus material as well as symbolic: how time, energy and labor are directed within institutions affects how they surface. Diversity workers aim to intervene in how the institution surfaces. (Ahmed 2012, 29)

As to how the creative precariousness of *Counting and Cracking* may 'surface' in the theatre world has been a case study in complexity, negotiation and persistence. In 2017 Shakthidharan could say, after more than 10 years, that the play was slated for 2019, and that, 'so far, so good, things are developing well and overall it's been a great experience':

> Eamon [Flack] is directing, I'm writing and co-directing. The creative process has been excellent as we've met as equals and developed the work with respect for what it needs to be. (S. Shakthidharan 2017, email)

This comment indicates that Shakthidharan's relational leadership and 'diversity worker' role, in combination with Belvoir's efforts, have been productive. Belvoir receives funding for their productions; however, *Counting and Cracking* required additional funding, suggesting that this type of work has yet to become 'business as usual':

> It has been tough raising the money for the work as it is so ambitious—it's a family epic with a big cast. Both companies are operating out of their 'business as usual' paradigms to make a project like this happen, which have required persistence and flexibility from both of us. (S. Shakthidharan 2017, email)

There is a danger that Shakthidharan is, to an extent, a 'volunteer creative' on the project. This common power imbalance in employment is yet to be righted for the majority of NESB artists.

Shakthidharan was the beneficiary of a Carriageworks residency that went the extra step when Havilah 'brokered' an introduction by recommending his work to Belvoir. In this sense, Shakthidharan and Havilah are both diversity practitioners—'people who want diversity *to go through the whole system*' (Ahmed 2012, 29, original emphasis). Shakthidharan wants to have his play produced on his terms on the mainstage and promoted as such. Havilah (2015, interview) claims that Carriageworks uniquely programs artworks across the spectrum of what constitutes 'diversity': 'I don't think, other than Carriageworks, there's a major cultural institution that holds diversity at its core. And I think that's a big issue'.

Counting and Cracking was presented by Belvoir (co-directed by Eamon Flack and S. Shakthidharan and co-produced by Belvoir Street and Co-Curious) at the 2018 Sydney Festival and at the 2019 Adelaide Festival of Arts. Testament to the persistence and creative leadership of those involved, the critical acclaim with which it was met was matched by industry accolades. *Counting and Cracking* went on to win seven out of eight national theatre awards at the 2019 Helpmann Awards, including Best Direction, Best Female Actor in a Supporting Role, Best Male Actor, Best Production and the overall award of Best New Australian Work (Helpmann Awards 2019). Shakthidharan (quoted in Boland 2019) commented:

> Eamon and I don't live in the same part of Sydney, we don't work for the same sort of companies, and we've had very different types of upbringings, but there's a strange power that emerges when people who aren't supposed to work together, work together.

> Australia is at a bit of a crossroads and everyone's telling us the
> best-case scenario is that we retreat into our tribes and tolerate
> each other or we can take a deep breath and keep walking along
> this type of path and embrace the messiness of solidarity.

This case study is one in which resilience and persistence have gone hand in hand—as has the vision and proactive brokerage on the part of Carriageworks and CoCurious with Belvoir. Persistence is a necessary attribute of the diversity practitioner (Ahmed 2012, 30). Shakthidharan, while working with Carriageworks and in his subsequent segue to Belvoir, was a recruit who could 'both renew and restore' the organisation (Ahmed 2012, 39). *Counting and Cracking* has the potential to renew the relevance of Australian theatre, extend to a broader audience and restore the creative dynamics in theatre production.

This illustrates Shakthidharan's relational leadership with a wide range of players, including his extended Tamil-Australian family, who are unused to 'Western style' theatre. The process of 'accompaniment' is present in the equal sharing of skills and knowledge between director and playwright. The process of 'attunement' is evident in the playwright working with his extended family to develop the play and, in particular, his attempt to bring their aesthetics and experiences to the mainstage. The overall intention appears to be one of establishing productive relations at the centre of both the creative project and the organisation.

Establishing Trust through Organisational Collaboration

The capacity to activate networks is viewed as a core leadership skill. Being isolated from arts sector and creative networks is a consistent theme articulated by NESB artists. This is supported by research conducted in 1998 that identified the need for peer support and artistic opportunities (Positive Solutions n.d.). These factors, coupled with a lack of contact between the fragile, overworked, state-based multicultural arts organisations, led to the Arts in a Multicultural Australia (AMA) 2000 policy initiatives aimed at alleviating these issues (Keating, Bertone and Leahy n.d.). This section analyses one such initiative: kultour, a national program that promoted the work of NESB artists and multicultural arts content and demonstrated capacity building for leadership in multicultural arts practices. I argue that the previous benefits to NESB artists and organisations through a dedicated national multicultural touring network are not entirely satisfied by occasional inclusion in mainstream arts touring programs.

The Funded Network: kultour

Kultour was one of the significant funded initiatives of AMA 2000 and 2006 that brought creative and organisational leadership elements together. This national network exchanged artworks as a way for organisations to support each other and to expand their experience and that of the artists through a working relationship (kultour 2015). Kultour was established to address the isolation of NESB artists and multicultural arts organisations through peer interaction and national touring programs. It existed as a network across Australia from 2001 to 2014 (Diversity Arts Australia [DARTS] 2018). The program was established to give legitimacy to NESB artists and their support organisations. The kultour network aimed to alleviate some of the tensions between the multicultural specific organisations and the better-resourced arts mainstream. It exemplifies distributed leadership in which members are called upon to play to their strengths and lead as the project requires. I suggest that being part of a network increases artists' confidence and helps them form functional relationships from which they can identify opportunities and form collaborations that lead to new creative endeavours. 'Network expertise' includes brokers who are 'located on the margins of communities or well-placed information keepers [who can identify] opportunities to broker' (Carmichael 2011, 49). This expertise 'represents relational competencies that emerge through co-evolution of individual and distributed cognitions' (Hakkarainen et al. quoted in Carmichael 2011, 49). In this context, kultour members can be seen as multi-sited brokers who distributed their knowledge to realise opportunities for creative presentation.

This national network brought together professional artists who performed, exhibited and developed community-based workshops to audiences and community groups via a structure that provided cross-cultural brokerage skills. Kultour presented an annual national and (occasional) international touring program in all disciplines of Australian contemporary multicultural arts from 2001 for 11 years. The program supported artists in professional development via opportunities for their work to reach new audiences. In turn, audiences were exposed to a wide range of art practices through a quality professional program.

In contrast to mainstage arts organisations, which tend to focus on a particular artform (e.g. literature, visual or performing arts), kultour worked with artists from different cultural backgrounds and across all artforms—an ability and burden that is often placed on multicultural arts organisations. Working across all artforms produces a wide range of understandings within a multicultural arts organisation; however, it also heightens the risk of diluting the creative attention given to any one form. This historical pattern of multi-artform multicultural organisations may stem from the low numbers of NESB artists across different artforms, but it reinforces their need for supportive relationships while pursuing an art career.

Initially, kultour comprised an informal national network; however, it soon became a company 'dedicated to the touring of innovative and unique Australian multicultural arts' (Kapetopoulos 2004, 13). Its membership of multicultural arts organisations remained stable between 2001 and 2007 and then grew and evolved. Northern Rivers Performing Arts chaired the network for many years and Multicultural Arts Victoria also played a significant leadership role as the network host by providing space, resources and professional advice. Carmichael (2011, 43) observes that, for 'networks to function and be sustained for any length of time, a key issue is that of trust'. Trust needed to accumulate between members and with touring venues, arts organisation and artists. Table 3 identifies the member organisations that established kultour in 2000.

Table 3: Member organisations of kultour in 2000

Company name	Location
Belconnen Community Arts	Canberra, Australian Capital Territory
Brisbane Ethnic Music and Arts Centre	Brisbane, Queensland
Browns Mart Theatre	Darwin, Northern Territory
Kulcha Multicultural Arts of Western Australia	Perth, Western Australia
IHOS Opera	Hobart, Tasmania
Multicultural Arts Victoria	Melbourne, Victoria
NEXUS Multicultural Arts Centre	Adelaide, South Australia
Northern River Performing Arts	Lismore, New South Wales

Source: Kapetopoulos (2004, 15).

Most of these organisations managed their own venue or had arrangements with partners and presented multi-arts programs. By 2004, the kultour network had expanded to include the NSW Carnivale Multicultural Arts Festival; Casula Powerhouse Arts Centre, Liverpool, NSW; Footscray Community Arts Centre, Victoria; and the Australian Asian Artists Association (Sydney) (Kapetopoulos 2004, 15).

The stated aim of kultour was to expand the professional experience of NESB artists and arts managers through a working relationship based on artistic exchange. The underlying intention was to develop and strengthen trust between state multicultural arts organisations, and to increase their capacity to identify their constituents' needs and straddle their organisational brokering roles. For example, the 2010 national kultour symposium included contributions from practitioners and organisers and raised issues of leadership. Alongside tensions about the benefits or otherwise of mainstreaming—'we should end this multiculturalism business and just be mainstream'—visual artist Khaled Sabsabi articulated the need for activism, claiming that 'arts leadership is a resistance against the way things are' (Anatolitis 2010, 42). The skill of the artist is to play to such contradictory elements; the skill of the network is to navigate them.

Another intention of kultour, as a national body dedicated to improving multicultural arts practice and profile, was to increase the legitimacy of multicultural arts organisations to artists and funding bodies. The knowledge they shared would provide mutual support, increase the profiles of artists and member organisations, and enhance the overall profile of multicultural arts more generally. Kultour thus demonstrated a holistic approach to participation, artist development and audience development (Keating, Bertone and Leahy n.d., 4). Kapetopoulos (2004, 14) found that this required a sophisticated blend of abilities: 'The network is held together by trust and knowledge. As a knowledge network, kultour members exhibit convergent mental models, adept at working in culturally complex environments'.

Each multicultural arts organisation would select artists' works to tour based on agreed quality, level of interest, capacity and logistics at an annual meeting. Touring was considered an opportunity to gauge creative developments in the field. Kultour meetings provided a rare occasion for members to meet face-to-face, raise issues and discuss and develop solutions. A review of the network in its first years conveys some of the complexity of these meetings:

> At meetings, members negotiate between style and genre;
> contemporary and traditional artforms and hybrids; their
> understanding of audiences and constituents; communication
> strategies; timing; presentation modes and most importantly
> budget. (Kapetopoulos 2004, 16)

Members' support and investment of time and effort stemmed from addressing the practical and perceptual aspects of kultour:

> As a touring network it is a good thing—I was surprised when the
> Australia Council initiated it. Playing Australia has gone down
> a mainstream path, and we need a touring network which can
> present quality work of a culturally diverse nature. It is a program
> which can redress some of the problems of the past in the areas
> of multicultural arts. When I think of kultour, I visualize quality
> multicultural arts. (kultour members quoted in Kapetopoulos
> 2004, 16)

One such 'quality multicultural arts' project, *Opposite My House is a Funeral Parlour*, was a solo dance piece by dancer and choreographer, Naree Vachananda. In 2006 kultour presented this work in Melbourne, Lismore, Fremantle and Campbelltown. *Opposite My House* contemplates a journey of death meditating on the Buddhist concept of the cyclical flow of life and death, with the performance structured using the journey of the Greek archetype, Persephone. The artist describes the connections:

> The idea of mortality is not only philosophical but also cultural.
> As a Buddhist trying to collect my thoughts about mortality,
> I looked at various streams of Buddhism … I found the Buddhist
> idea of cyclic flow of life and death was parallel to the myth of
> Persephone. (Vachananda 2004)

The publicity blurb described it as follows: 'Don't expect black costumes, white powder or saffron transcendence. This dance of death is uncompromisingly contemporary' (MAV 2006b). The work was a collaboration between Darwin-based composer Edward Kelly and multimedia designer Yeap Heng Shen from Malaysia. Author Jenny Joseph permitted the use of excerpts from her book *Persephone*, reinforcing the cross-cultural foundation of the work.

This dance work is one among many from the range of artforms presented by kultour. It conveys how artists experiment beyond the conventional binary of what constitutes either 'contemporary' or 'traditional' dance. Further, kultour acted as an intermediary, exercising combined organisational and creative leadership by delivering audience outreach and workshop presentations. Kulcha (then a Western Australian multicultural arts presenter) enhanced their community audience base and engaged two other companies in Perth and Fremantle, thus extending their cultural credibility and the repertoire and experience of their partners. While in Perth, Vachananda presented a workshop for dancers with the Strut Dance Company and performed in conjunction with Deckchair Theatre Company. The work attracted reviews in *RealTime Arts*, an arts review broadsheet:

> Vachananda is a daring, able choreographer with a strong presence and this work offers a provocative glimpse of the kinds of sustained solo work that can still exist outside the larger streams of dance in Australia. (Baily 2005)

The tour of *Opposite My House* exemplifies how kultour operated well beyond the norm of the 'fly-in fly-out' tour syndrome.

The next stage of kultour's development aimed to consolidate its role as a partnership broker between artists, major presenters and arts organisations by broadening the skills of its board of directors to include touring expertise and presenter influence. By its very structure, a network is stronger than the sum of its parts. Kultour's use of 'cultural sustainability through industry-based approaches' (Mar and Ang 2015, 23) was characteristic of its broader approach. Adopting an industry-based approach and demonstrating its capacity and legitimacy to manage and direct a tour strengthened the external perception of the organisation. As a national network, kultour also profiled the existence of a multicultural arts sector across each state and territory and enabled a platform for commentary on issues of cultural and political concern (kultour 2011, 2015).

Kultour's platform could not match the strength of other organisations in the industry, in part because the low levels of support afforded to multicultural arts organisation members resulted in a general economic fragility. The 2005 evaluation of AMA 2000 found that, despite the appropriateness of kultour being situated within multicultural arts organisations:

> There are inherent tensions when expectations of high quality are located within the context of an under-resourced sector. The funding base of some kultour organisations is precarious at times, where 'survival' issues overtake long-term strategic goals. (Keating, Bertone and Leahy n.d., 4)

The warning about the loss of small organisations to the network was prescient. Between 2000 and 2015, the number of multi-artform multicultural arts organisations across Australia reduced by over a third, as summarised in Table 4.

Table 4: Longevity of multi-artform multicultural arts organisations

Company name	State	Longevity
Footscray Community Arts Centre	Vic.	1974–present
Darwin Community Arts (formerly Brown's Mart)	NT	1970s–present
Carnivale Multicultural Arts Festival	NSW	1976–2004
Kulcha	WA	1983–2013
NEXUS Arts (formerly NEXUS Multicultural Arts Centre)	SA	1984–present
Multicultural Arts Alliance	NSW	1988–2000
Brisbane Ethnic Multicultural Arts Centre (merged with Queensland Multicultural Centre in 2013)	Qld	1990–present
Multicultural Arts Victoria	Vic.	1991–present
4A Centre for Contemporary Asian Arts (previously Asian Australian Artists Association 4A)	NSW	1996–present
Contemporary Asian Australian Performance (previously Performance 4A)	NSW	1998–present
kultour	Vic.	2000–14
Diversity Arts Australia (advocacy)	NSW	2015–present
Groundswell (advocacy)	NSW	2011–14

Table 4 shows 11 artform companies producing or presenting multicultural arts. Of these, seven remained in 2015; this represents a 36 per cent attrition rate and demonstrates the dismantling of dedicated creative entry points for many NESB artists. Around 2008, tension regarding the role of kultour came to the fore and continued during its lengthy transition into Diversity Arts Australia (DARTS), which was completed in early 2017. A former kultour manager saw the need to shift responsibility to the wider arts sector because of the exhaustion of doing all the 'heavy lifting' in circulating multicultural artworks (Mar and Ang 2015, 110). However, the challenges to DARTS are significant because the processes and politics of encouraging other organisations to increase their culturally diverse programming require (at a minimum) resources, influence, cooperation and a substantial change in current risk-averse attitudes. The issue of responsibility for multicultural arts characteristic of institutional settings is also found between organisations that struggle with issues of mainstreaming. This highlights the delicate nature of cooperation between creative and organisational leaders. Accompaniment and attunement can be useful processes in assisting this cooperation. To this end, DARTS has utilised social media platforms very effectively to support NESB artists and to increase the listening capacity of arts organisations. The increased access to a wide membership of artists and activists afforded through accessible social media provides DARTS with breakthrough network opportunities.

To Advocate or Practice

An organisation's ability to adapt to changing environments requires a particular type of responsive and visionary leadership. A former kultour member and Executive Officer of Darwin Community Arts Bong Ramilo (2015, interview) recalls that the Australia Council 'told kultour some years ago that it's no longer an initiative regarding touring'. Kultour was 'told' to transition from a network that linked 'cultural grassroots, the arts field, governance and policy spheres' to a 'new ambit' of advocacy (Mar and Ang 2015, 113).

The move to an advocacy role and away from the creative stimulation that had characterised kultour's remit did not happen lightly. The network resisted its new role, preferring instead to try and manage both roles, grounded in the:

> Fusion of quality aesthetic practice and the emergence of different practices and expressions, and using these stories in their arguments for inclusive arts practices that reflect the diversity of Australian society and its cultural contexts. That is perhaps why artist development continues as a key organisational interest, rather than pursuing a purely aesthetically neutral advocacy and service role. (Mar and Ang 2015, 113)

This shift into the politics of advocacy, while valuable, erodes the more difficult role in art production that argues that producing quality art is actually the best advocacy. As Ramilo (2015, interview) (see Image 21) states:

> You need to demonstrate that cultural diversity in the arts is a good thing. So me personally, I'd rather just make things. I'd rather have more productions, more recordings, more shows, more books— that demonstrate that this work is good.

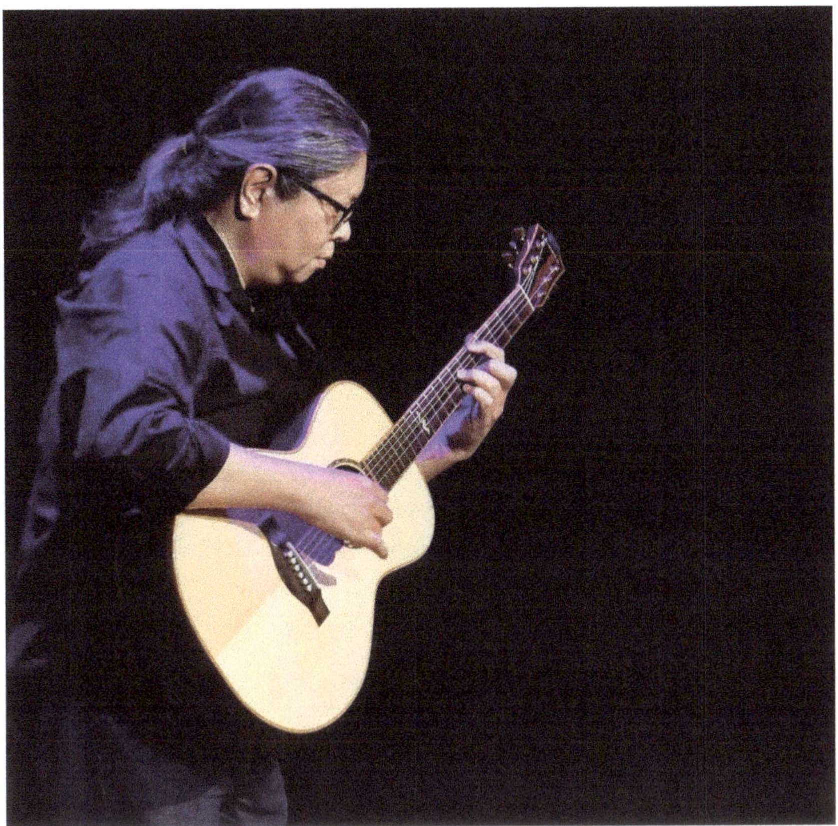

Image 21: Bong Ramilo, *Treasure Language Storytelling*, performance, 2016

Photographer: Aikuma Project

Part of kultour's role change can be tracked through the different sections of the Australia Council that managed their contract. Executive management decided to 'internally mainstream' the kultour initiative from the AMA policy manager to other departments. This resulted in varying degrees of comprehension by staff as to the needs kultour was meeting and, subsequently, varying responses as to the best approach. The danger of being an initiative of the Australia Council was that kultour was always beholden to them. Compromising with council generated friction between the members:

> Multicultural touring should be taken up by the other touring organisations also funded by Australia Council, which of course makes sense—they should be responsive to cultural diversity as well. I heard that Multicultural Arts Victoria, BEMAC [Brisbane

> Multicultural Arts Centre] and Nexus want to set up their own touring circuit, and I support that. They don't think that the other touring organisations will at this point meet all the needs and desires of the companies and artists who want to tour multicultural arts products. I don't know if Performing Lines and the other organisations are really up to it. I don't know how culturally diverse the decision-making bodies of these organisations are or whether they understand the need to represent cultural diversity or not, because I mean it doesn't come automatically. (B. Ramilo 2015, interview)

Performing Lines (PL) is a development, production and touring company for independent Australian performing artists (PL n.d.-a). Ramilo's statement questions the capacity of the 'mainstream' to comprehend and deliver on the aspirations of NESB artists and audience members who may or may not be attracted to, and/or familiar with, their work, and the tensions generated in such interactions.

Mainstream, Tributary or Edge

If there was adequate infrastructure to produce and present work by NESB artists, one could view the shift in kultour's mission as an important philosophical change that shifted the focus from a 'minority' multicultural sector to diversity across the entire arts sector. Certainly, the multifarious roles are supportive and include all aspects of a creative project from concept to audience response. The multicultural arts milieu would benefit from having a range of multicultural organisations, including ones that produce, tour *and* advocate. However, in the multicultural arts, it is often an 'either/or' scenario that indicates the limits of that milieu.

Who takes responsibility for, and leadership roles in, multicultural arts have been perennial issues in the arts sector since the 1970s. The low level of support for NESB artists by major companies reinforces the notion that 'mainstreaming' for multicultural practices is not 'automatic', and also highlights issues in the processes of inclusion and organisational leadership. Characteristic tensions for such artists include gaining entry to, and then 'fitting in' with, mainstream arts organisations, or finding creative networks that may have a lower profile but are more supportive. Artists in Far North Queensland, for example, expressed the value of a 'multicultural arts network' to support their 'artistic development' (Babacan 2011, 18). Even though it is expected of them, mainstream organisations may not yet have the capability. Ahmed's (2012, 138, original emphasis) comments, although ostensibly about universities, are relevant to mainstream arts organisations:

> Mainstreaming, even as an ideal, becomes a problem in the sense that universities are not ready for it: to act as if mainstreaming is the case, because it should be the case, can be counterproductive because the conditions are not available in the present *to make it the case.*

The issues of timeliness, context and conditions for cultural diversity are necessary precursors before an organisation's values and programs can be considered culturally diverse. Ramilo's statement that 'it doesn't come automatically' respects the myriad knowledges that are in play, at times under tension, within multicultural practices. Georgina Sedgwick of the Darwin Festival reveals how some practices developed and how networks were activated through kultour. These included careful observation and an ability to broker opportunities between artist experimentation, the local community and audience context:

> I can't just bring an artist in; get their trust; tour the work, and then after a year the engagement's over. You get to that point where you're a year or two into the engagement and you're just starting to get momentum and see the possibilities. (Sedgwick quoted in Mar and Ang 2015, 108)

In December 2014 kultour's board of directors closed their presence in Melbourne and announced a move to Western Sydney. The state of Victoria has at least two successful arts organisations dedicated to cultural difference: Multicultural Arts Victoria and the Footscray Community Centre. While a move to NSW might address the absence of a dedicated multicultural arts organisation in that state, and could attract different sources of funding, the high calibre of creative and organisational leadership for multicultural artists in Victoria was, arguably, key to kultour's successful functioning. The board responded to the lack of organisational support for culturally diverse artists in NSW by relocating to Western Sydney, an area with a high concentration of NESB artists (Hanna 2012).

Coupled with the remit of national advocacy (probably an impossibility for an under-resourced organisation), the challenge for kultour was to 'encourage' a range of subsidised touring organisations that were resistant to increasing diversity in their programming. In 2015 a multicultural arts centre staff and kultour member observed the unwillingness of touring agencies to diversify their marketing or audience. Market driven, such agencies were unconvinced that a market existed for multicultural programming. If one tour was not as successful as expected, the touring agency developed what the staff member described as a 'dampened enthusiasm' to showcase further multicultural artworks.

Another factor is the tension between the desire to remain a marginal artist and the push towards the 'mainstream', as Ramilo observes:

> Artists appreciated having an organisation that toured their work because possibly no one else will. No one else appreciated the importance of what kultour did. However, some of us—myself and Aaron Seeto in particular—said we don't want to be part of the mainstream, we like being on the margins. That's an aesthetic thing as well. Some of us don't want to be in the mainstream arts sector automatically. (B. Ramilo 2015, interview)

A previous touring partner, Artback NT, expressed a similar strategic position—namely, that being on the 'margins of things, is a far more interesting place to work' (quoted in Mar and Ang 2015, 111). The relationship between kultour and touring artists reflects trusting negotiations based on knowledge and processes focused on how to tour multicultural arts. This level of intercultural understanding underpins the potential for an artwork to be part of a capacity-building process that goes beyond solely being a presentation. By contrast, established touring companies such as PL develop work to sell into a mainstream arts market. Their website profiles the available work for international and national tours. In 2017 PL developed and promoted some NESB artists for touring: a dance work, *A Faint Existence*, by performer Kristina Chan; a multimedia work, *Crawl Me Blood*, by APHIDS; and *Layla Majnun* by illUMEnate, a performance in development with Western Australian PL Associate Producer Zainab Syed (PL n.d.-b).

These projects suggest that PL has taken up some of the 'heavy lifting' of touring and demonstrates that they value cultural difference in the arts. In later years, touring may form part of their contract with the Australia Council, which, as Ramilo (2015, interview) observes, is 'admirable and legitimate'. However, the mainstage touring approach taken by PL may compromise the extent to which artists can engage with local audiences. The previous description of Vachananda's tour and the reviews of kultour highlight the intense labour invested in their touring partnerships that went beyond a scheduled presentation in a particular venue (Kapetopoulos 2004; Keating, Bertone and Leahy n.d.).

The Australia Council's decision to terminate kultour's active touring role and transition it to an advocacy role meant that it was reclassified as a 'service' organisation, which some perceive as the least vital component in the arts system and, therefore, as less crucial in times of financial duress. An estimated 70 per cent reduction in funding to individual artists (Croggon 2016b) occurred in 2016. The S2M sector was also hard-hit and the DARTS (previously kultour) CEO confirmed that it had been 'unsuccessful for 4-year organisational funding announced in 2016' (L. Nahlous 2017, email).

Crucially, the great majority of funding is provided to MPAs. Shakthidharan criticised this Australia Council approach to funding, which assumes that major companies are more 'trustworthy' with funds. This creates the situation—or the perception of a situation—in which multicultural arts organisations with cultural expertise lose funding to major companies who deliver multicultural arts that are more palatable to mainstream audiences. A push–pull tension occurs regarding the value of 'going mainstream'. The risk is that it limits the multiplicities of practice that have characterised multicultural arts in the past and shrinks to a narrow perception of what mainstream companies and their usual audiences consider acceptable.

This case study of kultour exemplifies a history that is littered with the rise and demise of support for Australia's multicultural arts. Kultour was the only national multicultural, multi-artform organisation in Australia. It offered myriad artistic opportunities, including facilitating high-profile national tours of multicultural artworks, promoting creative leadership for artists and facilitating organisational leadership within member organisations. And yet, there was no effective support for kultour to reach its full potential. The legacy of kultour is that supportive relationships between remaining state-based multicultural organisations are in place and they may continue to work together. The structural potential for national multicultural organisational leadership is still viable, albeit in a different form. With this in mind, I argue in the next section that the link between creative production and organisational influence remains the most viable way to generate traction for multicultural arts practices, as exemplified by the partnership between CAAP and PWA.

Traction Gained through Confluence: Longer-Term Productive Partnerships

A mission to enter into dialogue with the arts mainstream and broader society formed the mandate of a small arts organisation established in 1996—the Asian Australian Artists Association. The Centre for Contemporary Asian Art (CCAA) is now the visual arts arm of this organisation while CAAP, which became a separate entity in 1998, is the performance arm. In 2015 CAAP began a partnership with PWA, a national company that develops new plays. Both organisations share the aim of developing and producing Asian-Australian performing arts content for the mainstage. The high level of trust established in this partnership generates traction on the mainstage.

Activist Beginnings

The predecessor to CCAA and CAAP, the Asian Australian Artists Association, also known as 4A, began in a humble upstairs room in Liverpool Street in Sydney's CBD. The impetus for its establishment was twofold. One motivation was to actively resist the rise of anti-Asian racism emerging in Australia at that time (Ang and Stratton 1998; Hage 2000; Marr 2017). Friction in the sociopolitical environment brought artists together to counter that negativity. Secondly, its creative aims were to promote Asian-Australian art in the context of increasing interest in Asian art and to critique the absence of Asian-Australian artists in the Queensland Art Gallery's inaugural 1996 Asia-Pacific Triennial. The friction between international interest and the lack of recognition by mainstream arts organisations domestically motivated Asian-Australian artists to build an alternative platform. These were 4A's 'unambiguously political and activist origins'; its persistent aim was to be a 'lightning rod' for Asian-Australian and international visual artists, academics and curators (Hore-Thorburn 2017). At the CCAA's twentieth anniversary symposium in late 2016 questions about the centre's relevance resurfaced. Nationalist politician Pauline Hanson had recently been re-elected and the current political climate was described as:

> 'A far darker situation' indicated by the enormous backlash against cosmopolitanism, diversity, and the ascendency of Trump, the Brexit movement and others. The present situation is in many ways more dangerous than it was in the nineties and more problematic. (Hore-Thorburn 2017)

One of the roles of organisations such as CCAA and CAAP is to provide counter-narratives to those of mainstream arts organisations and media. CCAA is the only funded visual arts organisation in Australia dedicated to cultural diversity. Its success is attributed, in part, to its artist-centred focus—or, as visual artist Lindy Lee put it, 'its fidelity to its artists and community' (Hore-Thorburn 2017). Such fidelity may be found within the agility of S2M arts organisations.

The Ripple Effect

The intense difficulties faced by Asian-Australian performers and live theatre producers, alongside low resourcing levels, to some extent explains why CAAP has taken longer than CCAA to establish itself. CAAP is a small organisation with a barely remunerated executive officer position, many volunteers and philanthropic support for project delivery to increase the number of Asian-Australian performances to reach broad audiences:

> CAAP is dedicated to making exceptional contemporary Asian Australian work for all audiences. We engender greater cultural diversity in Australian performing arts by producing cross art form theatrical works of the highest quality, in partnership with major festivals and flagship companies. (CAAP 2017)

Writer, performer, producer, dramaturg, 2021 Artistic Director of the OzAsia Festival and Executive Producer of CAAP Annette Shun Wah (2015, interview) (see Image 22) views the role of CAAP as telling stories and seeing different perspectives that 'examine what it is to be Asian-Australian in contemporary Australia. There's not very much work that reflects or explores that'.

The organisation's strength is its willingness and commitment to band together as a group of Asian-Australian artists, and to connect and match with like-minded creative and entrepreneurial partners. Shun Wah describes the company's influence as one that produces 'ripple' effects through their productions and partnerships. The impact of this 'ripple' both erodes the resistance to cultural diversity demonstrated by larger performance companies and generates the energy to produce more.

While CAAP is a clear example of the benefits of the 'banding together' approach criticised by Shakthidharan, Shun Wah nevertheless shares his view of the role of the activator (an artist who works productively with friction):

> We are only a tiny company, but it's good to be there, to influence
> and have that ripple effect through the sector. I know I can't do
> a great deal on my own. Our little company only makes one or
> two works a year. It's a fantastic effect if we can work with the
> other people who want to tick that [diversity] box but haven't
> quite worked out how to do it. (A. Shun Wah 2015, interview)

Shun Wah articulates an alternative perspective on the typically derogatory attitude towards, and assumed tokenism of, 'ticking the box' (DARTS 2017). In doing so, she signals her flexible style of leadership and openness to develop a range of partnerships. Her willingness to assist those who are interested in diversity shows her readiness to engage—a readiness that is likely to be reciprocated. She demonstrates transformational leadership in her charismatic personality, and relational leadership in the relationships that extend from the small organisation. CAAP engenders trust and increases traction when successful works are produced for the mainstage.

CAAP's success is evidenced in the list of its theatre productions programmed by the Sydney and Darwin festivals: *In Between Two*, *The Serpent's Table*, *Yasukichi Murakami—through a Distant Lens*, *Stories Then & Now* and *Who Speaks For Me?* Experienced commercial Asian-Australian artists such as web designers were involved in *The Serpent's Table*. For many, it was their first opportunity to explore their cultural heritage:

> The artists brought their personal backgrounds to the performance
> and found it so liberating because in the other work they've done
> until now they haven't been able to utilise any of that. (A. Shun
> Wah 2015, interview)

Shun Wah's statement points to the issue of creative isolation. Asian-Australian artists do not have a well-established historical record of performances and narratives to draw upon. The lack of a creative history of multicultural, cross-cultural or intercultural arts practices in Australia turns the discourse into a vicious cycle. CAAP, which became a resident company at Carriageworks in 2018, has devised a range of programs aimed at stimulating and sustaining artists and effecting change, including the Asian Australian Performance Directory, the Longhouse Networking Program and the Lotus Playwriting Project; the last undertaken in partnership with PWA (CAAP 2017). This well-crafted suite of programs supports artists in maintaining their creative stamina through professional development and peer support.

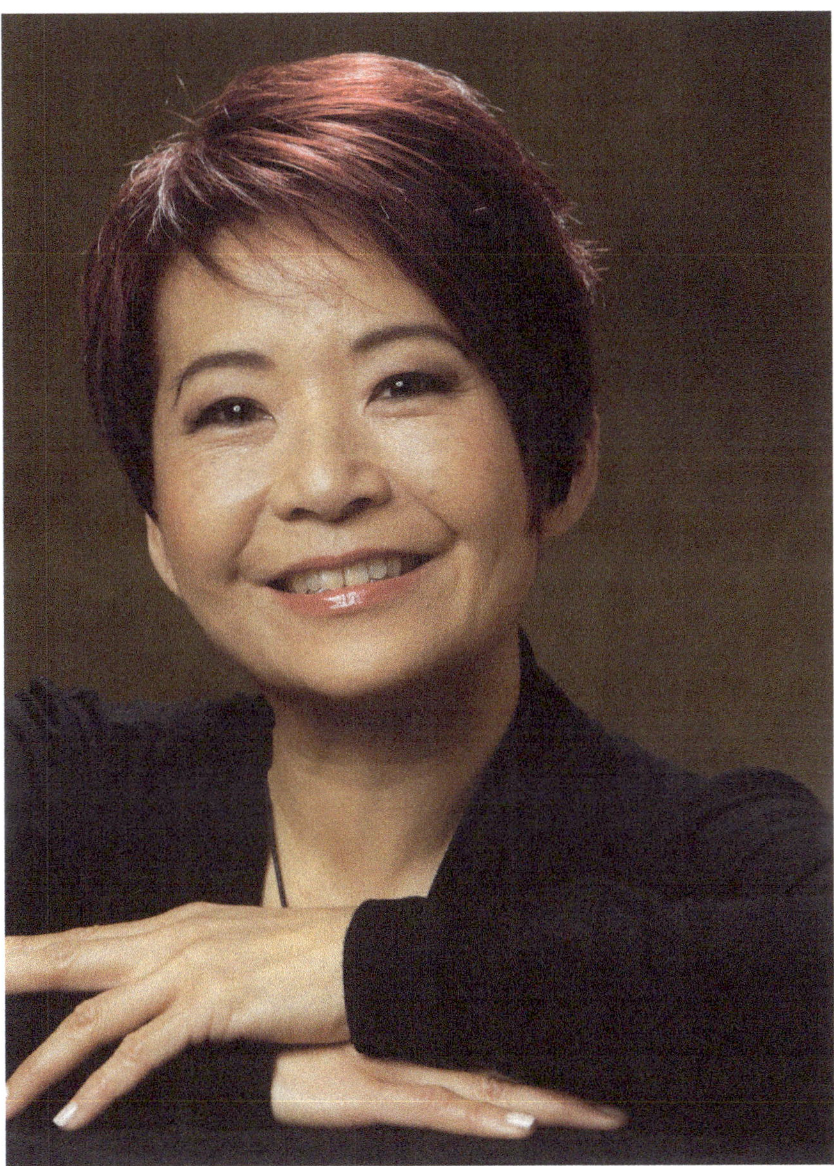

Image 22: Annette Shun Wah
Photographer: Brian Geach

Fundamental Change: Lotus Playwriting Project

The partnership between CAAP and PWA reflects UNESCO's 'culture cycles': each stage in the cycle is designed to contribute to culturally diverse art production leading to a final presentation. The work undertaken by CAAP flows through all those processes and addresses a criticism levelled at 'fashionable diversity', whereby 'diversity is restricted to aesthetic presentation, rather than a meaningful, committed, resourced, long-term process of shifting existing power-dynamics' (Canas 2017).

The shift in the arts towards increasingly diverse presentations requires structural change that is deemed to 'take a long time', according to CAAP's partner on the Lotus Playwriting Project (Lotus), PWA's Artistic Director, at the time, Tim Roseman:

> Our plays are very white, very middle class. Last year [2013] there were six plays on the Australian stage not written by white people. Every company I speak to is itching to put on a play by that Cambodian-Australian playwright, but it isn't there. (Radio National 2014)

Roseman's insights and enthusiasm are genuine and demonstrate elements of organisational leadership. However, the trope of time—'we want to make a fundamental change, but it will, of course, take time'—mitigates against the processes to make that change (Radio National 2014). Roseman appears to accept his colleagues' ignorance regarding structural problems captured by their 'itching to put on' what 'isn't there'. His colleagues may have been irritated by their lack of contemporary programming regarding that 'Cambodian-Australian playwright', but they neither took responsibility for the fact that they could not find such a play nor attempted to address the situation. Roseman saw a gap in the market that PWA could address, but he needed an expert partner—CAAP.

Lotus nurtures a new generation of Asian-Australian writers to address the low numbers of their published plays, which, currently, can be counted on 'the fingers of one hand' (A. Shun Wah 2015, interview). It develops the artists' trust in themselves via increased confidence and peer support. When their work reaches a certain stage, producers from mainstage organisations are able to trust their work and begin to work with those writers. In under a year, Lotus generated play readings from 12 writers at Brisbane's La Boite Theatre, Melbourne's Malthouse Theatre and Parramatta's Riverside Theatre. Shun Wah is confident that the combined programs run by CAAP will have another 12 completed, full-length plays by Asian-Australian writers in under three years (A. Shun Wah 2015, interview).

One aspect of a culture cycle is the research and development phase. Preparatory phases are needed to gain the interest and commitment of writers of Asian-Australian backgrounds to attend the program. The partnership between CAAP and PWA has been successful in part because the leaders of both organisations are committed to changing the face of Australian performance and because they straddle roles of creative development and service organisations. The following description of PWA could equally apply to CAAP: 'I think we're an artistic-led company, servicing the rest of the industry by providing them with amazing new plays' (T. Roseman 2015, interview).

This synergy deepens when Shun Wah's and Roseman's skills combine to work 'across cultures'. Roseman brings experience from the United Kingdom, which he sees as probably a 'good generation or so ahead of what's happening in Australia because they are moving away from the deficit model' (T. Roseman 2015, interview). PWA employ culturally diverse staff and uses a process of decision-making for programming that engages with artists of relevant cultural backgrounds. This collaborative approach is also evident in their business planning:

> In our last [strategic plan], we had a section called 'our diversity projects' and I've taken that out because as long as you have your work and your diversity work, you're silo-ing and you're still living in the realm of otherness. So we make a statement that all of our projects speak to cultural, linguistic, social, political, regional diversity. (T. Roseman 2015, interview)

This statement encapsulates the organisation's commitment to diversity and its plans for long-term change. When applying a 'diversity' label, PWA maintained such projects' status as a sidebar, an add-on. Changing its mission statement may assist the company to translate its plans into action, as expressing intention can activate 'hopeful performative' attention (Ahmed 2012, 67).

Roseman also knows that 'cultural parity [is yet to be achieved, and that PWA needs to] create programs that speak directly' to particular marginalised groups (T. Roseman 2015, interview). Further, he acknowledges the expertise that CAAP brings to delivering PWA's aims.

For example, whereas there was a poor response to a call-out by PWA for Asian-Australian artists to attend a workshop on playwriting, when CAAP did their call-out for the inaugural Lotus Project, over 30 people attended, and these numbers were replicated across capital cities. CAAP engages across a wide artistic spectrum that includes 'writers, bloggers, poets, actors, musicians' (A. Shun Wah 2015, interview). According to Roseman (2015, interview), 'the only rule of theatre is that content dictates form', which, for Lotus, relieves the pressure of making multicultural stories fit into what might be a mainstream canon or aesthetic. The style of the performance of the work will depend on the content that is being explored. Both parties, therefore, are bringing an open perspective to the playwriting process, which directly benefits the presentation outcomes.

An early presentation phase for Lotus is PWA's annual Playwriting Festival, which, in 2016, included four play readings developed through the Lotus program: *Site Rubiyah* by Katrina Irawati Graham, *Squint Witch* by Shari Indriani, *My Father Who Slept in A Zoo* by Ngoc Phan and *Entomology* by Natesha Somasundaram (PWA 2016). As well as delivering CAAP and PWA's joint aims for long-term change, crucially Lotus also highlights how creative capacities can build relatively quickly. The 2015 Lotus Project in Brisbane had works picked up by niche theatre company La Boite, new writing theatre Playlab and the mainstage Queensland Theatre Company—'even before we finished the second stage' (A. Shun Wah 2015, interview). *Blue Bones*, written by Merlyn Tong, was presented by Playlab and later won six Matilda Awards for Queensland theatre, including the Brisbane Lord Mayor's best new Australian work (Matilda Awards 2017). While the ensuing publicity could have acknowledged CAAP more roundly, successes such as these have placed their processes in the spotlight and are likely to inspire others. They challenge the 'it will take time' trope.

Industry accolades notwithstanding, the lack of tertiary recognition or accreditation for such informal professional development is a potential risk. Shun Wah responds to such concerns by pointing out the lack of playwriting courses in Australia and the lack of cultural depth on the curriculum. Professional training streams, where they do exist, tend not to engage in multicultural content development. Many NESB artists in tertiary education undertake parallel training, seeking out content that resonates and could lead to career opportunities. Some Asian-Australian artists who have completed courses at the National Institute of Dramatic Arts (NIDA), for example, also use Lotus in their careers:

> When I talk to students, who come fresh out of NIDA or wherever, they're full of optimism after just graduating, and don't think they need to bear the culturally diverse tag because they know they're smart and talented. But about two years later they come back [to me], having realised the opportunities that rightfully should be theirs, are not there. (A. Shun Wah 2015, interview)

Lotus is unique because it steps the writer through as many stages of development as possible: from writing to non-professional/professional readings to industry presentation. Recognising the value of Lotus, a philanthropic foundation committed three years of support. This will ensure program delivery and freedom from the rigours of grant applications for Australia Council and other funding with their associated criteria and constraints. The foundation's support will enable Lotus to be an 'in-depth, longer term, serious intensive workshopping and mentoring' program (A. Shun Wah 2015, interview) (see Image 23). Nevertheless, CAAP's low levels of remuneration serve to maintain the performing arts' inequitable power structure. CAAP creates content that is taken up by companies that are funded to present such work, but who do not (necessarily) contribute financially to CAAP's processes. In this way, well-resourced companies reap the benefits without (necessarily) contributing to the research and development processes of the playwright. It is philanthropic support to CAAP that enables the Lotus workshops to 'ripple through' the arts.

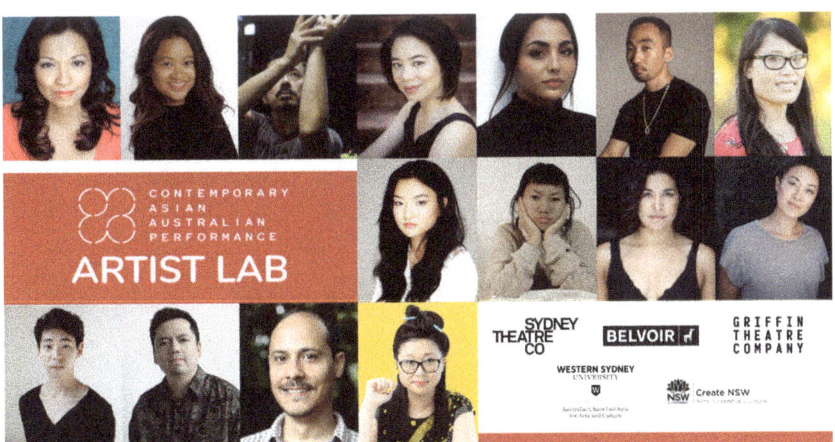

Image 23: Contemporary Asian Australian Performance Artists Lab brochure, 2020

Courtesy: Contemporary Asian Australian Performance

A Virtuous Cycle

The creative success of Lotus extends beyond the initial bipartisan partnership, delivering several phases in the culture cycle across many arts organisations. That joint vision extends the capabilities for CAAP and PWA to generate an engagement beyond the occasional, one-off experience. In this way, Lotus has led a virtuous cycle to increase the production of multicultural arts, the phases of which can be described as: artist > CAAP identifies a viable creative process for change > PWA recognises a diversity gap and seeks ways to address it > CAAP and PWA in partnership > initial play development > workshops > play reading by professional actors and directors > showcase to performing arts industry > selection by mainstage > public presentation > possible national or regional tour > increased profile of artists and companies > increased relevance to diverse audiences > contribution to a multicultural arts milieu > more Asian-Australian artists are involved. (See Appendix E for a graphic representation of this organisational change cycle.)

This cycle draws on relational and transactional leadership and uses the skills of attunement and accompaniment to develop an alternative trajectory in the Australian arts. The cycle depicts the practical outcomes when creative and organisational leadership work in concert. In the case of Lotus, the initial partnership seeks to widen Asian-Australian artists' capacity to link directly with 'industry' or the mainstage. Alongside Roseman's critical assessment of the situation in Australia, Shun Wah's leadership drives *Lotus* with skill, patience and perseverance:

> Big companies are now seeking our partnership or collaboration. The aim is for the entire sector, all of us, to respond and learn how to be more culturally diverse in what we do. To create work that's more relevant to the Australian society as it is today and, in doing that, maybe attract more diverse audiences. (A. Shun Wah 2015, interview)

Shun Wah's relational leadership is tangible. She creates opportunities for other artists beyond her immediate sphere and through CAAP programs on the mainstage. Her experience is also tangible—she has been working in the area of multicultural performance, presentation and writing since the mid-1980s, and draws on that experience to ensure long-term change. As such, she brings her extensive knowledge and experience as a cultural and creative broker to envisage, promote and enact change. In 2018

CAAP became a resident company at Carriageworks, which provides stable accommodation and a high-profile venue for their programs (Taylor 2017).

Despite their active partnership in changing the multicultural arts milieu, neither Shun Wah nor Roseman expressed a close link to the Australia Council's Cultural Engagement Framework (CEF) or arts policy. Because of her long-term engagement with multicultural arts practices, Shun Wah (2015, interview) is aware of the AMA policies, the loss of companies such as Carnivale and the retreat from multiculturalism as a government focus, which:

> Got replaced for a while by a push towards youth arts and so suddenly the big focus was on a lot of stuff for young people, which was fantastic. But then it's as if you can only deal with one priority at a time. And I think, as a nation, we could be a bit more sophisticated than that.

Shun Wah's vision for a multicultural arts milieu is one that extends across age, socio-economic and cultural backgrounds. To be sophisticated suggests a more complex conversation and exploration of how diversity is 'circulated' (Ahmed 2012, 81). Facilitating the circulation of creative diversity occupies Shun Wah and Roseman outside the realms of policy:

> I've never had a conversation about arts policy with any practitioner in the two and a half years that I've been in this job. A real problem regards the conditions of funding. The Australia Council believes that it's up to arts companies to decide what they want to do and how to spend their money. I firmly believe in quotas and not incentives. (T. Roseman 2015, interview)

Echoing debates articulated earlier between Marinos and Klika, Roseman identifies the combative friction between legislating for change and laissez-faire. He wants funding to be dependent on an organisation's strategies to alter the 'white hegemony of this culture, [which] is way more important than … risk management or marketing' (T. Roseman 2015, interview).

A cause for concern for Shakthidharan is the increasing direction of funds towards mainstage organisations—particularly given those organisations' risk-averse track record in terms of generating distinctive multicultural artworks. The Australia Council has adopted an incentive approach with regard to the MPAs; it offers a grant that only MPAs are eligible to apply for and requires them to deliver on one of the diversity options across the CEF. This apparent disregard for small multicultural organisations may go deeper. As a consequence of shrinking support to multicultural organisations, the ability of the next generation of NESB artists to gain the experience necessary to keep the multicultural arts baton active and in circulation will be severely limited.

The demographic context is changing rapidly in Australia. The country's increasingly culturally diverse population implies that what the 'multicultural arts sector' means today cannot be the same as in the 1980s. CAAP and PWA demonstrate an agile ambitiousness that responds to opportunities in the current society for Asian-Australian performance and opens up possibilities in a structured and detailed approach that is also fluid and creatively responsive to the interests of artists. This form of relational leadership can be seen in both Shun Wah's and Roseman's leadership styles, yet is differently nuanced. Shun Wah's version may be slightly more attuned, as she helps to bring the creative material into reality, while Roseman's may be more linked to accompaniment, as the steps taken lead towards presentation on stage. In these ways, a 'community takes shape through the circulation of diversity' (Ahmed 2012, 81) that expands the possibilities available in a multicultural arts milieu.

Conclusion

Artists and organisations take up a leadership mantle to devise new ways of working for, and in, the production and presentation of multicultural arts. Their methods of working combine both creative and organisational forms of leadership, whereby an exchange of knowledge occurs between artist, cultural broker and organisation. I argue that both creative leadership and organisational leadership working in tandem are pivotal to any new social and civil contract, and these need to be led by NESB artists who are essential contributors to a multicultural arts milieu. Creative leadership improves diverse art production and organisational leadership improves its dissemination; when working in concert, they extend those outcomes across each segment of the arts. Processes such as 'attunement' (Gibson 2005) and 'accompaniment' (Lynd and Lynd 2009) enable attentiveness that extends the modes of leadership. The observation that, in 'being spoken, and repeated in different contexts, a world takes shape around diversity' (Ahmed 2012, 81), contributes to the relational style of leadership most suited to achieve those outcomes. Ahmed articulates a principle relevant to an expanding multicultural arts milieu: that uptake needs to occur across the range of arts organisations and artists. However, multicultural arts practice can be a tremulous zone that spins on the head of a pin and requires persistent pushing into place. It is through the intercultural artistic processes used by NESB artists that increased participatory outcomes for diversity are shaped. Through the shared processes found in the modes of relational and distributed leadership, the arts can participate in the 'creation of a world'.

Epilogue: Towards a Supportive Multicultural Arts Milieu

Despite over 40 years of multicultural arts policy, my research shows that the issue of participation by non–English speaking background (NESB) artists and arts practices remains fraught. The term 'non–English speaking background' or 'NESB' has been critiqued because it positions those with that label as linguistically incomplete in terms of the dominant English language. While acknowledging this issue, I use it precisely because it positions the 'non' as a distinguishing factor and as a way to 'reinscribe the negativity' (Papastergiadis, Gunew and Blonski 1994, 128). Diverse notions of leadership have been considered so as to analyse the challenges faced by artists in a multicultural Australia, and to help foster greater participation by NESB artists and multicultural arts practices. My research aims to provide artists and arts workers with a record of their multicultural historical precedents and scalable options for professional pathways. It may also provide bureaucrats and decision-makers with theoretical discourses and case studies that demonstrate innovation.

Transactional, transformational, distributed and relational modes of leadership help to navigate the perennial issues associated with cultural difference in the arts and create a move towards a supportive and supported multicultural arts milieu. The practices of 'accompaniment' and 'attunement' enhance these leadership modes because they extend the possibilities of how trust can be established between individuals, institutions and organisations. Trust is seen as the hinge that alters the artists' experiences of friction to generate traction for change in multicultural arts policy and practices. The idea of a multicultural arts milieu helps to generate understanding of the cultural, social and political issues experienced by artists, and helps leaders to think differently about ways of increasing NESB participation in the arts.

Transactional, transformational, distributed and relational modes of leadership could be activated to realise the creative potential offered by Australia's ethnic diversity. Transactional leadership articulates expectations and ties the use of resources, including public funds, towards increasing the production and presentation of multicultural arts practices. I also suggest that funds should increasingly be directed towards NESB artists and groups rather than current practices that favour allocating 'diversity' funds to MPAs.

Transformational leadership employs charismatic personalities to effect change in groups or organisations by mobilising others' momentum towards high-profile, but often short-term, change. The charismatic personality in the multicultural arts sector is the representative who speaks up and out. Distributed leadership shares and alternates the lead role, depending on the skills needed to generate change. It can be found in multicultural arts groups or advocates whose resources are thinly spread, but who have a high degree of internal trust among group members, as was the case with kultour. Relational leadership results in longer-term change because it is based on relationship building across all levels of an organisation to identify and resource others to address specific issues. This mode of leadership is especially relevant in the institutional settings of policy development and implementation as in the Arts in a Multicultural Australia (AMA) 2000 policy process. Relational leadership can generate change in established arts organisations that are challenged to maintain attention towards cultural difference in the arts, as is the case with Contemporary Asian Australian Performance (CAAP) and Playwriting Australia's (PWA) Lotus program in relation to mainstage companies.

Each of these modes will benefit from 'accompaniment' and 'attunement'. The concept of accompaniment draws on Lynd and Lynd's (2009, 93) work; it recognises the skills and life experience that each person brings to the process of participation. In the case of a playwright and a mainstage theatre director, for example, this mutual recognition will enhance equitable knowledge sharing to benefit both artist and company. Attunement is adapted from Gibson's (2005, 272) observations concerning the complexity of understanding across multiple cultural experiences. Attunement provides a way into sensitive adjustments and amplification of issues and practices that also benefit intercultural practices. These modes and traits are all capabilities that develop through experience and supportive networks, and are most likely to be found in people in the arts already committed to seeing change in the multicultural arts milieu. The problem, then, is how best to see these capabilities develop to a greater extent as leadership capacities for multicultural arts practices.

Three domains of arts leadership have been considered: creative, institutional and organisational. Institutional leadership appears to be waning. Therefore, change towards a productive multicultural arts milieu is most effectively achieved through exercising creative leadership in combination with organisational leadership. Creative leadership refers to the role of individual artists in making new pathways for their colleagues. Organisational leadership refers to the role that leaders in arts organisations can bring to the extension of their programs and influence towards a productive and supportive multicultural arts milieu. The most productive types of leadership that generate this influence (and within a tangible timeframe) bring the creative leadership of NESB artists into partnership with resourced arts organisations resulting in organisational leadership for the arts in a multicultural Australia. This idea moves beyond the 'placement' method (where an artist resides for a time within an organisation) to a partnership model in which the knowledge, experience and networks of each partner are shared and work in tandem to produce and present artworks that reflect and respond to a multicultural Australia.

Policy, Problems and Practices

My analysis of the relationship between Australian arts and cultural policies and the fostering of creative practices among NESB artists leads me to conclude that there is no longer an explicit national policy directing attention to NESB artists. Consequently, many NESB artists have taken up the mantle for broader arts sector change through their own practices. It is worth exploring whether Australian multicultural arts policies enabled the 'mainstream' to change and/or whether artists continue to work in marginalised spaces. The AMA 2000 and 2006 policies aimed to address issues of participation of NESB artists through kultour, the Multicultural Arts Professional Development (MAPD) program and regular conferencing. These initiatives no longer exist; therefore, artists continue to drive change. Many artists, such as Shun Wah, Koukias and Valamanesh, prefer to be considered as part of the 'mainstream' while others, such as Ramilo, prefer to stay on the margins, which they view as a much 'more interesting place to be'. The role of focused multicultural arts organisations such as kultour (now Diversity Arts Australia) and CAAP is valuable in generating a supportive networked environment that can broker wider exposure for artists.

The ways in which artists maintain their arts practices and draw on their hybrid and multiple identities will describe, influence and critique Australia's cultural landscape. These art practices highlight the types of leadership that foster the expression of the complexity of identity in contemporary Australia.

As is to be expected, NESB artists participate to a greater extent in non–linguistic based artforms (Throsby and Petetskaya 2017, 147). However, fluctuating and low levels of participation are curiously found in the community arts sector (Throsby and Zednick 2010, 24; Throsby and Petetskaya 2017, 143). Data on community arts participation are in marked contrast to historical and current arts sector perceptions that NESB artists work predominantly in ethnic communities (Gonsalves 2017). Such data would benefit from further research, as they raise questions about changing levels of NESB artists' participation and how ethnic communities' arts engagement is being creatively facilitated.

Multicultural Arts Milieu

The idea of a 'multicultural arts milieu' represents a new use of a concept that refers to the social context of organisational and informal networks that encourage or constrain a creative environment. It is the environment that helps to define, organise and maintain the relations of interaction in any given context. A supportive multicultural arts milieu would resource and engage with the creative potential afforded by a multicultural society (see Image 24).

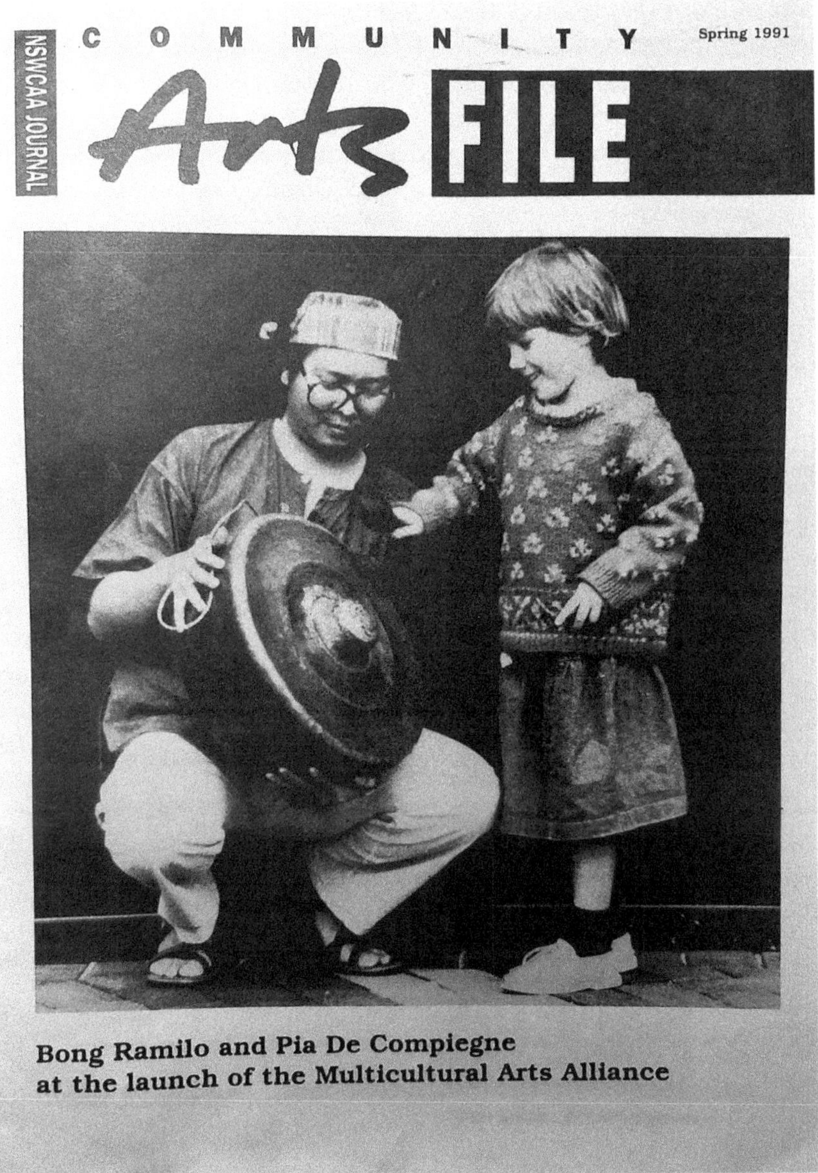

Image 24: Bong Ramilo with Pia De Compiegne, 1991, launch of the New South Wales Multicultural Arts Association

Photographer: New South Wales Community Arts Association

The idea of a multicultural arts milieu developed as a means of analysing the lack of change for inclusion in the arts expressed by many NESB artists. A milieu moves the discussion into a different register—beyond the focus on individuals' experiences, the responsibilities of arts organisations and/or the institutional relations that are typically foregrounded in arts governance. The artists who were interviewed for this project, regardless of the stage of their careers, appeared confident in their creative and personal identities, but articulated concerns about perception and the lack of knowledge about their arts practices in their arts environment. For example, they complained about being ethnically typecast on stage or screen or through their practice, and about having to balance expectations regarding the creative use of their cultural heritage in an industry that fails to understand their practices. Many also articulated a desire for peer and family support networks.

A multicultural arts milieu can be used to gauge changes within an arts environment, such as whether the milieu can encompass the increasing numbers of artists who express multiple identities and how artists keep pace with changes in intercultural arts practices. The concept of a multicultural arts milieu contests the perception that multicultural arts are outmoded and static, and provides a way to locate the dynamic shifts of arts practice. The idea opens up possibilities across the arts spectrum for practitioners to consider how they may wish to contribute to an environment that holds all the aspects of UNESCO's 'culture cycles' in play (Mar and Ang 2015, 11). A supportive multicultural arts milieu could become an open invitation to participate—to provide spaces for collaboration, negotiation, new ideas and active profiling of multicultural arts work.

The idea was also developed in part through the Australia Council's reluctance to engage in a transparent manner with multicultural issues. A supportive multicultural arts milieu does not deny the history of embattled discourse. Instead (and even if, for some artists, their experience may remain embattled), conceptually, it offers a chance for the Australia Council to exert an influential role beyond that of the 'instrumental' (Blonski 1992, 3). The most agile approaches contributing to the milieu are those discussed in Chapter 6, whereby creative and organisational leadership combines to make a systemic difference (these are also charted in Appendices 4 and 5) in the development, production and presentation of culturally diverse arts. The impetus for this particular case study's process was stimulated by the friction caused by the marginalised position of Asian-Australian actors and performance on the mainstage.

My conclusions reflect on the role of friction and the function of trust to generate traction towards sustained change in the arts, and the modes of leadership that can cultivate that traction.

Creative Use of Friction

The metaphor of 'friction' contains the potential for productive and creative results as a source of inspiration and innovation and I have used this metaphor to explain some of the creative, social and political experiences of NESB artists working in Australia today. The practices reveal creative choices across a complex spectrum of arts and artforms. Despite this, many mainstream major performing arts companies retain a heritage arts view of multicultural arts, which perpetuates a historical association with cultural maintenance, demarcating multicultural arts from mainstream arts (Blonski 1992; Hawkins 1993; Khan et al. 2013). Some NESB artists, even international experts in specific traditional artforms, feel that the arts industry sees them as relevant primarily to ethnic community cultural maintenance (Gonsalves 2017). One response to this is that, over the decades, NESB artists have explored artistic innovation through a spectrum of creative processes. The spectrum ranges from ethno-specific to intra-cultural to bicultural to intercultural to cross-cultural and, more recently, to transcultural categories. These 'multicultural arts' or 'hybrid' practices are at the forefront of collaborative practices that engage with the complex multiplicity of Australian ethnic and cultural identities. I argue that the creative developments of artists who engage across ethnically defined cultures dynamically increases the multicultural arts repertoire. The range of that repertoire, often developed through a creativity arising from friction between cultural forms, whether innovative or traditional, positions these practices into a more 'everyday' experience of how art-based cross-cultural interactions can occur.

Far from seeing friction as inherently problematic, the nature of artistic practice and multicultural challenges to settled notions of identity show how friction can be creatively, organisationally and politically productive. The frictions around multicultural arts policy recur in cycles, and these begin when artists critique their creative environments and funding institutions, which, nationally, is primarily the Australia Council, and when they acknowledge and direct attention to their issues. This attention invariably wanes when the Australia Council shifts its focus elsewhere;

historically, this cycle repeats itself when faced with the continuing issues raised by NESB artists. Television and stage actor and presenter Lex Marinos (2015, interview) notes that calls for change by practitioners within the performing arts industry occur every four or five years. The institutional cycle appears to take around 10 years, because each decade since the 1970s has seen a renewed push for change by practitioners. This cycle began again in 2017 (DARTS 2017).

The contributions that arise from discourse and advocacy are valuable; however, I argue that the most effective results stem from the presentation of artworks that successfully engage with Australian cultural difference. In this way, the artist takes on a sociopolitical as well as creative leadership role in the multicultural arts milieu that, in part, requires them to develop trusting relationships with any number of agencies and partners.

Establishing Trust

The productive nature of friction is most evident when there are established relations of trust between the multicultural arts milieu and the wider arts scene, between artists, and between artists and key organisations within the sector. This is a role for 'cultural brokers' (Kurin 1997, 17) and involves artists and dedicated multicultural arts organisations initiating and persisting with the brokering processes that establish trust.

In the way I have used it, trust functions to tease out some of the intercultural relationships as well as gaps between the NESB artist and the mainstream arts sector. Until recently, arts policy has been used to address those gaps but, increasingly, artists must manage those gaps as well as their creative practices. My research has explored the use of trust as a way to productively engage NESB artists' experiences in changing the dynamics of the arts sectors. Trust is most succinctly defined as a 'specific solution to risk' (Luhmann 2000, 95). This definition justifies the inclusion of trust across the full spectrum of the arts sectors, including artists, funding institutions and presenting organisations. In its most basic form, 'trust is established when you do what you say you would do' in an ethical manner and with all the relevant 'processes, platforms and people' in place (Punt and Bateman 2018, 39). Taken in an even wider sense, there is the potential for significant outcomes when trust is reciprocated because 'theories of trust can serve as a tool to become aware of the human ability to cooperate' (Weltecke 2008, 391).

The issues raised by the interviewees in this study highlight the need for more and better trust in the arts. Interviewees advised how they sometimes experienced lack of understanding on the part of 'arts gatekeepers' as lack of trust in their creative endeavours. This occurred across facets such as devising content, securing funding, presenting and marketing. The potential for a broader multicultural arts milieu expands when trust is evident between artists, institutional staff and advisers, arts organisations and the public.

Methods to Generate Trust

There are several methods that the arts can employ to increase the participation of NESB artists. Some methods suggest that simulacrums of trust are more suited to institutions and can be stimulated through transactional means such as conditions on funding. Other approaches stimulate more trusting working relationships through different means of organisational interactions.

For example, the Australian screen sector has successfully used quotas to improve gender parity (Castagna 2017). An approach adopted by Arts Council England (2018) stipulates the conditions of socio-economic inclusion in the awarding of a particular arts grant. The Australia Council has not used quotas for multicultural arts practice since the late 1990s. However, implicitly acknowledging their low levels of funding, a 2016 Australia Council strategic goal aims to grant 14 per cent of funding to culturally and linguistically diverse (CALD) artists and organisations by 2020.

Another method of trust combines transactional and relational forms of leadership, such as the protocols for non-Indigenous people working with Indigenous artists. These protocols address issues of respect, behaviour and intellectual property (Janke 2016), and are transparent and transactional because they explicitly articulate the conditions under which this kind of cross-cultural work can occur.

Trust can also be acknowledged through a relational mode of leadership. This can be seen in a memorandum of understanding (MoU), whereby the parties enter into an agreement that they jointly develop based on agreed and perceived mutual benefits. MoUs are developed after a period of familiarisation that has led to greater understanding and agreement between the parties.

Opportunities to increase familiarity may also establish trust through increased exposure. Recent AMA initiatives such as kultour and MAPD included aims of increased exposure. Likewise, the work of CAAP provides a conduit for trust between Asian-Australian writers and mainstream creative producers.

Trust needs to be evident between the artist and the institution. This can be generated through recruiting NESB artists as assessment and advisory peers. The Australia Council Multicultural Advisory Committee (ACMAC) was effective at developing generations of artist advocates and stimulating sector-wide critical discourse. This process of equipping NESB artists as peers and advocates within an institutional setting has yet to be replaced. The establishment of a structured program would be valuable to ensure those capacities can be well developed in future generations.

In these ways, trust acts as a hinge that articulates and enables communication between a range of players across any given multicultural art project. The results of establishing trust can generate traction towards a robust, ethnically diverse arts sector.

Generating Traction

Traction suggests both grip and movement. It can be generated through the creative use of friction in conjunction with a trusting environment. The processes that generate traction will lead to longer-term change and reduce cycles of limited change. It can be generated when NESB artists and arts organisations align their goals and work together, utilising and acknowledging their different sets of expertise, resources and influence. Long-term traction will also depend on issues of equitable resourcing and the development of platforms to enable the succession of leadership roles. Both issues are yet to be resolved for NESB artists and multicultural arts organisations. The work entailed in maintaining the partnership momentum must be financially validated, otherwise the NESB artist or multicultural arts organisation will always be the unsustainable 'volunteer' in the process. The persistence of the artist and cultural practitioner leads to creative, institutional and organisational change by revealing the dynamic nature of Australian identities and continually prompting the arts sector to engage with the creative potential of multicultural Australia.

The number of successful transitions into the mainstream afforded through the Lotus program highlights how swiftly creative capacities can build when the leaders of organisations share similar values and aims. The creative and organisational leadership roles demonstrated by CAAP and PWA provide symbolic value and expand the economic value chain proposition to include an awareness of audience reception based on presentation of form and marketing context. Most significantly, this process for the production of performing arts can be adapted to other art spheres to provide an alternative to the traditional 'placement' model of one NESB artist in a large organisation.

The 'pathway' processes and range of partnerships developed by CAAP and PWA in the Lotus program reinforce a productive phase towards the next step in a professional career, recognition by industry and programming that expands audiences. The creative and organisational skills of the artists share the characteristics of persistence, steadfast adherence to vision and flexibility in its realisation, highly nuanced negotiation skills and a commitment to change beyond their immediate sphere. The artists and the multicultural arts milieu to which they contribute form what Ahmed (2012, 139) describes as the 'backbone' of diversity work. Such artists take on the responsibility for diversity in the arts as they wish to see them, rather than engaging only with the often tokenistic options offered by institutions or mainstream organisations suffering from 'equity fatigue' (Ahmed 2012, 90, 139):

> Because diversity and race equality are not already mainstream—because everything is 'not okay'—we need support, specialisms and drivers. Practitioners or experts provide a backbone. When mainstreaming is taken up as if it describes what already exists, then mainstreaming is used by the organisations to avoid appointing specialists in the area, or indeed to avoid giving diversity and equality the additional support that it needs.

The avoidance of mainstreaming applies to the scaling back of dedicated multicultural arts programs that began in 2008 with the end of ACMAC and the low participation rates of NESB artists. Methods that successfully intervene in the prevailing temporary 'one-off project' nature of multicultural arts practice in Australia establish more visible pathways. These pathways, which are examples of creative and organisational leadership working in concert, demonstrate a new version of the 'backbone' of Australian multicultural arts practice in which a more robust multicultural arts milieu could emerge. The NESB artists are the ones who show leadership and 'make a new door' to gain entrance to the arts industry (Badami 2017).

The types of consultations that occur with artists as leaders and peers at the institutional site of the Australia Council cause a range of frictions. The significant redirection of federal and state funding away from multicultural arts organisations (see Table 4) is compounded by the absence of an identifiable national creative centre or hub for producing art in a multicultural Australia. Therefore, NESB artists and groups must locate receptive arts organisations that have the capacity and capability to produce work from multicultural Australia.

Recent History of the Arts in a Multicultural Australia

The gap in the published history of AMA since the late 1990s is addressed in this text through the account of the aims, results and issues arising from the AMA 2000 and AMA 2006 policies. A summary timeline of the development of the arts in a multicultural Australia is provided in Appendix B. AMA 2000 brought together tradition and innovation and profiled individual artists' practices as well as their roles in the arts and the wider community. By taking this focus, the policy attempted to alter perceptions of multicultural artists as only being relevant in cultural community settings. As such setting have a low status in the arts world, this was a purposeful shift (Rentschler, Le and Osborne 2008, iv). The various prongs of this policy addressed a spectrum of issues through the professional and creative development program of MAPD, the national multicultural arts organisation network of kultour that toured multicultural arts practices, and two international conferences with associated publications and expert roundtable discussions. AMA 2006 identified a renewed focus in the areas of leadership, participation and creative production, including between Indigenous and NESB artists. The Australia Council allocated three years of funding to three multicultural arts organisations to increase their presentation and promotion skills and hosted symposium events. Making Creative Cities: The Value of Cultural Diversity in the Arts, held in conjunction with the British Council in 2008, was the last formal AMA international event. The forum pointed out the value of different leadership modes for cultural difference in the arts that I have extended to encompass relevant modes of leadership across creative, institutional and organisational domains.

Creative Leadership

Artists demonstrate creative leadership in their capacity for social, creative and political agency within the Australian arts sector. Alongside their hybrid identities, NESB artists also develop capacities to navigate differences arising from intercultural (in terms of artistic practice as well as ethnicity), intergenerational and linguistic spheres. Their navigation of the arts industry is often from a marginal position that, in the past, has prompted an almost inevitably political response towards change in the arts. These political responses include pushing the boundaries of traditional/conventional perceptions of the canon and creative adaptations of cultural heritage. These elements are aspects that define a multicultural arts milieu. Creative leaders take on the additional mantle to shift that milieu to one that provides greater support and understanding of their arts practices.

The theme of creativity from friction identifies creative leadership as a key driver contributing to a multicultural arts sector. Artists who lead 'just by making art' are creative leaders, as visual artist Valamanesh observed. However, creative leadership is more evident in those who also create spaces or pathways for other artists, whether as mentors, through peer networks or by establishing arts organisations to increase creative opportunities for NESB artists. Individual artists are often seen as torchbearers of cultural translation, a perception that both reifies and implicitly limits how many artists of NESB backgrounds can carry such a torch. Papastergiadis (2000, 134) observes that arguments for expanding the 'cultural boundaries of art [are accompanied by a] fetishization of the alterity' of the marginalised artist who acts as translator between the periphery and the centre. He also observes that recognition of the influence of those individual artists has not been met with similar arts educational and industry frameworks to understand the significance of cultural differences (Papastergiadis 2000, 134).

Creative leadership is demonstrated when the artist recognises the need to forge some of those frameworks and, in doing so, goes beyond their own practice. In this way, the charismatic and transformational form of leadership mostly associated with individual practitioners is altered through a closer attentiveness to the needs of other artists. This suggests that the iterative communication process of 'attunement' (Gibson 2005, 271)—a process relevant across all domains of leadership—is particularly appropriate in the complex environments that stimulate the practices of NESB artists.

Institutional Leadership

The conceptual understanding of institutional leadership refers to modes needed for both management and advocates. Transactional leadership clarifies responsibilities and relational leadership is likely to generate a culture that will see those responsibilities embedded in the most effective ways. Both of these modes apply to the internal management responses of the Australia Council and how NESB artists' interactions led to policy responses for the arts in a multicultural Australia. Three traits can be discerned from the 1970s to the 2010s. First, multicultural issues are discarded in times of financial constraint and internal instability, which suggests that the arts in a multicultural Australia is not a core area of concern. When the will is present to address uneven responses to the creative potential of multicultural Australia, it is linked to a second trait of sustained support for, and use of, multicultural advisory committees (Blonski 1992, 1–5). A third trait demonstrates sustained engagement by the Australia Council in multicultural arts; this occurred when ACMAC and NESB artists were central to the institution's overall strategic direction, as was the case with AMA 2000.

During the implementation stage of AMA 2006, the Australia Council concluded its historical relationship of sustained engagement with NESB artists as artform board appointments and expert policy advisers. Regardless of how fraught or fruitful that engagement had been, ACMAC was a mainstay of the Australia Council's work and made a space for complex and creative policy discourse. ACMAC served as a conduit between the arts sector and the Australia Council, contributed significantly to the discourse of multicultural arts and was central to the direction taken by the institution. It appears that the council's decision to end ACMAC in 2008 and its subsequent decline as a leader in multicultural arts are linked. A policy response from the Australia Council regarding the arts in a multicultural Australia has yet to be fully articulated.

When a history is neither documented nor critically reflected upon, the risk of unproductive circular debates and repetitive institutional responses increases. When I began this research in 2014, AMA 2006 was the Australia Council's extant statement on its approach to the arts in a multicultural Australia. By the end of the study in mid-2018, all references to multicultural arts policy had disappeared from the Australia Council's website, reinforcing their institutional retreat from this area. The goal to increase grants to CALD artists was not accompanied by a published 'cultural diversity' plan. Unless and until a change of leadership prompts a different institutional approach, it seems that AMA 2006 was the Australia Council's final policy on the arts in a multicultural Australia.

Organisational Leadership

Cross-cultural competencies have been shown as essential skills for navigating a 'hyper-diverse' multicultural Australia, and cultural aspects, such as the arts and media, demonstrate the most resistance to long-term inclusion. It is the artists from diverse ethnic backgrounds who continue to take responsibility for increasing the level of culturally diverse creative production. This is most effectively achieved when leaders of arts organisations form partnerships to equitably share knowledge and resources to develop and present new multicultural arts content.

Traction can be generated in several ways, as shown in the leadership modes evident throughout the case studies explored in this book. For example, the writer and director Shakthidharan drew on the infrastructure of a major arts presenter, Carriageworks, and, subsequently, Belvoir Street Theatre. The development phase of his play, *Counting and Cracking*, took more than a decade; it was finally presented at the Sydney Festival in 2019. This points to Shakthidharan's persistence in negotiations with mainstage companies to co-direct his play. Coupled with his charismatic personality, it demonstrates transformational leadership. This case exemplifies the erosion of resistance and development of equitable trust through persistent friction. The caveat is that the trust will not be equitable until the issue of remuneration is addressed for NESB artists.

Kultour, a successful example of distributed leadership that activated networks, foundered in the face of funders' expectations around 'mainstreaming'. By contrast, the small performing arts company CAAP, led by actor and director Shun Wah in collaboration with arts industry organisation PWA, led by arts manager Roseman, explored how to fast-track the work of Asian-Australian writers into the performing arts mainstage arena. Shun Wah demonstrates creative leadership in the form of accompaniment through creative enabling processes. Both Shun Wah and Roseman display organisational and transformational leadership through the partnerships developed on behalf of aspiring artists.

Conclusion

The concept of a more productive multicultural arts milieu forms from the space that is opened up through multicultural arts practices and discourse. It is also partly formed by having to address the inadequacies within this space, whether in the area of policy, discourse or practice. The milieu holds a number of tensions in play: institutional and mainstream diversity 'fatigue', which leads to occasional token responses rather than systemic change; low financial and creative participation rates of NESB artists; continued advocacy by NESB artists; and the formation of delicate partnerships between organisations dedicated to improving conditions for NESB artists. A productive shift can be discerned in theatre through the increased numbers of scripts from NESB writers that are presented on stage. This shift, which is partly documented in this book, has been led by a handful of determined NESB artists over the past several years to address their ongoing marginalised position in the arts.

The creative responses of artists include their interactions through governance in the federal arts institution and organisational partnerships that foster opportunities for swift change in the profile of creative content. The projects I have presented here are not large in scale but they are influential in the scope of their potential. Their ability to scale up is dependent on understandings of the finesse of their niche approaches. Taken one by one, each project can be seen as small wins; in combination they show the resilient capacity of artists to continue the 'fight' and, in confluence with mainstream organisations, energise a productive multicultural arts milieu.

Hitherto conventional methods of placing NESB artists into mainstream arts organisations or the national funding agency as part-time 'champions' have achieved limited success. The significance of the partnership between CAAP and PWA is that both companies maintain their specific creative and organisational identities and capabilities to achieve mutual aims.

Multicultural Arts Victoria (MAV) is the most successful multicultural arts organisation in Australia, both in terms of its longevity and its ability to secure recurrent funding that provides appropriate remuneration for staff and artists (MAV 2018). A national equivalent for multicultural arts practices could expand the MAV remit and partnership approach into a national focus. A national equivalent could take the form of an artform 'flagship' company, as envisioned by Paul (2018) in her ambitions for her *Theatre of Rhythm and Dance* project, or take up the blueprint of the far broader Art + Cultural Difference + Global Collaboration workshop (outlined in Appendix D), which proposed that academics, bureaucrats, artists and organisations partner in dialogue and action to see a more supportive multicultural arts milieu.

General leadership courses are proliferating in the arts in Australia; these would benefit from a critical assessment of the extent to which they address the arts in a multicultural Australia or merely replicate the standard management practices of the arts industry. The UK's Clore Foundation arts leadership program has diversity as its central aim (Clore Leadership Foundation n.d.). Among the range of leadership issues to be addressed in Australia are the capabilities required as an NESB peer assessor and multicultural arts adviser. The opportunity to gain such experience has diminished significantly with the disbanding of ACMAC and the introduction of short-term peer assessors, resulting in a diminution of long-term, arts sector–based knowledge.

Capacity building within an arts institutional setting is accompanied by a palpable need for NESB artist networks. Access to supportive peers continues to be raised specifically by NESB artists (Stevenson et al. 2017, 54). The reinvigoration of national opportunities to develop current critical discourse could go part way towards addressing this issue. The conferences and publications supported by ACMAC in the early 2000s remain a key legacy, but these have not been revisited on a similar international scale since 2004. The artistic opportunities afforded through the friction of an increasingly diverse society remain at the cutting edge of cultural production that would benefit from more well-curated conferencing and publications.

Despite the proactive and creative energies of artists, the findings of this research indicate that the issues for the arts in a multicultural Australia have not diminished. The NESB artists in this research lead the arts sector across creative, institutional and organisational activities in several ways.

They do the 'work' that symbolises the complexity of cultural identities. They also do the 'work' to negotiate with mainstage and gallery directors and to engage diverse audiences. They are entrepreneurial. They have to be, as there is limited government support for their work. They carry the burden and take the risk of untangling the representation of complex Australian lives.

Meta-themes of leadership across three domains of the arts frame the relationship between practice, policy and the environment that surrounds the artist. The experiences and creative endeavours of artists and how their artworks articulate complex understandings show how they creatively lead as artists, citizens, activists, 'ethnics' and Australians. Organisational leadership is found in situations in which artists and arts organisations work towards a supportive multicultural arts milieu that expands the aesthetic canon of the arts to include their practices and also a different Australia, which is both more inclusive of difference and more open to engagement with creative work. Institutional leadership for AMA policies articulates a quest for change, but the processes need to be carefully tailored, well supported and continual. By paying 'detailed attention to the very *process* of creating a sense of "we" in the face of our heterogeneity' (Ang 2003a, 33, original emphasis), I argue that it is artists who make creative meaning from the 'friction' caused by the contestations and negotiations of multicultural Australia. It is artists who gain the trust to generate traction for structural change.

Appendix A: Participant Biographies

Interviewees

Jennifer Bott. Interview date: 20 May 2015.

Bott is a former director of the Portrait Gallery, Canberra, ACT, and CEO of the Australia Council.

Panos Couros. Interview date: 9 September 2016.

Couros is a sound designer, media artist and cultural producer.

Lisa Havilah. Interview date: 27 May 2015.

Havilah is the CEO of the Museum for Arts and Applied Sciences and was a former CEO of Carriageworks, a contemporary multi-arts centre based in Redfern, Sydney.

Su Hoyle. Interview date: 7 July 2015.

Hoyle was the director of England's Clore Leadership Programme.

Abid Hussain. Interview date: 7 July 2015.

Hussain is Senior Manager for Diversity at Arts Council England, the national development agency for the arts in England.

Deborah Klika. Interview date: 8 May 2015.

Klika is an academic, author and television comedy scriptwriter. Her 2018 text *Situation Comedy, Character, and Psychoanalysis: On the Couch with Lucy, Basil and Kimmie* was published by Bloomsbury Academic, New York. She is a former chair of the Australia Council's Community Cultural Development Board (CCDB), Multicultural Advisory Committee (ACMAC) and Youth Arts programs.

Konstantin Koukias. Interview date: 17 August 2015.

Koukias is a 'Greek-Tasmanian' composer and the artistic director of the experimental opera company IHOS Opera, now based in Amsterdam.

Anna Lau. Interview date: 17 August 2015.

Lau is a playwright and blogger and a young woman of Taiwanese-Malaysian parentage. She was working as a receptionist at the Sydney Theatre Company at the time of her interview.

Sean Ly. Interview date: 28 May 2015.

Ly, a 24-year-old Cambodian-Australian, was a youth arts organiser for Fairfield Council and assistant director on CuriousWorks' feature film *Riz*. Ly has since enrolled in a tertiary and further education course to gain a youth worker certificate.

Lex Marinos. Interview date: 12 May 2015.

Marinos is a Greek-Australian actor, presenter, writer and director for screen, stage and radio. He is a former deputy chair of the Australia Council, and former chair of CCDB and ACMAC.

Pino Migliorino. Interview date: 5 April 2017.

Migliorino is Chair and Managing Director of the Cultural Perspectives Group.

Vinh Nguyen. Interview date: 28 May 2015.

Nguyen is a 24-year-old freelance videographer who studied at University of Technology Sydney and whose parents came to Australia as Vietnamese refugees.

Frank Panucci. Interview date: 20 May 2015.

Panucci is a former executive director of Arts Funding and Engagement at the Australia Council.

Annalouise Paul. Interview date: 5 May 2015.

Paul is a dancer, choreographer and actor who has been practising internationally for over 30 years. She established Groundswell in NSW in 2011.

Bong Ramilo. Interview date: 6 May 2015.

Ramilo is the executive officer of Darwin Community Arts and a musician. He was a member of kultour.

Tim Roseman. Interview date: 9 June 2015.

Roseman is a former CEO of Playwriting Australia. He is a director, dramaturg and producer.

S. Shakthidharan. Interview date: 5 May 2015.

Shakthidharan is a community engaged artist and playwright/co-director of *Counting and Cracking*. He is the founder and director of Kurinji. He is the founder and was the creative director of CuriousWorks until 2018.

Annette Shun Wah. Interview date: 3 June 2015.

Shun Wah is Executive Producer at Contemporary Asian Australia Performance, Sydney. She is a broadcaster and writer, and a producer of television and theatre.

Nicholas Tsoutas. Interview date: 5 April 2017.

Tsoutas is a visual arts curator and was a member of ACMAC.

Sandar Tun. Interview date: 9 December 2015.

Tun is an emerging community arts worker at Darwin Community Arts.

Hossein Valamanesh. Interview date: 9 December 2015.

Valamanesh is a visual artist. He was born in Iran and graduated from the School of Fine Art, Tehran, in 1970. He exhibits frequently in Australia and overseas.

Email Correspondence

Annette Blonski is a scriptwriter and film director. Her email communication was received on 9 September 2017.

Linda Cooper is Director of Ninti One and was a member of ACMAC. Her email communication was received on 14 December 2016.

Teresa Crea is a research associate at the Centre for Creative and Cultural Research at the University of Canberra and was a member of ACMAC. Her email communication was received on 19 December 2016.

Kon Gouriotis is the editor and managing director of *Artist Profile* and was a member of ACMAC. His email communication was received on 28 February 2017.

Connie Gregory is a literary editor and was a member of the Literature Board and ACMAC. Her email communication was received on 19 December 2016.

Fotis Kapetopoulos manages Kape Communications and was a member of ACMAC. His email communication was received on 4 December 2016.

Tiffany Lee-Shoy is Senior Strategic Project Leader (Culture Strategy) at the City of Parramatta. She was previously a manager at Fairfield City Council and was a member of ACMAC. Her email communication was received on 19 December 2016.

Lex Marinos's email communication was received on 14 September 2020.

Lena Nahlous is Director of Diversity Arts Australia. Her email communication was received on 30 August 2017.

S. Shakthidharan's email communication was received on 19 October 2017.

Appendix B: Chronology

Table 5: Chronology of multicultural arts policy at the Australia Council

Year	Multicultural arts policy stage at the Australia Council
1967	Prime Minister Harold Holt establishes the Australian Council for the Arts as part of the Prime Minister's Department with an allocation of AU$4.6 million (Gardiner-Garden 2009, 1).
1968	First meeting of the Australian Council for the Arts. Chair: Dr H. C. Coombs.
1973	Prime Minister Gough Whitlam establishes the Australia Council (based on the British and Canadian models) with 24 councillors and seven boards: Aboriginal arts, crafts, film and television, literature, music, theatre and visual arts, with funds of AU$14 million (Gardiner-Garden 2009, 2).
1974	An Ethnic Arts Committee is formed and chaired by Evasio Costanzo (Gardiner-Garden 1994, 16).
1974–75	The Community Arts Committee distributes AU$44,682 to 'ethnic projects', 4.5 per cent of the total budget for 1974–75 (Hawkins 1993, 42).
1975	The Australia Council Act is legislated as a statutory body. The Ethnic Arts Committee is disbanded (Gardiner-Garden 1994,16).
1976	Australia Council staff support ethnic arts (Blonski 1992, 7).
1977	Prime Minister Malcolm Fraser announces a Community Arts Board (Gardiner-Garden 1994, 15).
1978	The *Galbally Report: A Review of Post-Arrival Programs and Services for Migrants* finds the Australia Council 'deficient' and recommends increased connections with 'ethnic communities' to redress budgetary inequalities for 'ethnic arts' (Gardiner-Garden 1994, 16).
1980	A committee meets twice to consider the Arts Council's response to the Galbally Report but does not institute 'programs or policy initiatives' (Blonski 1992, 7).
1982	Institute of Multicultural Affairs finds that Galbally's recommendations have not been addressed (Blonski 1992, 6).
1982	The Arts Council accepts Galbally's recommendations and employs an ethnic arts officer. AU$250,000 is dedicated to ethnic arts activity to be matched by the boards (Australia Council 1982, 17–18).

Year	Multicultural arts policy stage at the Australia Council
1985	Terminology shifts from 'ethnic' arts to 'multicultural' arts, coinciding with the establishment of the Multicultural Advisory Committee. The central Incentive Fund allocation for multicultural arts is reported to be AU$1,030,000 in 1984–85 (Australia Council 1985, 36).
1986	Multicultural arts are defined during this time as the 'practice of artistic traditions (popular, folk or high arts) of immigrants and people descendant [*sic*] from non-English speaking backgrounds'. AU$1.3 million, or 3 per cent of Arts Council funding, supports the multicultural arts policy (Jupp quoted in Bennett 2001, 269).
1988	A national conference, Arts Policy for a Multicultural Australia, is held in Adelaide, a joint initiative of the Multicultural Artworkers Committee of South Australia, the Community Cultural Development Unit and the Office of Multicultural Affairs (Australia Council 1988, 22–23).
1990	The Australia Council Multicultural Advisory Committee (ACMAC) is established by membership of each artform board and Aboriginal and Torres Strait Islander Arts to develop policy (Australia Council 1991, 12).
1991–92	The Arts Council's overall Arts for a Multicultural Australia expenditure is 8.8 per cent (Australia Council 1992, 21).
1991–92	The Australia Council and the Office of Multicultural Affairs co-sponsors the National Arts for a Multicultural Australia Working Party composed of all state arts funding authorities and ethnic affairs commissions to develop Arts for a Multicultural Australia policies across Australia. This is endorsed by the Cultural Ministers' Council and the Immigration and Ethnic Affairs Ministers' Council (Australia Council 1992, 22).
1993	New Arts for a Multicultural Australia policy released. 'It is increasingly acknowledged that Australia derives enormous advantages from its cultural diversity' (Australia Council 1994, 27).
1999	The Arts Council releases a draft discussion paper in the lead up to the next Arts for a Multicultural Australia policy. ACMAC notes that 'over the past decade the field, and even the definition and use of the term multiculturalism has broadened to encompass a wide variety of arts practice and content' (Jupp quoted in Bennett 2001, 270).
2000	New Arts in a Multicultural Australia (AMA) policy launched. The key characteristics include a five-year strategic vision that is outwardly focused and applies real investments in the field (Australia Council 2001, 21–22).
2000–05	More than AU$2 million in dedicated funds to AMA initiatives is expended (Keating, Bertone and M. Leahy n.d.).
2002	Globalisation, Art + Cultural Difference international conference held in Sydney. (Convened by Tsoutas and Papastergiadis, resulting in Papastergiadis ed. 2003. *Complex Entanglements: Art, Globalisation + Cultural Difference.*)
2003	Empires, Ruins and Networks international conference held in Melbourne, resulting in McGuire and Papastergiadis, eds. 2004. *Empires, Ruins and Networks: The Transcultural Agenda in Art.*

Year	Multicultural arts policy stage at the Australia Council
2004	A review of the AMA policy is commenced to assess the extent to which its objectives have been achieved, current issues in the field and strategies for 2005 (Australia Council 2004, 17).
2004	The Australia Council meets all applicable key performance indicators against *The Charter of Public Service in a Culturally Diverse Society* (Australia Council 2004, 50).
2004	'AMA 2000 Evaluation' presented to the Arts Council.
2006	ACMAC develops AMA 2006. Australia Council ratifies AMA 2006 with AU$600,000 over three years (Australia Council 2007).
2007	Multicultural Arts: Cultural Citizenship for the 21st Century held at Parliament House in November. Senior bureaucrats from each state and territory, academics and artists attend (Australia Council 2007).
2007	ACMAC is disbanded in December (Australia Council 2009, 20).
2008	The Cultural Engagement Framework is introduced and includes the arts in a multicultural Australia (Australia Council 2009, 20).
2009–11	The Australia Council and the Human Rights and Equal Opportunity Commission partner in an AU$660,000 initiative with Muslim Australians to build cultural participation, skills and mutual respect (Australia Council 2009, 20).
2011	The Australia Council's Corporate Plan contains two 'multicultural' references. 'Diverse', however, occurs many times and with reference to a range of administrative, strategic or artistic pursuits (Australia Council 2011, 39, 42).
2014	Increased participation in the arts in under-represented communities includes regional Australia, disability, young people, cultural diversity, emerging communities, Indigenous people, and remote Indigenous communities (Australia Council 2014a, 24).
2016	The Corporate Plan aims for a 14 per cent target of culturally and linguistically diverse artists (Australia Council 2016b).
2017	Major Performing Arts companies can apply for increased funds to work with artists across all diversity areas (Australia Council n.d.-e).
2018	The AMA policies are no longer found on the Australia Council website.

Appendix C: Governance

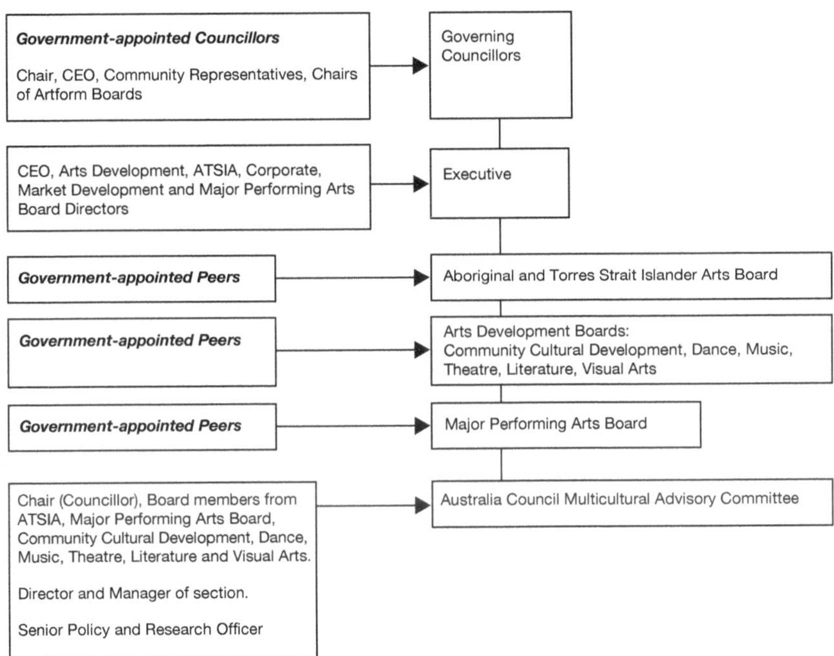

Figure 1: Governance structure of the Australia Council, 2006–11

Appendix D: Art + Cultural Difference + Global Collaboration

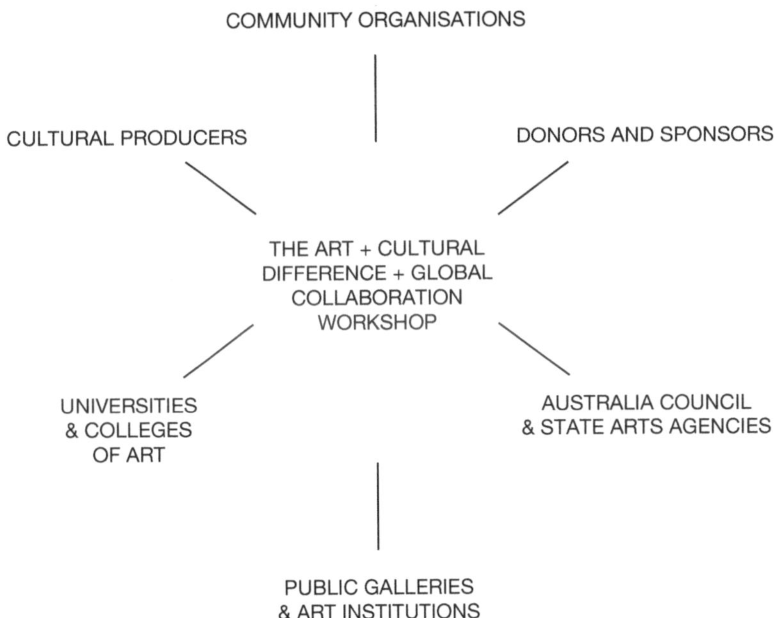

Figure 2: Art + Cultural Difference + Global Collaboration workshop

Source: Australia Council Multicultural Advisory Committee (n.d.-b)

Appendix E: Cycle of Change

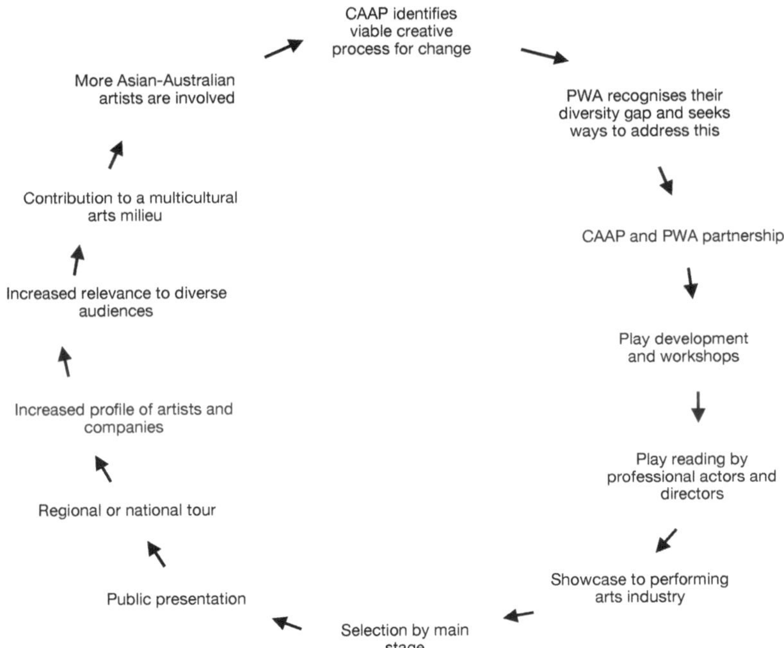

Figure 3: Contemporary Asian Australian Performance and Playwriting Australia. Cycle of change using creative and organisational leadership

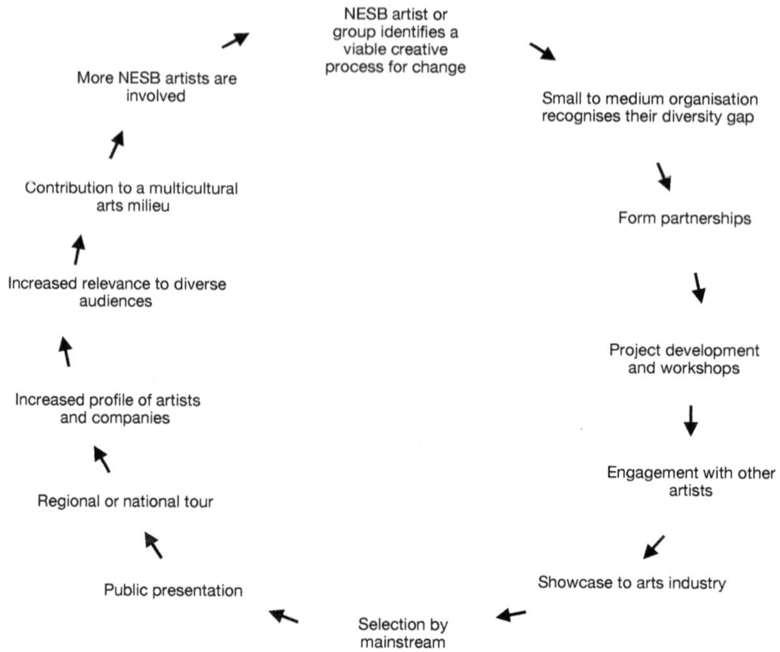

Figure 4: Cycle of change using creative and organisational leadership

References

4A Centre for Contemporary Asian Art. 2017. 'About 4A'. Accessed 20 April 2018. www.4a.com.au/about-4a/.

Adelaide Festival Centre. 2007. *OzAsia 07*. Accessed 7 February 2018. www.ozasia festival.com.au/media/2218/ozasia-2007-brochure.pdf.

Ahmed, S. 2012. *On Being Included: Racism and Diversity in Institutional Life*. Durham: Duke University Press. doi.org/10.1515/9780822395324.

Anatolitis, E. 2010. 'Multicultural Arts: Always Already Mainstream'. *Real Time Arts*, no. 98. Accessed 19 April 2015. www.realtimearts.net/article/issue98/9954.

Andrew, P. 2011. 'Bagryana Popov'. *Australian Stage*, 1 July. Accessed 18 April 2017. www.australianstage.com.au/201106304527/features/melbourne/bagryana-popov.html.

Ang, I. 2001. *On Not Speaking Chinese: Living Between Asia and the West*. London: Routledge.

Ang, I. 2003a. 'Cultural Translation in a Globalised World'. In *Complex Entanglements: Art, Globalisation and Cultural Difference*, edited by N. Papastergiadis, 30–41. London: Rivers Oram Press.

Ang, I. 2003b. 'Together-in-Difference: Beyond Diaspora into Hybridity'. *Asian Studies Review* 27 (2): 141–54. doi.org/10.1080/10357820308713372.

Ang, I. 2011. 'Navigating Complexity: From Cultural Critique to Cultural Intelligence'. *Continuum* 25 (6): 779–94. doi.org/10.1080/10304312.2011.617873.

Ang, I. 2015. 'Stuart Hall and the Tension between Academic and Intellectual Work'. *International Journal of Cultural Studies* vol. 19 (1): 29–41. doi.org/10.1177/1367877915599609.

Ang, I., J. Brand, G. Noble and J. Sternberg. 2006. *Connecting Diversity: Paradoxes of Multicultural Australia*. Robina, Qld: Bond University.

Ang, I., J. Brand, G. Noble and D. Wilding. 2002. *Living Diversity: Australia's Multicultural Future*. Robina, Qld: Bond University.

Ang, I., G. Hawkins and L. Dabboussy. 2008. *The SBS Story: The Challenge of Cultural Diversity*. Sydney: UNSW Press.

Ang, I. and Stratton, J. 1998. 'Multiculturalism in Crisis: The New Politics of Race and National Identity in Australia', *TOPIA: Canadian Journal of Cultural Studies* 2 (22): 22–41. doi.org/10.3138/topia.2.22.

Anheier, H. and Y. Isar. 2007. *The Cultures and Globalization Series 4: Heritage, Memory & Identity*. London: SAGE Publications.

Appignanesi, R. 2010. *Beyond Cultural Diversity: The Case for Creativity*. Third Text. Accessed 12 February 2015. www.thirdtext.org/case_for_diversity_in_britain.

Araeen, R. 2013. 'Cultural Diversity, Creativity and Modernism'. In *Debates in Art and Design Education*, edited by N. Addison and L. Burgess, 95–110. London: Routledge, London.

Art in Society. n.d. 'Empires, Ruins + Networks: Art in Real Time Culture'. Accessed 6 August 2017. www.art-in-society.de/AS2/ArtNews/Melbourne.shtml.

Artlink. 1991. 'Arts in a Multicultural Australia'. *Artlink* 11 (1/2).

Artlink. 2011. *Diaspora* [special issue], *Artlink* 31 (1). Accessed 28 February 2018. www.artlink.com.au/issues/3110/diaspora/.

Arts Council England (ACE). 2011. 'Creative Case: What is the Creative Case for Diversity?' Accessed 21 June 2014. www.artscouncil.org.uk/diversity/creative-case-diversity.

Arts Council England (ACE). 2016. *Equality Diversity and the Creative Case: A Data Report, 2015–16*. Accessed 12 January 2018. www.artscouncil.org.uk/publication/equality-diversity-and-creative-case-2015-16.

Arts Council England (ACE). 2018. *Equality Diversity and the Creative Case: A Data Report, 2016–17*. Accessed 15 January 2018. www.artscouncil.org.uk/publication/equality-diversity-and-creative-case-data-report-2016-17.

Arts Council England (ACE). n.d.-a. 'Supporting Arts, Museums and Libraries'. Accessed 12 January 2018. www.artscouncil.org.uk/what-we-do/supporting-arts-museums-and-libraries.

Arts Council England (ACE). n.d.-b. 'Diversity'. Accessed 12 January 2018. www.artscouncil.org.uk/how-we-make-impact/diversity-and-equality.

Arts Council England (ACE). n.d.-c. 'Elevate'. Accessed 21 January 2018. www. artscouncil.org.uk/funding-finder/elevate.

Australia Council for the Arts. 1982. *Annual Report 1981–82*. North Sydney: Australia Council for the Arts.

Australia Council for the Arts. 1985. *Annual Report 1984–85*. North Sydney: Australia Council for the Arts.

Australia Council for the Arts. 1988. *Annual Report 1987–88*. North Sydney: Australia Council for the Arts.

Australia Council for the Arts. 1991. *Annual Report 1990–91*. Redfern, NSW: Australia Council for the Arts.

Australia Council for the Arts. 1992. *Annual Report 1991–92*. Redfern, NSW: Australia Council for the Arts.

Australia Council for the Arts. 1993. *Policy on Arts for a Multicultural Australia*. Accessed 19 March 2018. www.multiculturalaustralia.edu.au/doc/auscouncil arts_3.pdf.

Australia Council for the Arts. 1994. *Annual Report 1993–94*. Redfern, NSW: Australia Council for the Arts.

Australia Council for the Arts. 2000. *Arts in a Multicultural Australia Policy 2000*. Strawberry Hills, NSW: Australia Council for the Arts.

Australia Council for the Arts. 2001. *Annual Report 2000–01*. Strawberry Hills, NSW: Australia Council for the Arts.

Australia Council for the Arts. 2002. *Annual Report 2001–02*. Strawberry Hills, NSW: Australia Council for the Arts. Accessed 11 May 2018. www.australia council.gov.au/workspace/uploads/files/news/australia_council_annual_ report-2001-02.pdf.

Australia Council for the Arts. 2004. *Annual Report 2003–04*, Strawberry Hills, NSW: Australia Council for the Arts.

Australia Council for the Arts. 2005. *Annual Report 2004–05*. Strawberry Hills, NSW: Australia Council for the Arts.

Australia Council for the Arts. 2006a. *Arts in a Multicultural Australia*. Accessed 19 March 2018. www.multiculturalaustralia.edu.au/doc/austcouncil_arts policy.doc.

Australia Council for the Arts. 2006b. *Annual Report 2005–06*. Strawberry Hills, NSW: Australia Council for the Arts.

Australia Council for the Arts. 2007. 'Multicultural Arts: Cultural Citizenship for the 21st Century'. Accessed 25 November 2020. www.australiacouncil. gov.au/news/media-centre/speeches/multicultural-arts-cultural-citizenship-for-the-21st-century/.

Australia Council for the Arts. 2009. *Annual Report 2008–09*. Strawberry Hills, NSW: Australia Council for the Arts. Accessed 27 October 2016. www.australia council.gov.au/workspace/uploads/files/news/australia_council_annual_report_2008-09.pdf.

Australia Council for the Arts. 2011. *Annual Report 2011–12*. Strawberry Hills, NSW: Australia Council for the Arts. Accessed 15 April 2018. www.australia council.gov.au/workspace/uploads/files/news/australia_council_annual_report_2011-12.pdf.

Australia Council for the Arts. 2014a. 'A Culturally Ambitious Nation'. Accessed 25 November 2020. www.australiacouncil.gov.au/strategic-plan/.

Australia Council for the Arts. 2014b. *Annual Report 2013–14*. Strawberry Hills, NSW: Australia Council for the Arts. Accessed 15 April 2018. www.australia council.gov.au/workspace/uploads/files/news/annual-report-2013-14.pdf.

Australia Council for the Arts. 2016a. *Annual Report 2015–16*. Strawberry Hills, NSW: Australia Council for the Arts.

Australia Council for the Arts. 2016b. 'Cultural Engagement Framework'. Accessed 18 November 2016. www.australiacouncil.gov.au/about/cultural-engagement-framework/.

Australia Council for the Arts. 2017a. *Annual Report 2016–17*. Strawberry Hills, NSW: Australia Council for the Arts. Accessed 11 May 2018. www. australiacouncil.gov.au/workspace/uploads/files/australia-council-for-the-arts-5a1b80d5da897.pdf.

Australia Council for the Arts. 2017b. *Australia Council Corporate Plan 2017–21*. Strawberry Hills, NSW: Australia Council for the Arts. Accessed 11 May 2018. www.australiacouncil.gov.au/workspace/uploads/files/aca-corporate-plan-2017-21-fin-59a7a7d06a67f.pdf.

Australia Council for the Arts. 2017c. 'Connecting Australians: Results of the National Arts Participation Survey, June 2017'. Accessed 17 January 2018. www.australiacouncil.gov.au/research/connecting-australians/.

Australia Council for the Arts. 2017d. *Making Art Work: A Summary and Response by the Australia Council for the Arts*. Accessed 20 November 2017. www.australiacouncil.gov.au/workspace/uploads/files/making-art-work-companion-repo-5a05105696225.pdf.

Australia Council for the Arts. 2017e. 'The National Arts Participation Survey: Culture Segments Australia'. Accessed 14 January 2018. www.australiacouncil.gov.au/research/connecting-australians-culture-segments/.

Australia Council for the Arts. n.d.-a. 'Four Year Funding for Organisations'. Accessed 24 October 2016. www.australiacouncil.gov.au/funding/funding-index/four-year-funding-for-organisations/ (site discontinued).

Australia Council for the Arts. n.d.-b. 'IETM-Australia Council for the Arts Collaboration Project'. Accessed 23 March 2018. www.australiacouncil.gov.au/news/media-centre/media-releases/ietm-australia-council-for-the-arts-collaboration-project/.

Australia Council for the Arts. n.d.-c. 'Leadership Program'. Accessed 25 January 2018. www.australiacouncil.gov.au/programs-and-resources/leadership-program/ (site discontinued).

Australia Council Multicultural Advisory Committee (ACMAC). n.d.-a. 'Australia Council Multicultural Advisory Committee Meeting Minutes November 1999'. Unpublished internal Australia Council document.

Australia Council Multicultural Advisory Committee (ACMAC). n.d.-b. 'Australia Council Multicultural Advisory Committee Meeting Minutes April 2004'. Unpublished internal Australia Council document.

Australian Bureau of Statistics (ABS). 2013. '4102.0 – Australian Social Trends, April 2013'. Accessed 10 April 2014. www.abs.gov.au/AUSSTATS/abs@.nsf/Previousproducts/4102.0Main%20Features1April%202013.

Australian Bureau of Statistics (ABS). 2017. '2071.0 – Census of Population and Housing: Reflecting Australia – Stories from the Census, 2016'. Accessed 20 November 2017. www.abs.gov.au/ausstats/abs@.nsf/Lookup/by%20Subject/2071.0~2016~Main%20Features~Cultural%20Diversity%20Data%20Summary~30.

Australian Institute of Aboriginal and Torres Strait Islander Studies (AIATSIS). n.d. 'Indigenous and Torres Strait Isalnder people'. Accessed 25 July 2020. aiatsis.gov.au/explore/indigenous-australians-aboriginal-and-torres-strait-islander-people.

Babacan, H. 2011. '"Multi Is My Culture": Critical Reflections on Multicultural Arts in Tropical Australia'. *eTropic: Electronic Journal of Studies in the Tropics* 10. doi.org/10.25120/etropic.10.0.2011.3401.

Badami, S. 2017. 'Of All Things Qualifying Us to Make Art, Where We "Really" Come from Shouldn't Define Us'. *Guardian*, 16 August 2017. Accessed 22 October 2017. www.theguardian.com/global/commentisfree/2017/aug/16/of-all-things-qualifying-us-to-make-art-where-we-really-come-from-shouldnt-define-us.

Baily, J. 2005. 'Death Danced around and through'. *RealTime* 68. Accessed 20 April 2015. www.realtimearts.net/article/68/7941.

BDL Museum. 2018. 'Asymmetrical Objects'. Accessed 11 February 2018. www.bdlmuseum.org/exhibitions/2018/asymmetrical-object.html.

Bell, D and K. Pahl. 2018. 'Co-Production: Towards a Utopian Approach'. *International Journal of Social Research Methodology* 21 (1): 105–17. doi.org/10.1080/13645579.2017.1348581.

Belvoir. n.d. [Home Page]. Accessed 5 September 2017. belvoir.com.au/.

Bennett, T., M. Emmerson and J. Frow. 2001. 'Social Class and Cultural Practice'. In *Culture in Australia: Policies, Publics and Programs*, edited by T. Bennett and D. Carter, 193–216. Melbourne, Cambridge University Press.

Berger, J. 1992. *Keeping a Rendezvous*. London: Granta.

Bertone, S. 2002. 'Productive Diversity in Australia: Bureaucratic Aspirations and Workplace Realities'. In *Culture, Race and Community: Making It Work in the New Millennium*, edited by D. Gabb and T. Miletic, n.p. Melbourne: VTPU.

Bertone, S., C. Keating and J. Mullaly. 1998. *The Taxidriver, the Cook and the Greengrocer: The Representation of Non-English Speaking Background People in Theatre, Film and Television*. Redfern, NSW: Australia Council for the Arts.

Blonski, A. 1992. *Arts for a Multicultural Australia, 1973–1991: An Account of Australia Council Policies*. Redfern, NSW: Australia Council.

Blonski, A. 1994. 'Persistent Encounters: The Australia Council and Multiculturalism'. *Culture, Difference and the Arts*, edited by S. Gunew and F. Rizvi, 192–208. St Leonards, NSW: Allen & Unwin.

Boland, M. 2019. 'Helpmann Awards Show Theatre Is Winning Diversity Race in Australian Entertainment'. *ABC News*, 16 July. Accessed 10 August 2020. www.abc.net.au/news/2019-07-16/helpmann-awards-hannah-gadsby-new-comedy-wins/11310632.

Bourdieu, P. 1984. *Distinction: A Social Critique of the Judgement of Taste*. Harvard: Routledge & Kegan Paul.

Bourdieu, P. and L. Wacquant. 1992. *An Invitation to Reflexive Sociology*. Chicago: University of Chicago Press.

Bowen, C. 1997. 'Cultural Diversity in the Arts: Potentials and Problems'. In *Cultural Policy Case Studies*, edited by J. Craik, 1–14. Nathan, Qld: Australian Key Centre for Cultural and Media Policy, Griffith University.

British Council. 2008. *Making Creative Cities: The Value of Cultural Diversity in the Arts*. Melbourne: British Council.

Burke, C., D. DiazGranados and E. Sales. 2011. 'Team Leadership: A Review and Look Ahead'. In *The SAGE Handbook of Leadership*, edited by A. Bryman, D. Collinson, K. Grint and M. Uhl-Bien, 338–51. London: SAGE Publications.

Camillus, J. 2008. 'Strategy as a Wicked Problem'. *Harvard Business Review*, May. Accessed 27 April 2016. hbr.org/2008/05/strategy-as-a-wicked-problem.

Canada Council for the Arts (CCA). 2017. *Equity Policy*. Accessed 29 December 2020. canadacouncil.ca/about/governance/corporate-policies.

Canada Council for the Arts (CCA). 2018. 'InfoSource 2018'. Accessed 7 September 2020. canadacouncil.ca/about/public-accountability/info-source.

Canada Council for the Arts (CCA). 2019. *A Shared Future. Annual Report 2018–2019*. Canada Council for the Arts.

Canada Council for the Arts (CCA). n.d. 'Board Members'. Accessed 19 July 2020. canadacouncil.ca/about/governance/board-members.

Canas, T. 2017. 'Diversity is a White Word'. *ArtsHub Australia*, 9 January. Accessed 20 April 2017. www.artshub.com.au/education/news-article/opinions-and-analysis/professional-development/tania-canas/diversity-is-a-white-word-252910.

Caprar, D. 2018. 'Part of What Australians Think is Good Leadership, Might Just Be Anglo Traits'. *Conversation*, 19 April. Accessed 20 April 2018. theconversation.com/part-of-what-australians-think-is-good-leadership-might-just-be-anglo-traits-94969.

Carmichael, P. 2011. *Networking Research: New Directions in Educational Enquiry*. London: Continuum International Publishing Group.

Carriageworks. n.d. [Home Page]. Accessed 23 April 2018. carriageworks.com.au/.

Castagna, F. 2017. 'From Ticking Boxes to Thinking Outside the Square'. Diversity Arts Australia. Accessed 8 December 2020. diversityarts.org.au/ticking-boxes-thinking-outside-square/. Originally published by ArtsHub.

Castells, M. 2010. *The Rise of the Network Society: Economy, Society, and Culture Volume 1*. Oxford: Wiley-Blackwell.

Clore Leadership Foundation. n.d. [Home Page]. Accessed 7 May 2018. www.clore leadership.org/.

Collins, J. 2013. 'Multiculturalism and Immigrant Integration in Australia'. *Canadian Ethnic Studies* 45 (3): 133–49. doi.org/10.1353/ces.2013.0037.

Concise Oxford Dictionary. 1982. 'Friction'. Oxford: Oxford University Press.

Conger, J. 2011. 'Charismatic Leadership'. In *The SAGE Handbook of Leadership*, edited by A. Bryman, D. Collinson, K. Grint, B. Jackson and M. Uhl-Bien, 86–102. London: SAGE Publications.

Contemporary Asian Australian Performance (CAAP). 2017. [Home Page]. Accessed 20 April 2018. www.caap.org.au/.

Cope, B. & M. Kalantzis. 1997. *Productive Diversity A New, Australian Model for Work and Management*. Annandale, NSW: Pluto Press.

Cope, B., M. Kalantzis and C. Ziguras. 2003. 'Multimedia, Multiculturalism and the Arts: A Discussion Paper from the Australia Council'. Accessed 14 March 2018. www.researchgate.net/publication/242706448.

Couros, P. 2017. [Home Page]. Accessed 26 October 2017. panx.com.au/.

Craik, J. 2007. *Re-Visioning Arts and Cultural Policy: Current Impasses and Future Directions*. Canberra: ANU Press. doi.org/10.22459/RACP.07.2007.

Create NSW. 2015. 'Create in NSW: The NSW Arts and Cultural Policy Framework'. Accessed 20 July 2020. www.create.nsw.gov.au/category/arts-in-nsw/create-in-nsw/.

Creative Victoria. 2016. *Creative State Victoria's First Creative Industries Strategy 2016–2020*. Accessed 20 July 2020. creative.vic.gov.au/__data/assets/pdf_file/0005/110948/creativestate-4.pdf.

Croggon, A. 2016a. 'Culture Crisis: The Arts Funding Cuts are Just a Symptom of a Broader Malaise in Australia'. *Monthly*, October. Accessed 4 July 2017. www.themonthly.com.au/issue/2016/october/1475244000/alison-croggon/culture-crisis#mtr.

Croggon, A. 2016b. 'The 70% Drop in Australia Council Grants for Individual Artists is Staggering'. *Guardian*, 19 May. Accessed 1 July 2016. www. theguardian.com/culture/2016/may/19/the-70-drop-australia-council-grants-artists-funding-cuts.

Cubitt, S. 2005. 'Citizens, Consumers and Migrants'. In *Empires, Ruins and Networks. The Transcultural Agenda in Art*, edited by S. McQuire and N. Papastergiadis, 304–19. Carlton, Vic.: Melbourne University Press.

CuriousWorks. n.d. 'Counting and Cracking Project'. Accessed 5 September 2017. www.curiousworks.com.au/project/a-counting-cracking-of-heads/ (site discontinued).

CuriousWorks. 2021a. 'About Us'. Accessed 21 July 2021. curiousworks.com.au/ what-we-do/.

CuriousWorks. 2021b. 'Artists'. Accessed 21 July 2021. curiousworks.com.au/ artists/.

D'Andrea Marisol, J. 2017. 'Symbolic Power: Impact of Government Priorities for Arts Funding in Canada'. *The Journal of Arts Management, Law, and Society* 47 (4): 245–58. doi.org/10.1080/10632921.2017.1340209.

Deleuze, G. and F. Guattari. 1987. *A Thousand Plateaus: Capitalism and Schizophrenia*. Minneapolis: University of Minnesota Press.

Department of Communications and the Arts. 1994. *Creative Nation: Commonwealth Cultural Policy, October 1994*. Accessed 16 September 2017. apo.org.au/node/29704.

Department of Culture and the Arts (DCA). 2016. *Strategic Directions 2016–2031*. Accessed 20 July 2020. www.dlgsc.wa.gov.au/docs/default-source/ culture-and-the-arts/arts-leadership-group/arts-leadership-group-strategic-directions-2016-2031.pdf?sfvrsn=8446dc6b_2.

Department of the Premier and Cabinet. 2019. *Arts and Culture Plan South Australia 2019–2024*. Accessed 29 December 2020. www.dpc.sa.gov.au/ responsibilities/arts-and-culture/arts-plan.

Diversity Arts Australia (DARTS). 2017. 'Beyond Tick Boxes. A Symposium on Cultural Diversity in the Creative Sector in Sydney'. Accessed 15 June 2017. diversityarts.org.au/event/beyond-tick-boxes/.

Diversity Arts Australia (DARTS). 2018. 'Our History'. Accessed 3 March 2018. diversityarts.org.au/about/our-history/.

Donovan, T. 2011. '5 Questions (for Contemporary Practice) with Tania Bruguera'. *Art21 Magazine*, 14 April. Accessed 5 September 2017. magazine. art21.org/2011/04/14/5-questions-for-contemporary-practice-with-tania-bruguera/#.X88AgmgzbIU.

Edge of Elsewhere. n.d. 'About Edge of Elsewhere'. Accessed 29 January 2018. edgeofelsewhere.wordpress.com/about/.

Eltham, B. 2015. 'Brandis is Wrong'. *Crikey*, 18 September. Accessed 17 April 2017. www.crikey.com.au/2015/09/18/brandis-is-wrong-small-arts-orgs-deliver-much-greater-bang-for-govt-buck/.

Eltham, B. 2016. *When the Goal Posts Move*. Platform Papers 48. Strawberry Hills, NSW: Currency House.

Enwezor, O. 2002. *Documenta 11, Platform 5: Exhibition Catalogue*. Ostfildern-Ruit: Hatje Cantz.

Fatona, A. M. 2011. '"Where Outreach Meets Outrage": Racial Equity at The Canada Council for the Arts (1989–1999)'. PhD thesis, University of Toronto.

Fisher, J. 2010. 'Cultural Diversity and Institutional Policy'. In *Beyond Cultural Diversity. The Case for Creativity*, edited by R Appignanesi, chapter 3. London: Third Text Publications.

FORM Dance Projects. n.d.-a. 'Fostering Dance Culture in Western Sydney'. Accessed 23 March 2018. www.form.org.au/.

FORM Dance Projects. n.d.-b. 'Mother Tongue'. Accessed 23 March 2018. www.form.org.au/mother-tongue/.

Foucault, M. 1991. 'Governmentality'. In *The Foucault Effect*, edited by G. Burchell, C. Gordon and P. Miller, 87–104. Chicago: University of Chicago Press.

Fuata, B. 2011. 'Wrong Solo'. *Diaspora* [special issue], *Artlink* 31 (1): 22–23.

Gardiner-Garden, J. 1994. 'Arts Policy in Australia. A History of Commonwealth Involvement in the Arts'. Background Paper no. 5. Department of the Parliamentary Library. Accessed 14 May 2018. www.aph.gov.au/binaries/library/pubs/bp/1994-95/94bp05.pdf.

Gardiner-Garden, J. 2009. 'Commonwealth Arts Policy and Administration'. 7 May. Parliament of Australia. Accessed 14 May 2018. www.aph.gov.au/About_Parliament/Parliamentary_Departments/Parliamentary_Library/pubs/BN/0809/ArtsPolicy.

Gardner, L. 2017. 'Diversity is the Real Winner in Arts Council England's New Round of Funding'. *Guardian*, 28 June. Accessed 13 January 2018. www.theguardian.com/stage/theatreblog/2017/jun/27/diversity-arts-council-england-funding-national-portfolio-organisations.

Gerber, A. 2017. *The Work of Art: Value in Creative Careers*. California: Stanford University Press. doi.org/10.1515/9781503604032.

Gertsakis, E. 1994. 'An Inconstant Politics: Thinking about the Traditional and the Contemporary'. In *Culture, Difference and the Arts*, edited by S. Gunew and F. Rizvi, 35–53. St Leonards, NSW: Allen & Unwin.

Gibson, R. 2005. 'Attunement and Agility'. In *Empires, Ruins + Networks. The Transcultural Agenda in Art*, edited by S. McGuire and N. Papastergiadis, 269–78. Melbourne: Melbourne University Publishing.

Glow, H. 2013. 'Cultural Leadership and Audience Engagement. A Case Study of the Theatre Royal Stratford East'. In *Arts Leadership: International Case Studies*, edited by J. Caust, 131–43. Prahran, Vic.: Tilde University Press.

Gonsalves, R. 2017. 'Some Observations in Three Colours on "Beyond Tick Boxes"'. *Southern Crossings*, 14 August. Accessed 24 October 2017. southerncrossings.com.au/arts-and-culture/some-observations-in-three-colours-on-beyond-tick-boxes/.

Grint, K. 2005. *Leadership Limits and Possibilities*. Houndmills, UK: Palgrave Macmillan.

Gunew, S. 1994. 'Arts for a Multicultural Australia: Redefining the Culture'. In *Culture, Difference and the Arts*, edited by S. Gunew and F. Rizvi, 1–12. St Leonards, NSW: Allen & Unwin.

Gunew, S. 2003. 'Multicultural Sites: Practices of Un/Homliness'. In *Complex Entanglements: Art, Globalisation and Cultural Difference*, edited by N. Papastergiadis, 178–204. London: Rivers Oram Press.

Gunew, S. 2004. *Haunted Nations: The Colonial Dimensions of Multiculturalism*. London: Routledge.

Gunew, S. 2017a. 'Written Response to *In Short Measures*'. *Sydney Review of Books*, 11 July. Accessed 13 November 2017. sydneyreviewofbooks.com/review-review-correspondence/.

Gunew, S. 2017b. *Post-Multicultural Writers as Neo-Cosmopolitan Mediators*. London: Anthem Press. doi.org/10.2307/j.ctt1kft8bw.

Gunew, S., B. Olubas, M. Chakraborty, D. Trimboli and P. Muraca. 2017. 'Discussion: Post-Multicultural Writers as Neo-Cosmopolitan Mediators'. *Journal of Intercultural Studies* 38 (5): 586–97. doi.org/10.1080/07256868. 2017.1375182.

Gunew, S. and F. Rizvi, eds. 1994. *Culture, Difference and the Arts*. St Leonards, NSW: Allen & Unwin.

Hage, G. 1997. 'At Home in the Entrails of the West: Multiculturalism Ethnic Food and Migrant Home-Building'. Academia. Accessed 18 January 2018. www.academia.edu/12916012/At_Home_in_the_Entrails_of_the_West_ Multiculturalism_Ethnic_Food_and_Migrant_Home-Building.

Hage, G. 2000. *White Nation. Fantasies of White Supremacy in a Multicultural Society*. 2nd edn. New York: Routledge.

Hall, S. 1997. *Representation: Cultural Representations and Signifying Practices*. London: SAGE in association with the Open University.

Hanna, K. 2012. *Environmental Scan of Culturally and Linguistically Diverse Artists, Arts Workers and Projects in NSW*. Create NSW. Accessed 26 October 2014. www.create.nsw.gov.au/news-and-publications/publications/environmental-scan-of-culturally-and-linguistically-diverse-artists-arts-workers-and-projects-in-nsw/.

Harms, L. 2011. 'Iran: Scripts of Despair and Love: Nasim Nasr & Siamak Fallah'. *Diaspora* [special issue], *Artlink* 31 (1): 44–47.

Hawkins, G. 1993. *From Nimbin to Mardi Gras: Constructing Community Arts*. St. Leonards, NSW: Allen & Unwin.

Helpmann Awards. 2019. '2019 Nominees and Winners'. Accessed 10 July 2020. www.helpmannawards.com.au/2019/nominees-and-winners/theatre.

Hewison, R. and J. Holden. 2011. *The Cultural Leadership Handbook. How to Run a Creative Organisation*. London: Routledge. doi.org/10.4324/9781315 615196.

Ho, C. 2013. 'From Social Justice to Social Cohesion: A History of Australian Multicultural Policy'. In *'For Those Who've Come across the Seas…': Australian Multicultural Theory, Policy and Practice,* edited by A. Jakubowicz and C. Ho, 31–41. North Melbourne: Australian Scholarly Publishing.

Holmes, J., M. Marra and B. Vine. 2011. *Leadership, Discourse and Ethnicity*. Oxford: Oxford University Press. doi.org/10.1093/acprof:oso/978019973 0759.001.0001.

Hore-Thorburn, I. 2017. 'Foundations and Corollary Actions: 4A's Twenty Years Symposium'. Centre for Contemporary Asian Art. Accessed 22 May 2017. www.4a.com.au/4a_papers_article/foundations-corollary-actions-4as-twenty-years-symposium/.

Hosking, D. 2011. 'Moving Relationality: Mediations on a Relational Approach to Leadership'. In *The SAGE Handbook of Leadership*, edited by A. Bryman, D. Collinson, K. Grint, B. Jackson and M. Uhl-Bien, 455–67. London: SAGE Publications.

Idriss, S. 2018. *Young Migrant Identities. Creativity and Masculinity.* Abingdon, UK: Taylor and Francis. doi.org/10.4324/9781315308159.

IMDb. 2003. 'The Finished People [by K. Do]'. Accessed 11 October 2017. www.imdb.com/title/tt0400434/.

Institute of International Visual Arts (iniva). 2017. [Home Page]. Accessed 6 August 2017. www.iniva.org/.

Jackson, B. and K. Parry. 2011. *A Very Short, Fairly Interesting and Reasonably Cheap Book about Studying Leadership.* Los Angeles: SAGE.

Jacobs, M. 2014. 'Cultural Brokerage, Addressing Boundaries and the New Paradigm of Safeguarding Intangible Cultural Heritage. Folklore Studies, Transdisciplinary Perspectives and UNESCO'. *volkskunde 2014* 3: 265–91.

Jakubowicz, A. and C. Ho. 2013. 'Conclusion: An Agenda for the Next Decade'. In *'For Those Who've Come across the Seas…': Australian Multicultural Theory, Policy and Practice*, edited by A. Jakubowicz and C. Ho, 277–89. North Melbourne: Australian Scholarly Publishing.

James, P. 2014. *Globalization and Politics, Volume 4: Political Philosophies of the Global.* London: SAGE Publications.

Janke, T. 2016. *Indigenous Protocols and the Arts.* Rosebery, NSW: Terri Janke & Co. Accessed 26 February 2017. www.terrijanke.com.au/indigenous-cultural-protocols-and-arts.

Johanson, K. and R. Rentschler. 2002. 'The New Arts Leader: The Australia Council and Cultural Policy Change'. *International Journal of Cultural Policy* 8 (2): 167–80. doi.org/10.1080/1028663022000009524.

Kalantzis, M. and B. Cope. 1994. 'Vocabularies of Excellence: Rewording Multicultural Arts Policy'. In *Culture, Difference and the Arts*, edited by S. Gunew and F. Rizvi, 13–34. St Leonards, NSW: Allen & Unwin.

Kalantzis, M., S. Castles and B. Cope. 1993. *Access to Excellence: A Review of Issues Affecting Artists and Arts from Non-English Speaking Backgrounds, Vol. 1 Overview*. Canberra: Office of Multicultural Affairs.

Kape Communications. n.d. 'International Speakers Dr. Kurin'. Accessed 7 February 2018. www.kape.com.au/kurin.html.

Kape Communications. 2010. 'Multicultural Arts Professional Development'. Accessed 21 July 2021. kape.com.au/mapd/aboutmapd.html.

Kapetopoulos, F. 2004. *Who Goes There?: National Multicultural Arts Audience Case Studies*. Strawberry Hills, NSW: Australia Council for the Arts.

Kapetopoulos, F. 2009. *Adjust Your View Toolkit*. Surry Hills, NSW: Australia Council for the Arts. Accessed 26 November 201. www.kape.com.au/adjustyrview/Adjust%20Your%20View%20Toolkit.pdf.

Karavas, R. 2009. 'Rembetika Masterclass'. *Neos Kosmos*, 2 September. Accessed 21 February 2016. neoskosmos.com/news/en/Rembetika-masterclass-.

Keating, C., S. Bertone and M. Leahy. n.d. 'Evaluation of the Arts in a Multicultural Australia 2000 Policy'. Unpublished internal consultant report for Australia Council for the Arts.

Kefala, A. 2016. *Fragments*. Artarmon, NSW: Giramondo Publishing Company.

Kelly, V. ed. 1998. *Our Australia Theatre in the 90s*. Atlanta: Rodopi.

Khan, R. 2010. 'Going 'Mainstream': Evaluating the Instrumentalisation of Multicultural Arts'. *International Journal of Cultural Policy* 16 (2): 184–99. Accessed on 30 May 2014. doi.org/10.1080/10286630902971561.

Khan, R., D. Wyatt and A. Yue. 2014. 'Making and Remaking Multicultural Arts: Policy, Cultural Difference and the Discourse of Decline'. *International Journal of Cultural Policy* 21 (2): 219–34. doi.org/10.1080/10286632.2014.890603.

Khan, R., D. Wyatt, A. Yue and N. Papastergiadis. 2013. 'Creative Australia and the Dispersal of Multiculturalism'. *Asia Pacific Journal of Arts and Cultural Management* 10 (1). Accessed 21 July 2021. www.academia.edu/31293546/.

Khan, R., A. Yue, N. Papastergiadis and D. Wyatt. 2017. *Multiculturalism and Governance: Evaluating Arts Policies and Engaging Cultural Citizenship*. Parkville, Vic.: University of Melbourne. Accessed 9 February 2018. mcag.esrc.info/objects/D00000017_Final_Report.pdf.

Knight, K. 2013. *Passion Purpose Meaning-Arts Activism in Western Sydney*. Ultimo, NSW: Halstead Press.

Knights, M. and I. North. 2011. *Hossein Valamanesh: Out of Nothingness*. Kent Town, SA: Wakefield Press.

Koubaroulis, K. 2014. 'Groundswell Arts NSW—Supporting Cultural Diversity in the Arts'. Chuffed. Accessed 2 March 2018. www.chuffed.org/project/supportgroundswellartsnsw/.

kultour. 2011. *Submission to the National Cultural Policy*. Canberra: Australian Government.

kultour. 2015. *Annual Report 2015*. Melbourne: kultour. Accessed 13 September 2015. diversityarts.org.au/app/uploads/kultour_annualreport2015.pdf.

Kurin, R. 1997. *Reflections of a Culture Broke*. Washington, DC: Smithsonian Institution Press.

Kwai, A. n.d. [Bio]. Accessed 21 July 2021. www.ajakkwai.com/bio.

Latour, B. 1987. *Science in Action*. Cambridge, MA: Harvard University Press.

Lau, A. n.d. 'How Likely are Asian Kids to attend Performing Arts Schools?' Unpublished blog.

Lee, J. 2014. 'We Need More Asian American Kids Growing Up to be Artists, Not Doctors'. *Guardian*, 16 March. Accessed 18 February 2018. www.theguardian.com/commentisfree/2014/mar/16/asian-american-jobs-success-myth-arts.

Lewis, L. 2007. *Cross-Racial Casting: Changing the Face of Australian Theatre*. Platform Papers 13. Strawberry Hills, NSW: Currency House.

Luhmann, N. 2000. 'Familiarity, Confidence, Trust: Problems and Alternatives'. In *Trust: Making and Breaking Cooperative Relations*, edited by D. Gambetta, 94–107. Oxford: Department of Sociology, University of Oxford.

Lynd, A. and S. Lynd. 2009. *Stepping Stones: Memoirs of a Life Together*. Lanham, MD: Lexington Books.

Macdonnell, J. 1992. *Arts, Minister?: Government Policy and the Arts*. Paddington, NSW: Currency Press.

Macdonnell, J. n.d. 'AMA Options Paper A 2008'. Unpublished internal consultant report for Australia Council for the Arts.

Machiavelli, N. and N. Thompson. 1992. *The Prince*. New York: Dover Publications.

Mar, P. and I. Ang. 2015. *Promoting a Diversity of Cultural Expression in Arts in Australia*. Strawberry Hills, NSW: Australia Council for the Arts.

Marinos, L. 2014. *Blood and Circuses. An Irresponsible Memoir.* Crows Nest, NSW: Allen & Unwin.

Markus, A. 2016. *Australians Today: The Australia @2015 Scanlon Foundation Survey.* Caulfield East, Vic.: Monash University. Accessed 11 September 2016. scanlonfoundation.org.au/wp-content/uploads/2018/10/2016-Mapping-Social-Cohesion-Report-FINAL-with-covers.pdf.

Markus, A. 2017. *Mapping Social Cohesion: The Scanlon Foundation Surveys 2017.* Caulfield East, Vic.: Monash University. Accessed 3 May 2018. scanlonfoundation.org.au/wp-content/uploads/2018/10/ScanlonFoundation_MappingSocialCohesion_2017-1.pdf.

Marr, D. 2017. 'The White Queen. One Nation and the Politics of Race'. *Quarterly Essay* 65. Melbourne: Black Inc.

Mason, R. 2010. 'Australian Multiculturalism: Revisiting Australia's Political Heritage and the Migrant Presence'. *History Compass* 8, no. 8 (August): 817–27. Accessed 17 May 2018. doi.org/10.1111/j.1478-0542.2010.00721.x.

Matarasso, F. 2010. 'Francois Matarasso Part 1: The Parliament of Dreams: Why Everything Depends on Culture'. *YouTube.* Accessed 23 January 2018. www.youtube.com/watch?v=IC_rDA0NCRI.

Matilda Awards. 2017. 'Award Recipients'. Accessed 5 February 2018. www.matildaawards.com.au/recipients/.

McMaster, B. 2008. *Supporting Excellence in the Arts: From Measurement to Judgement.* London: Department for Culture, Media and Sport. Accessed 15 January 2018. webarchive.nationalarchives.gov.uk/+/http:/www.culture.gov.uk/images/publications/supportingexcellenceinthearts.pdf.

McNeilly, J. 2014. 'Mother Tongue'. *RealTime Arts* 124: 33. Accessed 26 May 2017. www.realtimearts.net/article/issue124/11780.

McPhee, H. 1995. 'Cultural Identity in the Arts'. In *Global Cultural Diversity Conference.* Canberra: Australian Government. Accessed 6 August 2014. www.dss.gov.au/our-responsibilities/settlement-and-multicultural-affairs/programs-policy/a-multicultural-australia/programs-and-publications/1995-global-cultural-diversity-conference-proceedings-sydney/culture-education-and-language/cultural-identity-in-the-arts (site discontinued).

McQuire, S. and N. Papastergiadis, eds. 2005. *Empires, Ruins + Networks. The Transcultural Agenda in Art.* Carlton, Vic.: Melbourne University Press.

Melbourne Theatre Company (MTC). 2014. 'MTC Connect'. Accessed 15 December 2017. www.mtc.com.au/about/key-initiatives/artist-access/mtc-connect/ (site discontinued).

Melbourne Theatre Company (MTC). n.d. [Home Page]. Accessed 5 September 2017. www.mtc.com.au/.

Mendonca, M. and R. Kanungo. 2007. *Ethical Leadership*. Maidenhead: McGraw-Hill/Open University Press.

Meyrick, J. 2007. 'Comments'. Responses to Lee Lewis's 'Cross-Racial Casting: Changing the Face of Australian Theatre'. Currency House. Accessed 23 July 2015. currencyhouse.org.au/node/58.

Migliorino, P. 1998. *The World is Your Audience*. Redfern, NSW: Australia Council for the Arts.

Mirza, M. 2009. 'Aims and Contradictions of Cultural Diversity Policies in the Arts: A Case Study of the Rich Mix Centre in East London'. *International Journal of Cultural Policy* 15 (1): 53–69. doi.org/10.1080/10286630802562593.

Mitchell, T. 1998. 'Maintaining Cultural Integrity: Teresa Crea, Doppio Teatro Italo-Australian Theatre and Critical Multiculturalism'. In *Our Australian Theatre in the 1990s*, edited by V. Kelly, 132–51. Amsterdam: Rodopi.

Morató, A., M. Zarlenga and M. Zamorano. 2015. *How Does Cultural Diversity Contribute to Cultural Creativity in Europe*. Accessed 27 January 2018. www.academia.edu/22364732/How_does_cultural_diversity_contribute_to_cultural_creativity_in_Europe.

Morellini, M. 2015. '2015 Sydney Film Festival'. *AltMedia*. Accessed 21 September 2017. www.altmedia.net.au/2015-sydney-film-festival/105693 (site discontinued).

Morris Hargreaves McIntyre. 2013. *Audience Atlas Australia Report*. Auckland: Morris Hargreaves McIntyre.

Mosquera, G. 2003. 'Alien-Own/Own Alien'. In *Complex Entanglements: Art, Globalisation and Cultural Difference*, edited by N. Papastergiadis, 18–29. London: Rivers Oram Press.

Multicultural Arts Victoria (MAV). 2006a. 'Ajak Kwai—Multicultural Arts Victoria Event'. Accessed 21 February 2015. www.multiculturalarts.com.au/events2006/ajakkwai.shtml (site discontinued).

Multicultural Arts Victoria (MAV). 2006b. 'Opposite My House is a Funeral Parlour—Multicultural Arts Victoria Event'. Accessed 20 April 2015. www.multi culturalarts.com.au/events2006/oppositemyhouse.shtml (site discontinued).

Multicultural Arts Victoria (MAV). 2018. [Home Page]. Accessed 28 February 2018. multiculturalarts.com.au/.

Musica Viva. 2018. '75 Years of Making Australia a More Musical Place'. Accessed 9 December 2020. musicaviva.com.au/about-us/company/.

Nadon, C. 2013. *Enlightenment and Secularism: Essays on the Mobilization of Reason*. Plymouth UK: Lexington Books.

NEXUS Arts. n.d. [Home Page]. Accessed 28 February 2018. nexusarts.org.au/.

Noble, G. 2009. 'Everyday Cosmopolitanism and the Labour of Intercultural Community'. In *Everyday Multiculturalism*, edited by A. Wise and S. Velayutham, 46–65. Hampshire: Palgrave Macmillan. doi.org/10.1057/9780230244474_3.

Noble, G. 2011. '"Bumping into Alterity": Transacting Cultural Complexities'. *Continuum* 25 (6): 827–40. doi.org/10.1080/10304312.2011.617878.

Noble, R. 2012. *Utopias*. London: Whitechapel Gallery.

Nwachukwu, T. and M. Robinson. 2011. *The Role of Diversity in Building Adaptive Resilience*. London: Arts Council England. Accessed 3 May 2018. culture hive.co.uk/wp-content/uploads/2013/07/Diversity_and_adaptive_resilience _public-1.pdf.

Papastergiadis, N. 2000. *The Turbulence of Migration*. Cambridge, UK: Polity Press.

Papastergiadis, N. 2003. *Complex Entanglements: Art, Globalisation and Cultural Difference*. London: Rivers Oram Press.

Papastergiadis, N. 2005. 'Hybridity and Ambivalence'. *Theory, Culture & Society* 22 (4): 39–64. doi.org/10.1177/0263276405054990.

Papastergiadis, N. 2010. *Spatial Aesthetics: Art, Place and the Everyday*. Amsterdam: Institute of Network Cultures.

Papastergiadis, N. 2013a. 'Why Multiculturalism Makes People So Angry and Sad'. In *Space Place & Culture* by Future Leaders, 1–25. www.futureleaders. com.au/book_chapters/pdf/Space-Place-Culture/Nikos-Papastergiadis.pdf.

Papastergiadis, N. 2013b. 'Hospitality, Multiculturalism and Cosmopolitanism: A Conversation between Christos Tsiolkas and Nikos Papastergiadis'. *Journal of Intercultural Studies* 34 (4): 387–98. doi.org/10.1080/07256868.2013. 769935.

Papastergiadis, N. 2013c. *Cosmopolitanism and Culture*. New York: John Wiley & Sons.

Papastergiadis, N., S. Gunew and A. Blonski. 1994. *Access to Excellence: A Review of Issues Affecting Artists and Arts from Non-English Speaking Backgrounds, Vol. 2 Writers*. Canberra: Office of Multicultural Affairs.

Parliament of Australia. 2013. *Creative Australia: National Cultural Policy 2013*. Accessed 17 May 2018. www.nck.pl/upload/attachments/302586/creative australiapdf2.pdf.

Parliament of Australia. 2015. 'An Inquiry into the Impact of the 2014 and 2015 Commonwealth Budget Decisions on the Arts—Submissions'. Accessed 11 August 2017. www.aph.gov.au/Parliamentary_Business/Committees/ Senate/Legal_and_Constitutional_Affairs/Arts_Funding/Submissions.

Paul, A. 2010. 'About Groundswell'. Groundswell Arts NSW. Accessed 30 November 2017. groundswellctcs.blogspot.com.au/p/about-groundswell. html.

Paul, A. 2015. '"Mother Tongue" Audience Vox Pop'. *YouTube*. 18 January. Accessed 26 May 2016. www.youtube.com/watch?v=OEibbThfF54.

Paul, A. 2018. 'Mother Tongue'. Accessed 2 March 2018. www.annalouisepaul. com/mother-tongue/.

Performing Lines (PL). n.d.-a. [Home Page]. Accessed 20 April 2015. www. performinglines.org.au/.

Performing Lines (PL). n.d.-b. 'Layla Majnun'. Accessed 31 December 2020. www.performinglines.org.au/projects/laylamajnun/.

Playwriting Australia (PWA). 2016. 'npf16 lotus'. Accessed 12 September 2017. www.pwa.org.au/npf16-lotus/ (site discontinued).

Pledger, D. 2017. 'Australia's Cultural Revolution—It's Time to Remake the Australia Council'. *Daily Review*, 13 April. Accessed 13 April 2017. dailyreview.com.au/alternative-facts-cultural-revolution/58375/.

Positive Solutions. n.d. *Professional Development for Arts Administrators Working for the Arts in a Multicultural Australia*. Unpublished internal consultant report for Australia Council for the Arts commissioned in 1999.

Punt, W. and A. Bateman. 2018. 'Now We Have to Get Practical on the Problem of Trust'. *Financial Review*, 3 April. Accessed 4 April 2018. www.afr.com/opinion/ now-we-have-to-get-practical-on-the-problem-of-trust-20180403-h0y9qq.

Putnam, R. 2000. *Bowling Alone: The Collapse and Revival of American Community*. New York: Simon and Schuster. doi.org/10.1145/358916.361990.

PWA—see Playwriting Australia.

Radio National. 2014. 'Australian Stories for the Stage'. *Weekend Arts*, 10 May. Accessed 20 August 2015. www.abc.net.au/radionational/programs/archived/weekendarts/tim-roseman/5437024.

Radio National. 2015. 'Joseph Tawadros: Lamentations'. Accessed 11 February 2016. www.abc.net.au/radionational/programs/earshot/joseph-tawadros/6916482.

Radio National. 2017. 'Triple Treat: Jasper Jones Comes to the Big Screen'. 21 February. Accessed 22 March 2017. www.abc.net.au/radionational/programs/booksandarts/jasper-jones-the-film/8268252.

Reckwitz, A. 2014. 'Creativity as Dispositif'. In *Culture, Communication, and Creativity: Reframing the Relations of Media, Knowledge, and Innovation in Society*, edited by H. Knoblauch, M. Jacobs and R. Tuma, 23–33. Frankfurt: PL Academic Research.

Rentschler, R. 2006. *MixItUp Project Report: Building New Audiences*. Melbourne: Deakin University.

Rentschler, R. 2015. *Arts Governance: People, Passion, Performance Routledge*. England: Abingdon. doi.org/10.4324/9781315818016.

Rentschler, R., H. Le and A. Osborne. 2008. *Western Australia Intercultural Arts Research Project: An Investigation into Issues Faced by Culturally and Linguistically Diverse Artists in Western Australia*. Burwood, Vic.: Deakin University. Accessed 1 May 2017. dro.deakin.edu.au/eserv/DU:30018731/le-wainterculturalarts-2008.pdf.

Richens, F. 2017. *Pulse Report—Part 1: Diversity in the Arts Workforce—What Needs to Change?* Cambridge, UK: Arts Professional. Accessed 21 February 2017. www.artsprofessional.co.uk/pulse/survey-report/pulse-report-part-1-diversity-arts-workforce-what-needs-change.

Rittel, H. and M. Webber. 1973. 'Dilemmas in a General Theory of Planning'. *Policy Sciences* 4 (2): 155–69. doi.org/10.1007/BF01405730.

Rizvi, F. 2003. 'Looking Back and Looking Forward'. In *Complex Entanglements: Art, Globalisation and Cultural Difference*, edited by N. Papastergiadis, 229–38. London: Rivers Oram Press.

Robb, P. 2012. *Lives*. Sydney, NSW: Read How You Want.

Rowe, D., G. Noble, T. Bennett and M. Kelly. 2016. 'Transforming Cultures? From Creative Nation to Creative Australia'. *Media International Australia* 158 (1): 6–16. doi.org/10.1177/1329878X16629544.

Rowse, T. 1985. *Arguing the Arts. The Funding of the Arts in Australia*. Ringwood, Vic.: Penguin.

Sammers, C. 1999. 'Political Will or Political Won't'. Migration Heritage Centre Forum. Accessed 17 April 2017. www.migrationheritage.nsw.gov.au/mhc-reports/forum99/sammers.html.

Sawrikar, P. and I. Katz. 2009. 'How Useful Is the Term "Culturally and Linguistically Diverse (CALD)" in the Australian Social Policy Discourse?' Social Policy Research Centre, University of New South Wales. Accessed 30 May 2016. www.researchgate.net/publication/304849108_Sawrikar_P_Katz_I_2009_How_useful_is_the_term_Culturally_And_Linguistically_Diverse_CALD_in_the_Australian_social_policy_discourse_Refereed_Conference_Paper_Australian_Social_Policy_Conference_ASPC_20.

Screen Australia. 2016. *Seeing Ourselves: Reflections on Diversity in Australian TV Drama*. Sydney: Screen Australia. Accessed 8 September 2016. www.screenaustralia.gov.au/getmedia/157b05b4-255a-47b4-bd8b-9f715555fb44/TV-Drama-Diversity.pdf.

Screen Australia. 2017. *Gender Matters*. Sydney: Screen Australia. Accessed 31 January 2018. www.screenaustralia.gov.au/sa/media-centre/backgrounders/2017/11-30-gender-matters.

Seeto, A. 2011. 'Transcultural Radical'. *Diaspora* [special issue], *Artlink* 31 (1): 28–31.

Shopfront. 2017. 'The Company'. Accessed 28 October 2017. shopfront.org.au/the-company (site discontinued).

Sirkin, H., P. Keenan and A. Jackson. 2005. 'The Hard Side of Change Management'. *Harvard Business Review*, October. Accessed 15 April 2018. hbr.org/2005/10/the-hard-side-of-change-management.

Smith, T. 2006. 'Contemporary Art and Contemporaneity'. *Critical Enquiry* 32, no. 4 (Summer): 681–707. doi.org/10.1086/508087.

Sorenson, G., G. Goethals and P. Haber. 2011. 'The Enduring and Elusive Quest for a General Theory of Leadership: Initial Efforts and New Horizons'. In *The SAGE Handbook of Leadership*, edited by A Bryman, D Collison, K Grint, B Jackson & M Uhl-Bien, 29–38. London: SAGE Publications.

Sorsa, V., H. Merkkiniemi, N. Endrissat and G. Islam. 2017. 'Little Less Conversation, Little More Action: Musical Intervention as Aesthetic Material Communication'. *Journal of Business Research* 85 (April): 365–74. doi.org/10.1016/j.jbusres.2017.10.014.

Soutphommasane, T. 2016. 'Cultural Diversity in Leadership'. Australian Human Rights Commission, 8 September. Accessed 20 November 2016. www.humanrights.gov.au/news/speeches/cultural-diversity-leadership.

Soutphommasane, T. 2017. 'Cultural Diversity and the Arts'. Australian Human Rights Commission, 29 June. Accessed 3 May 2018. www.humanrights.gov.au/news/speeches/cultural-diversity-and-arts.

Stevenson, D. 2000. *Art and Organisation: Making Australian Cultural Policy*. St Lucia: University of Queensland Press.

Stevenson, D., D. Rowe, J. Caust and C. Cmielewski. 2017. *Recalibrating Culture: Production, Consumption, Policy*. Parramatta, NSW: University of Western Sydney. Accessed 24 November 2017. www.westernsydney.edu.au/__data/assets/pdf_file/0006/1239999/recalibrating-culture-report.pdf.

Sutton, B. and T. Seellig. 2017. 'The Do's and Don'ts of Creative Friction'. Stanford: Stanford Innovation Lab, Stanford University. Accessed 28 January 2018. ecorner.stanford.edu/podcasts/the-dos-and-donts-of-creative-friction/.

Svašek, M. and B. Meyer. 2016. *Creativity in Transition*. New York: Berghahn Books. doi.org/10.2307/j.ctvr695js.

Taylor, A. 2017. 'Carriageworks Boldly Goes Where Other Venues Fear to Tread in its 2018 Program'. *Sydney Morning Herald*, 17 November. Accessed 1 December 2017. www.smh.com.au/national/nsw/carriageworks-boldly-goes-where-other-venues-fear-to-tread-in-its-2018-program-20171117-gznvz2.html.

Throsby, D. and V. Hollister. 2003. *Don't Give Up Your Day Job: An Economic Study of Professional Artists in Australia*. Strawberry Hills, NSW: Australia Council. Accessed 12 November 2017. www.australiacouncil.gov.au/workspace/uploads/files/research/entire_document-54325d2a023c8.pdf.

Throsby, D. and N. Petetskaya. 2017. *Making Art Work: An Economic Study of Professional Artists in Australia*. Strawberry Hills, NSW: Australia Council. Accessed 12 November 2017. www.australiacouncil.gov.au/workspace/uploads/files/making-art-work-companion-repo-5a05105696225.pdf.

Throsby, D. and A. Zednick. 2010. *Do You Really Expect to Get Paid? An Economic Study of Professional Artists in Australia.* Strawberry Hills, NSW: Australia Council for the Arts. Accessed 12 August 2014. www.australiacouncil.gov.au/workspace/uploads/files/research/do_you_really_expect_to_get_pa-54325a3748d81.pdf.

Tomlinson, B. and G. Lipsitz. 2013. 'American Studies as Accompaniment'. *American Quarterly* 65 (1): 1–30. doi.org/10.1353/aq.2013.0009.

Totaro, P. 1991. 'Cultural Diversity: Media and the Arts: Discussion Paper from Forum 11'. In *National Ideas Summit.* Redfern, NSW: Australia Council for the Arts.

Trimboli, D. 2016. 'Mediating Everyday Multiculturalism: Performativity and Precarious Inclusion in Australian Storytelling'. PhD thesis, University of British Columbia.

Tsing, A. 2005. *Friction: An Ethnography of Global Connection.* Princeton: Princeton University Press. doi.org/10.1515/9781400830596.

Tsing, A. 2015. *The Mushroom at the End of the World: On the Possibility of Life in Capitalist Ruins.* New Jersey: Princeton University Press. doi.org/10.2307/j.ctvc77bcc.

Tsiolkas, C. 2013. 'Message to the ASRC'. Asylum Seeker Resource Centre. Accessed 9 February 2018. www.asrc.org.au/wp-content/uploads/2013/05/ctsiolkas.pdf.

Tsoutas, N. 2010. 'Curator's Statement'. In *Australian,* 6–7. Liverpool, NSW: Casula Powerhouse.

Usher, R. 2005. 'Disquiet over Australia Council Changes'. *Age,* 4 July. Accessed 1 May 2017. www.theage.com.au/entertainment/art-and-design/disquiet-over-australia-council-changes-20050408-gdzxr1.html.

UNESCO. 2001. Universal Declaration on Cultural Diversity. Accessed 29 December 2020. portal.unesco.org/en/ev.php-URL_ID=13179&URL_DO=DO_TOPIC&URL_SECTION=201.html.

Vachananda, N. 2004. 'Opposite My House is a Funeral Parlour'. Accessed 20 April 2015. www.nareevachananda.com/opposite-my-house-is-a-funeral-parlour.

Van de Vyver, J. and D. Abrams. 2017. 'The Arts as a Catalyst for Human Prosociality and Cooperation'. *Social Psychological and Personality Science* 9 (6): 664–74. doi.org/10.1177/1948550617720275.

van Teeseling, I. 2011. 'Literary Migrations: White, English-Speaking Migrant Writers in Australia'. PhD thesis, University of Wollongong.

Vertovec, S. 2010. 'Towards Post-Multiculturalism? Changing Communities, Conditions and Contexts of Diversity'. *International Social Science Journal* 61 (199): 83–95. doi.org/10.1111/j.1468-2451.2010.01749.x.

Weltecke, D. 2008. 'Trust: Some Methodological Reflections'. In *Strategies of Writing. Studies on Text and Trust in the Middle Ages*, edited by P. Schulte, M. Mostert and I. van Renswoude, 379–92. Turnhout: Brepols Publishers. doi.org/10.1484/M.USML-EB.3.4274.

Werbner, P. 2006. 'Understanding Vernacular Cosmopolitanism'. *Anthropology News*, 24 December. doi.org/10.1525/an.2006.47.5.7.

Westwood, M. 2017. 'Koukias Brings Opera Before the Flame Goes Out to Hobart'. *Australian*, 14 January.

Wilson, E. 2017. *The Origins of Creativity*. London: Penguin Random House.

Wise, A. 2009. 'Everyday Multiculturalism: Transversal Crossings and Working Class Cosmopolitans'. In *Everyday Multiculturalism*, edited by A. Wise and S. Velayutham, 21–45. Chippenham: Palgrave Macmillan. doi.org/10.1057/9780230244474_2.

Wise, A. and S. Velayutham. 2013. 'Conviviality in Everyday Multiculturalism: Some Brief Comparisons between Singapore and Sydney'. *European Journal of Cultural Studies* 17 (4): 406–30. doi.org/10.1177/1367549413510419.